Bob Vila's Guide to Historic Homes of the South

Bob Vila's Guides to Historic Homes of America

Bob Vila's
Guide to Historic Homes of the South

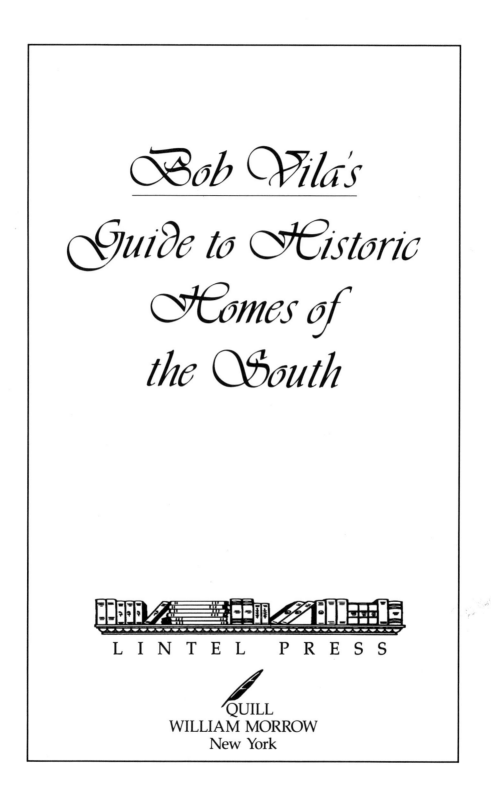

LINTEL PRESS

QUILL
WILLIAM MORROW
New York

It is the policy of William Morrow and Company, Inc., and its imprints and affiliates, recognizing the importance of preserving what has been written, to print the books we publish on acid-free paper, and we exert our best efforts to that end.

Bob Vila's guide to historic homes of the South.

Library of Congress Catalog Card Number 93-083607

ISBN 0-688-12492-5

Printed in the United States of America

First Quill Edition

1 2 3 4 5 6 7 8 9 10

MANAGING EDITOR— SUSAN RYAN
LAYOUT AND DESIGN BY EVA JAKUBOWSKI

Acknowledgment

$\mathcal{I}$ would like to acknowledge all of the people who helped make the idea of this book become a reality. To my wife Deborah who shares my enthusiasm for everything about history and whose idea of a vacation is incomplete without visiting every historic house along the way. Her encouragement and determination to see every room in every house gave me the idea for this series of guides.

To Ron Feiner who brought us all together long ago and by doing so enriched us all. To Bob Sann and Hugh Howard whose path findings led us to our publishers, a special thanks for enabling us to be spared the normative agony of attempting to get published. Through Hugh's excellent relationships we hope to benefit all.

To my brother, whose expertise in the publishing business facilitated my limited understanding of the industry.

To Susan Ryan and Kim Whelan who worked so tirelessly and professionally to make this a reality. I could not have found more skillful people whose strengths complemented my weaknesses.

To my partner Barry Weiner, whose unfailing support allowed us to open the checkbook when the possibility of returns were vague.

To Eva Jakubowski, who makes books and computers come together. If I ever figured out what you do I'd probably thank you even more.

And finally, to my mother, who aside from being a librarian demonstrated to me at a very early age that a universe of knowledge could be found between the covers of that most marvelous and wonderful of all things...books.

— *Jonathan Russo*
Lintel Press

Table of Contents

Publisher's Note

We hope that this book will serve as more than a conventional guide to historic homes. For while we set out to create a detailed, informative, and unique guide, devoted exclusively to historic houses, we also had higher goals. For those among you who enjoy, and are devoted to, preservation, architecture, decorative and fine arts, what we have attempted will be self-evident. For those who are first becoming interested in the world of historic Americana, we will try to give you a helping hand. For all those venturing across these historic thresholds, we invite you in, knowing that you will not be disappointed.

The following pages contain a wealth of information on the fascinating people—both the famous and not so famous—who lived in these houses, as well as descriptions of the houses and their remarkable collections. What can also be found within this book, beyond the listings of locations, hours, and tour information, is the most elusive of all things—wonder. For behind each and every house listing lies a world of wonder. Not the manufactured kind, packaged and sold to replace the imagination. Not the superficial kind which manipulates the emotions at the expense of the intellect. But wonder on a higher plane.

The first wonder is that any of these houses still exist and that anyone cares at all. Our society has often achieved its enviable position of affluence by focusing on the new and disposing with the old. The desire for the latest architectural styles, furnishings, and conveniences has often meant a bulldozing of the past, to the point where even the recent past is endangered. Of course, this has always been so; Colonial homes were remodeled into Greek Revivals at the expense of their original architecture. But the changes are far more devastating now, instead of remodeling the houses, we are tearing them down altogether. Time after time, when we went to a historic house in a small city or village, our guide's first statement was that the historic society had been formed to prevent the house from being torn down, often to make room for a parking lot. Historic houses have been made into rooming houses, beauty parlors, or high rises. As we walked through a fifteen room, four-story house built in 1840, complete with irreplaceable architectural details, the enormity of the "let's tear it down" mentality became overwhelming.

Of course the houses themselves possess more wonder than anything else. It is a sorrowfully calloused person who cannot experience the past in a historic house. To tour the prosperous ship captain's house in historic Newport, Rhode Island is to wonder at the riches of furniture, decorations, textiles and food stuffs that ships and winds provided. To tour the 18th-century stone houses of Washington, Pennsylvania with their two-foot thick walls is to wonder at the fortitude of their inhabitants as they struggled against attacks and defended themselves against the cold winters. The very cosmopolitanism of mercantile families in Greenwich Village, New York permeates the air of the historic houses there. One can sense the refinement these people must have felt when they sipped brandy and smoked cigars in their impressive parlors. To be told why people used fireplace screens —so that the wax women used as a cosmetic to fill in their pockmarked faces would not melt—is an explanation of a common object that brings the past alive in a personal and wonderful way. The treasures of art, architectural details, furniture, household implements, and costumes contained in these homes also makes us pause in reflection. Things were viewed very differently when they were made by hand and scarce. There is an education for all of us living in a throw-away culture.

So it is to the individuals, organizations and societies who are saving, preserving and displaying historic America that our sense of wonder and gratitude is directed. Sometimes, we would drive by a mall and see endless cars, stores and shoppers, and know that the energy of the town was now clearly centered at the mall. Then we would arrive at our destination, the local historic house, and find we were the only visitors. Despite this daunting competition from today's faster paced entertainments, our guide was cheerful, patient and full of enthusiasm for the wonder of the house.

We admire the volunteers who fundraise, lobby, catalogue, lecture, and guide their fellow citizens. As visitors, we enrich ourselves because of the efforts of the organizations and individuals who have labored to restore and revitalize these fine houses. We wish to thank the individuals who have given us their time and energy on these tours, and have given us their cooperation in putting this book together. If, in some small way, this guide helps you in your efforts, please consider it a thank you.

— *Jonathan Russo*
Lintel Press

Editor's Note

*T*hanks to everyone who filled out our questionaire and sent the vast amounts of brochures and booklets which provided the basis for the book. All of the information about the houses has been supplied by the historical organizations and societies themselves; we have tried to reproduce the descriptions, biographical information, and schedule information as accurately as possible. Since many of the houses are subject to uncertain funding, and their hours and activities for visitors vary from season to season, we encourage people to call in advance to verify the information. Wherever possible, we have mentioned other houses located in the same town or village for which we do not have a complete listing. Finally, please contact us if there are other houses you would like to see listed in the next edition.

 *Introduction*

A ll buildings have character, some seem friendly while others have a forbidding feel. Many big buildings demand your attention, while more than a few small ones seem content to let you pass by them unnoticed. Buildings can be eccentric, exotic, familiar, unassuming, warm and welcoming, or cold and sinister; but their individuality is there for all who choose to recognize it.

Since the Bicentennial celebration, millions of Americans have come to appreciate another element of the architectural personality. Like people of a certain age, antique buildings have survived wars and changes and visitors, wanted and unwanted alike. Their very characters are reflections of times past. Some buildings, like some people, have aged gracefully; some have seen happy and sad times, but all of them have something to teach us, about their histories and even ourselves. The truth is that all old houses have something in common with your house and mine.

I fell in love with houses and buildings early in my life—I studied architecture long before *This Old House* and *Bob Vila's Home Again* introduced millions to some intriguing rehabilitation jobs with which I've been involved. My fondness for buildings in general and my experience with old houses in particular only heightens my appreciation of the houses you'll meet in these pages, and the uncompromising approach the many historical societies, community organizations, individuals, and groups have taken to getting the houses restored just right.

These houses represent an immense range of the American experience. Every one has a story to tell, whether it's of the people who built the house or those who lived there; the community that is the context for the place; or even the events that led to its preservation; which so often involve battles with developers or others insensitive to the value and merit in a tumbledown, antique structure.

Each of these houses provides a unique opportunity to step back in time, to learn about how our ancestors lived. Which is another way of saying, these houses offer a glimpse of history, that wonderful state of mind that explains, in part, why and who we are today. I hope in some way we can help inspire you to visit these houses and those other eras that have so much to teach us.

—Bob Vila

Alabama

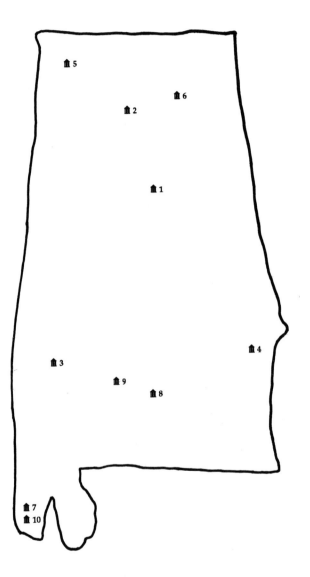

1. **Birmingham**
   Arlington

2. **Decatur**
   The Old State Bank

3. **Demopolis**
   Bluff Hall

4. **Eufaula**
   Shorter Mansion
   Hart House

5. **Florence**
   Pope's Tavern
   W.C. Handy House

6. **Huntsville**
   Weeden House

7. **Mobile**
   Bragg-Mitchell Mansion
   Oakleigh Period House Museum
   Bernstein-Bush House
   Carlen House Museum

8. **Montgomery**
   First White House of the Confederacy
   Scott & Zelda Fitzgerald Museum

9. **Selma**
   Sturdivant Hall

10. **Theodore**
    Bellingrath Gardens and Home

Arlington

Contact: Arlington Historical Association
Open: Tues.-Sat. 10 a.m.–4 p.m.;
  Sun. 1–4 p.m.; closed major holidays
Admission: Adults $3; students $2.
  Guided tours by appointment.
Suggested Time to View House: 45 minutes
Facilities on Premises: Gift shop, book
  store, luncheons for groups (12 or more)
Best Season to View House: Spring
Number of Yearly Visitors: 18,000
Year House Built: c. 1850
Style of Architecture: Greek Revival
Number of Rooms: 9

On-Site Parking: Yes **Wheelchair Access:** Yes

Description of House

William S. Mudd, the original owner, was a judge, an Alabama legislator, and one of the founders of the city of Birmingham in 1872. Henry DeBardeleben, the second owner, was the son-in-law of noted antebellum Alabama industrialist Daniel Pratt and Henry was also the first to build a post-war iron furnace in Birmingham. Robert S. Munger purchased the house around 1895 and made extensive Colonial Revival interior renovations. He also planted the Edwardian gardens which adorn the house. It was at Arlington that General James Wilson of the Union Army made plans to destroy the Alabama iron furnaces which supplied iron for the Confederate arsenal in Selma. Wilson's ranks divided at Arlington with one detachment moving to Tuscaloosa, where they destroyed the campus of the University of Alabama in April, 1865.

From the front of the house, visitor's will notice Arlington's graceful symmetry, typical of Greek Revival architecture. This style was popular in the South because of its structural suitability to the hot southern climate. The numerous windows and central hallway, both upstairs and downstairs, permitted effective cross ventilation, necessary to combat the summer heat in an era before air conditioning. Furnishings form a collection of American decorative art (1780 to 1880). Much of the collection has been obtained through the generosity of local donors.

Notable Collections on Exhibit

The collected furniture belonged to prominent Alabamians during the pre Civil War era. A portrait of Seminde Chieftain Osceola by William Laning painted at Fort Moultrie, South Carolina in 1838 hangs on the wall. There are also excellent collections of silver, porcelain, paintings, and textiles on exhibit.

The Old State Bank

925 Bank Street NE
Decatur, AL 35602
(205) 350-5060

Contact: City of Decatur/Old Bank Board of Directors

Open: Mon.-Fri. 9:30 a.m.–12 p.m., 1–4:30 p.m.; weekends and other hours by advance notification

Admission: Free, donations accepted. Guided tours, lecture series, various workshops, Christmas tour.

Suggested Time to View House: 30 minutes

Facilities on Premises: Sales desk

Description of Grounds: Period herb garden, "Pedestrian Hall" and "Founder's Park"

Style of Architecture: Classic Revival (blends elements of late Federal with early Greek Revival)

Best Season to View House: Summer

Number of Yearly Visitors: 6,000

Number of Rooms: 8

Year House Built: 1833

On-Site Parking: Yes **Wheelchair Access:** Yes

Description of House

Through 158 years of often turbulent history, the Old State Bank has survived as a proud monument to Decatur's past. Built in 1833 to house the Tennessee Valley branch of the state bank, the building is important not only for the rich history associated with its diverse uses, but also for its contribution to the architectural history and landscape of Alabama. It's hard to imagine anyone calling a bank home, but for reasons of security a cashier's apartment was placed over the bank. Research continues on the histories of the many cashiers who lived in this unusual dwelling.

The Old State Bank is an early forerunner of the Greek Revival style in Alabama, and influenced the design of other buildings in the state until the outbreak of the Civil War. Originally, the building was meant to employ the Federal style but the addition of the cashier's apartment resulted in a change of design. The building features a first floor bank lobby complete with the original walk-in vault and a replica of the teller's cage. The second floor, which contains the residence, was not only used as an apartment, but also as an area to entertain and house prospective clients. It now exhibits period furnishings. The apartment was considered an outpost of elegance during the days when Decatur was on the Alabama frontier.

Notable Collections on Exhibit

Most furnishings are of the Empire style, but are simple, less elaborate pieces that were common in this frontier location.

Bluff Hall

North Commissioners Avenue
P.O. Box 159
Demopolis, AL 36732
(205) 289-1666

Contact: Marengo County Historical Society
Open: Tues.-Fri. 10 a.m.–5 p.m.; Sun.
2–5 p.m., closed major holidays
Admission: Adults $3, youths (6-18) $1.
Suggested Time to View House: 1 hour
Facilities on Premises: Gift shop
Description of Grounds: Landscaped
grounds surround the mansion
Best Season to View House: Summer
Year House Built: 1832
Style of Architecture: Federal with Greek
Revival additions
Number of Rooms: 15
On-Site Parking: Yes
Wheelchair Access: Partial

Description of House

Francis Strother Lyon, a lawyer, cotton planter, and respected politician and statesman, built this impressive house in 1832. The house was named for the high chalk bluff on which it stands, overlooking the Tombigbee River. Lyon served in both the United States and the Confederate Congress. During the Civil War, Bluff Hall received many Confederate officers as guests and President Jefferson Davis himself was entertained here in October of 1863.

Bluff Hall represents two major trends in the architecture of the antebellum South. The original rectangular brick structure was a plain Federal townhouse. By 1850, the columned front portico and the large rear wing were added, and the entire exterior painted white—changes which reflect a shift in taste to the more fashionable Greek Revival style. Today the house contains a number of period rooms with furnishings representing Empire and early Victorian styles. In addition, there is a small museum of local history exhibiting the collections of the society.

Notable Collections on Exhibit

Bluff Hall showcases an impressive collection of antique clothing in addition to the period furniture.

Additional Information

Visitors to Demopolis should not miss the opportunity to visit Gaineswood (on Cedar Avenue), a stately Greek Revival mansion constructed around a two-room log cabin.

Shorter Mansion

340 North Eufaula Avenue
Eufaula, AL 36027
(205) 687-3793

Contact: Eufaula Heritage Association
Open: Mon.-Sat. 10 a.m.–4 p.m. CST; Sun.
1–4 p.m.; closed national holidays
Admission: $3. Annual Pilgrimage (first
weekend in April)
Suggested Time to View House: 45 minutes
Facilities on Premises: Historical books
available
Best Season to View House: Mid March
Number of Yearly Visitors: 10,000
Year House Built: 1906
Style of Architecture: Neo Classical
Number of Rooms: 22

Description of House

The Shorter Mansion was built by Eli Sims Shorter II, a cotton planter, and his wife, Wileyna Lamar Shorter, an heiress from Macon, Georgia. The mansion is recognized as an exceptional example of Neo-Classical Revival Architecture and one of the most outstanding homes in Alabama. Corinthian columns support an ornate entablature, and the frieze is of delicately molded icanthus leaves and scrolls. This gracious home now houses the collections of the local historical society as well as a fine selection of period furnishings.

Notable Collections on Exhibit

The exhibits features Waterford crystal and cut-glass chandeliers, a double-pedestal Regency banquet table, Regency sideboard and wine server, twelve English Chippendale chairs, painted photographs of antebellum homes, portrait of Fannie Shorter Upshaw (wife of a local leading citizen), antique mirror (c. 1860-80), Rosewood square grand piano, and portraits of the six Alabama governors from Barbour County.

Additional Information

Like many Southern cities, Eufaula hosts an annual pilgrimage in April which celebrates the antebellum mansions and customs of the Old South. Each year many privately-owned historic houses are open to the public and other celebrations take place in the city. Contact the Chamber of Commerce for more information at (205) 687-6664.

Hart House

211 North Eufaula Avenue
Eufaula, AL 36027
(205) 687-9755

Contact: Historic Chattahoochee
  Commission
Open: Mon.-Fri. 8 a.m.–5 p.m. CST;
  closed state holidays
Admission: Free
Suggested Time to View House: 15 minutes
Facilities on Premises: Book store
Number of Yearly Visitors: 1,500 plus
Year House Built: c. 1850
Style of Architecture: Greek Revival
Number of Rooms: 12
On-Site Parking: Yes
Wheelchair Access: Yes

Description of House

The house was built by John Hart, who moved to Eufaula from New Hampshire and became a prominent merchant and farmer. This beautiful Greek Revival structure is noted for its outstanding purity of line. When first constructed, the house was on the western edge of the town, but as the town grew it soon became part of the downtown area. The Hart House was one of only five Eufaula buildings recorded by the Historic American Building Survey in 1935. The building was also entered on the National Register of Historic Places in 1973 as part of the Seth Lore Historic District. Hart House was purchased by the Historic Chattahoochee Commission for use as its headquarters in 1985.

Some furnishings on exhibit are original to the house, others have been collected and are appropriate for the mid 19th century. Also of interest is an unusual back-lit display of photographs.

Additional Information

Visitors to Eufaula should also try to include a stop at the Sheppard Cottage (East Barbour Street), another home of a transplanted northerner, Dr. Edmund Shorter. Built in 1837, the cottage is considered one of the oldest dwellings in the city. It now houses the Eufaula Chamber of Commerce.

Pope's Tavern

203 Hermitage Drive
Florence, AL
(205) 760-6439

Contact: Florence Department of Arts and Museums

Open: Tues.-Sat. 10 a.m.–4 p.m.

Admission: Adults $2; youths (under 18) $.50. Guided tours, annual Frontier Day Celebration with music by the Shoals Dulcimer Society held first weekend in June.

Suggested Time to View House: 30 minutes

Facilities on Premises: Sales desk

Description of Grounds: A lovely lawn surrounds the house

Year House Built: 1811

Style of Architecture: Southern Colonial Vernacular

Number of Rooms: 8

On-Site Parking: Yes **Wheelchair Access:** Yes

Description of House

This one-time stagecoach stop, tavern, and inn is one of the oldest structures in Florence. Christopher Cheatham, a native of Scotland, is said to have built this tavern for LeRoy Pope and Thomas Bibb. The building's convenient location on Military Road (now called Hermitage Drive) made it an ideal center for commerce. Local legend recounts that General Andrew Jackson stopped here in 1814 on his march to battle the British at New Orleans. The tavern was also used as a hospital by both Confederate and Union troops during the Civil War. Pope's Tavern was later known as the Lambeth House for its most recent owners. Felix Lambeth, Sr. acquired the house in 1874 and it remained in the Lambeth family until it was purchased by the city in 1965.

The brick exterior of this modest structure was constructed of hand-made bricks baked in a kiln on the site. A veranda stretches the full length of the front and is supported by poplar columns. The large windows have nine panes to the sash and were fashioned from some of the first glass manufactured in this country. The tavern is completely furnished with period furniture and also exhibits Civil War memorabilia.

Additional Information

Visitors to Florence are also encouraged to tour the W.C. Handy House, home to the well-known musician and composer, and the Oscar Kennedy House (303 North Pine Street), one of the oldest Federal-style structures in the region.

W.C. Handy House

620 W. College Street
Florence, AL 35630
(205) 760-6434

Contact: Florence Historical Board
Open: Tues.-Sat. 9 a.m.–12 p.m. and
1–4 p.m., closed major holidays
Admission: Adults $2; children (under 12)
$.50. Annual W.C. Handy Music Festival
held first week in Aug.
Suggested Time to View House: 30 minutes
Facilities on Premises: Sales desk, library

Description of Grounds: Small lawn and
garden surrounding house
Best Season to View House: Summer-fall
Year House Built: 1870
Style of Architecture: Log cabin
Number of Rooms: 3
On-Site Parking: Yes

Description of House

The man known as the "Father of the Blues", W.C. Handy, was born in this simple log cabin on November 16, 1873. Handy is best known as the composer of "St. Louis Blues" and "Memphis Blues", but in his lifetime he wrote more than 150 secular and sacred musical compositions. He was the son and grandson of ministers and his father hoped that W.C. would follow in his footsteps to the pulpit. Young Handy had different ideas. He studied music for eleven years as a child in the local black public school and at the age of eighteen left his home in Florence and soon went on to write the songs that would make him famous. He later opened Handy Brothers Music Company, a music publishing firm in New York, which he managed through two onsets of blindness, the second of which was permanent. W.C. Handy died in New York City on March 28, 1958.

The Handy House features the original hand-hewn logs and appears much as it did during Handy's childhood in the late 19th century. The three rooms are devoted to showing his life and house the most complete collection of Handy's personal papers and artifacts in the world. Many of the furnishings are original; others have been collected to represent the period of Handy's youth.

Notable Collections on Exhibit

The extensive collection of Handy memorabilia includes his famous trumpet, his personal piano, handwritten sheet music, his library, citations from well-known people, photographs, and other artifacts. In addition, the library houses valuable resources for the study of black history and culture.

Additional Information

The W.C. Handy Music Festival is held each year in Florence during the first week in August. Sponsored by Music Preservation, Inc., this annual event pays tribute to Handy's musical legacy as "Father of the Blues."

Weeden House

300 Gates Avenue, S.E.
Huntsville, AL 35801
(205) 536-7718

Contact: Twickenham Historic Preservation
District Association
Open: Tues.-Sun. 1–4 p.m.
Admission: Adults $2; seniors $1.50;
children (under 12) $1. Guided tours.
Suggested Time to View House:
30–60 minutes
Facilities on Premises: Small gift shop
Description of Grounds: Small yard
Best Season to View House: Spring
Number of Yearly Visitors: 5,000-7,000
Year House Built: 1819
Style of Architecture: Federal
Number of Rooms: 7
On-Site Parking: Yes

Description of House

The house was the birthplace and lifelong home of poet and artist Maria Howard Weeden. Impoverished by the Civil War, she turned to writing and art to supplement her income and lived to see her talents acknowledged far beyond the confines of her native city. Four volumes of her verse were published, each of them illustrated by the writer herself despite frail health and failing eyesight. She died in 1905.

The Weeden House is a superb example of Federal architecture, with such notable exterior features as roof cornice medallions, a frieze below the front eave, and its doorway surmounted by a remarkable leaded-glass fanlight. Inside the entrance, a spiral staircase leads gracefully upward. The elaborate woodwork with its delicate reeding and fluting is handcarved, as are the three intricately carved Federal mantels. Aside from a Greek revival period door and two mantels installed about 1845 and the kitchen (c. 1870) now used as an office, the house stands today as it was originally built. Walls and mantels are painted in authentic early 19th-century colors. Most of the furnishings are collected and appropriate for the period, including a few items that belonged to the Weeden family.

Notable Collections on Exhibit

On display is a comprehensive collection of Maria's works, large and small, ranging from early illustrations and practice oils to the fully-realized paintings of her maturity, notably her affectionate watercolor portraits of local people. Also noteworthy are her studies of wildflowers, painted in their natural settings.

Bragg-Mitchell Mansion

1906 Springhi
Mobile,
(205)

Open: Mon.-Fri. 10 a.m.–4 p.m.,
Sun. 1–4 p.m.

Admission: Adults $3; children $2. Guided
tours, luncheons for groups (30 or more).

Suggested Time to View House: 1 hour

Description of Grounds: Small sculpture
garden

Best Season to View House: March-Dec.

Number of Yearly Visitors: 10,000

Year House Built: 1855

Style of Architecture: Greek Revival

Number of Rooms: 20

On-Site Parking: Yes **Wheelchair Access:** Yes

Description of House

The original owner of this impressive mansion, Judge Bragg, came from
North Carolina to Mobile in 1835 and started a law practice. He was soon a
big success and in 1842 he was elected circuit judge, a post he held for nine
years. In 1852, he was elected to the U.S. Congress. Later, in 1931, the
mansion was purchased by Mr. and Mrs. A.S. Mitchell who restored and
maintained the house and gardens for many years.

The house has eighteen rooms, all built on a grand scale. The ceilings
throughout the downstairs are fifteen-feet high. The spacious entrance hall
which extends the full length of the house ends with a sweeping curved
staircase. The T-shaped plan of the house allows for maximum ventilation
during hot Gulf Coast summers. The furnishings are of the period from 1855
to 1910.

Notable Collections on Exhibit

Exquisite damask draperies, a hundred year-old sterling tea service,
hand carved Chippendale chairs, and a pair of rare cobalt-blue Sevres urns
decorate this attractive mansion.

Oakleigh House Museum and Complex

350 Oakleigh Place
Mobile, AL 36604
(205) 432-1281

Contact: Historic Mobile Preservation Society
Open: Mon.-Sat., 10 a.m.–4 p.m. ;
Sun. 2–4 p.m.
Admission: Adults $4; children (6-18) $1;
students (with ID) $2; seniors $3; groups
(10 or more) $3. Guided tours, candlelight
Christmas (first weekend in Dec.)
Suggested Time to View House: 45 minutes
Facilities on Premises: Gift shop

Description of Grounds: 3½ landscaped
acres include a walk through the Memory
Garden of pear trees, azaleas and
dogwoods. Many oaks are over
150 years old.
Best Season to View House: March and April
Number of Yearly Visitors: 18,465
Year House Built: 1833
Style of Architecture: Greek Revival
Number of Rooms: 11
On-Site Parking: Yes

Description of House

The Oakleigh Mansion has been home to many prominent citizens of Mobile since it was first built in 1837 by James Roper. Roper was a successful merchant and his taste is evident in the beautiful details of the house. In 1955, the Mobile Preservation Society acquired the antebellum mansion for use as a historic site.

Oakleigh is museum noted for its architectural design and unique features. This raised creole cottage was typical of the modest middle-class city dwellers along the Gulf Coast. Oakleigh is a fine example of the T-shape, off-center hall plan, with lovely proportions and Greek Revival detail. The main portion of the house is of hand-hewn lumber; tool marks can still be seen in some areas of the house. The bricks used in the masonry walls on the ground floor were made on the property from clay dug from the grounds. The excavation that resulted is now the Sunken Garden. All visitors enter the museum by the cantilever stairway which is the original entrance to Oakleigh. The furnishings are of the same period of the house, however not original to Oakleigh. The many portraits on display are of prominent Mobilians or of others who have figured in the history of the region.

Notable Collections on Exhibit

The mansion exhibits an eclectic array of furnishings and decorative arts. All upper level furnishings are Empire, Regency and early Victorian while the art objects, including a painting by Thomas Sully, are mainly French and English in origin. The mirrors, chandeliers and the marble mantels were salvaged from old Mobile homes. The draperies in the twin parlors were woven in France of silk and eighteen-karat gold filament. The clocks are English, French and American timepieces, many of which are kept running today. Carnival memorabilia can be seen in the Mardi Gras Room. The textiles are mostly hand woven of the type used during this period. An unusual collection of hair jewelry can be seen in the Batre Bedroom.

Additional Information

The archives building is open to study original clippings, photographs, books and maps concerning the Mobile area which a collection that dates as far back as the 1820s.

‚tein-Bush House

Contact: Museums of the City of Mobile
Open: Tues.-Sat. 10 a.m.–5 p.m.,
  Sun. 1–5 p.m.
Activities: Guided tours; audio cassettes

Best Season to View House: Year round
Year House Built: 1872
Style of Architecture: Italianate
On-Site Parking: Yes

Description of House

The Bernstein-Bush House, a graceful Italianate townhouse built in 1872, has witnessed much of the city's fascinating history. As the state's only seaside port and the site of the oldest Mardi Gras celebration in America, the museum has a lot to offer visitors new to the city.

The collections span every period of history from the time of prehistoric Indian tribes to the present. The Colonization Room represents the periods of French, English, Spanish, and, finally, American rule with documents, artifacts and paintings. The Civil War Room displays uniforms, documents, paintings, models and weapons, including the sword of the Confederate hero Raphael Semmes. The Rutherford Carriage Room contains beautiful horse drawn carriages of days gone by. There are also comprehensive exhibits devoted to prehistoric artifacts, ship models, and an unusual display of early 20th-century women's fashions.

Notable Collections on Exhibit

While all of the exhibits are of interest, the Staples Gallery is unique in that it traces the history of Mardi Gras and displays the elaborate coronation gowns worn by Mardi Gras queens from 1960 to the present.

Carlen House Museum

355 Government Street
Mobile, AL 36602
(205) 434-7620

Contact: Museums of the City of Mobile
Open: Tues.-Sat. 10 a.m.–5 p.m.,
  Sun. 1–5 p.m.
Activities: Guided tours; audio cassettes
Best Season to View House: Year round
Year House Built: 1842
Style of Architecture: Creole Cottage
On-Site Parking: Yes

Description of House

The Carlen House is a beautiful example of the style of architecture unique to this area—the "Creole Cottage." Located on the campus of Murphy High School, well within the city, the Carlen House was a day's wagon ride to town when built in 1842 by Michael Carlen. The house features full-length galleries in front and back, a central hall, a kitchen filled with curious primitives, and random-width pine floors that still show the saw marks.

Outfitted with 19th-century furnishings and showcasing period fashions, the Carlen House is a charming step back in time. The cottage is also surrounded by decorative gardens filled with azaleas, magnolias, crepe myrtle and other plantings.

Additional Information

Visitors to Mobile should also make time for the Richards D.A.R (256 N. Joachim), an antebellum townhouse built by a ship captain. The house exhibits an excellent collection of early Victorian furnishings and features a walk through beautiful formal gardens as part of the guided tour.

First White House of the Confederacy

664 Washington Avenue
P.O. Box 64
Montgomery, AL 36130
(205) 242-1861

Contact: White House Association of
Alabama
Open: Mon.-Fri. 8 a.m.–4:30 p.m., Sat.-Sun.
9 a.m.–4:30 p.m.
Admission: Donation. Guided tours.
Suggested Time to View House: 1 hour
Description of Grounds: Landscaped lawn
Best Season to View House: Spring-fall
Year House Built: 1832
Style of Architecture: Federal
On-Site Parking: Yes

Description of House

This unpretentious two-story structure served as the first Executive Mansion for the Confederacy in 1861 by decree of the first Provisional Congress. President-elect Jefferson Davis and his wife lived here for just a few short months before moving to Richmond, Virginia, but the historical importance of the house lives on in its finely furnished period rooms and exhibits related to the Confederacy.

Before it became the White House, the house had been built and occupied by William Sayre (a relative of F. Scott Fitzgerald's wife Zelda) and several other prominent Montgomerians. The original Federal architecture was renovated in the fashionable Italianate style by a later occupant, Colonel Winter. The refined entranceway leads to a spacious interior with reception halls, double parlors, and a grand dining room suitable for entertaining and socializing. The house will always be remembered, however, for its importance in the Confederate cause, and the enduring legacy of the Civil War.

Notable Collections on Exhibit

Today the house displays a large amount of original furnishings both from the Davis period of occupancy and others that have been collected from other sources. The President's bedroom exhibits a special "button" bed made specifically for Davis, personal artifacts such as a walking stick and a valise, and the last photograph of Davis taken before he died. Each of the other rooms displays furniture used by the Davis's at this house, at Beauvoir (his final home), or other places that they visited during their travels. The relic room has many rare documents and artifacts related to the Confederacy.

Scott & Zelda Fitzgerald Museum

Felder Avenue
Montgomery, AL 36101
(205) 262-1911

Contact: Scott & Zelda Fitzgerald Museum
Association

Open: Wed.-Fri. 10 a.m.–2 p.m., Sat.-Sun.
1–5 p.m.

Admission: Donation. Guided tours,
lectures, films, special events related to
the Fitzgeralds' life.

Suggested Time to View House: 1 hour

Description of Grounds: Located in the
Cloverdale section of Montgomery

Best Season to View House: Spring-fall

Year House Built: 1910

On-Site Parking: Yes

Style of Architecture: Georgian vernacular

Description of House

One of America's most distinguished literary couples, Scott and Zelda Fitzgerald, lived in this modest brick home with their daughter, Scottie, from October, 1931 through the following spring. Those interested in the history of American literature will enjoy a visit to this house where Scott worked on one of his most famous novels, *Tender is the Night*, and Zelda wrote portions of her only published novel, *Save Me the Waltz*. The couple met and courted in Montgomery when Scott was stationed nearby during World War I. They were married in New York in 1920, and returned to live here together briefly after spending many years in New York and France during which time Zelda had begun to show signs of mental illness. She spent the rest of her years in either Montgomery, where she lived with her mother, or in a mental institution in Ashville, North Carolina, where she died in a fire in 1948. Although *Tender is the Night* was well-received, it was not a financial success and Scott moved to Hollywood in the early 1930s to try his luck as a screenwriter. Unfortunately, he never was able to reclaim the notoriety he achieved during the 1920s and died of a heart attack in 1940 at the age of 44.

The museum has been restored due to the hard work and determination of a local couple who learned that the house was to be torn down in order to build condominiums in 1987. In addition to restoring the house to its original appearance, a tremendous effort was made to collect Fitzgerald artifacts and memorabilia. The museum is a tribute to the couple who embodied the Jazz Age for many Americans and for literature lovers around the world.

Notable Collections on Exhibit

Among the many items of Fitzgerald memorabilia on display are two marble-topped tables from Zelda's childhood home, several of Zelda's paintings, a number of books from the Fitzgerald's contemporaries bearing his inscription, and two old typewriters resembling the ones used by the writers. In addition, there is an extensive exhibit of portraits and photographs as well as reproductions of the couple's correspondence.

Sturdivant Hall

713 Mabry Street
Selma, AL 36701
(205) 872-5626

Contact: Sturdivant Museum Association
Open: 9 a.m.–4 p.m., closed Mon.
Admission: Adults $5; students $2. Tours
on the hour, special events include
annual pilgrimage of historic homes-last
week in March, re-enactment of Selma
Ball-April, Riverfront Market and Tale
Tellin-2nd week Oct.
Suggested Time to View House: 1 hour
Facilities on Premises: Gift shop
Description of Grounds: Lovely lawn and
back courtyard
Best Season to View House: Summer-fall
Number of Yearly Visitors: 15,000
Number of Rooms: 10
On-Site Parking: Yes

Year House Built: 1852
Style of Architecture: Greek Revival
Wheelchair Access: Partial

Description of House

Sturdivant Hall, located in the historic area of Selma, is considered one of the state's outstanding historic homes open to the public. Construction began on this large Greek Revival mansion in 1852 by Colonial Edward Watts, a local resident. The architect was Semian Thomas Helm Lee, a cousin of Robert E. Lee. The next owner, John McGee Parkman, was an industrious and ambitious young man who rose rapidly from bank teller to bank president during the 1860s. Unfortunately, the bank suffered huge losses in cotton speculation and Parkham was imprisoned for his actions. He died while trying to escape from prison at the very young age of twenty-nine and so was never able to return to his lovely mansion.

This brick and marble structure has been described as "the finest Greek Revival neo-classic antebellum mansion in the Southeast." The building underwent substantial restoration in 1957 and visitors today will be able to see detailed ceiling freezes made of plaster and an unusual spiral staircase leading from the third floor to the widow's walk. The house is named for Mr. and Mrs. Robert Sturdivant who made a large donation to the city in 1957 in order to use the mansion to house their impressive collection of Southern antiques.

Notable Collections on Exhibit

The handsome furnishings represent a fine ensemble of period furniture, portraits, silver, dolls, and toys. The kitchen, which is separate from the house, has a large assortment of antebellum utensils and other kitchen and household novelties.

Bellingrath Gardens and Home

12401 Bellingrath Gardens Road
Theodore, AL 36582
(205) 973-2217

Contact: Bellingrath-Morse Foundation

Open: 8 a.m.–6 p.m., in winter last tour starts at 3:30 p.m.

Admission: Combination house and garden: Adults $14, children (6-11) $11, under 6 $8; Garden only: adults $6.50; children (6-11) $3.25. Guided tours, special exhibitions.

Suggested Time to View House: 1 hour–house, 2½ hours–house and gardens

Facilities on Premises: Gift shop, cafeteria, pet motel

Description of Grounds: The 65-acre grounds feature a magnificent array of camellias, rose bushes, azaleas, and chrysanthemums

Best Season to View House: The different varieties of flowers bloom at various seasons of the year.

Number of Yearly Visitors: 10,000

Year House Built: 1935

Style of Architecture: Brick mansion

Number of Rooms: 15

On-Site Parking: Yes

Wheelchair Access: Partial

Description of House

Bellingrath is best known for its magnificent gardens which cover over sixty-five acres. The property belonging to Mr. and Mrs. Walter Bellingrath was originally the site of a small fishing camp on the banks of the Fowl River. The Bellingraths began planting azaleas and camellias for their own pleasure in 1927; soon the gardens had become so extensive and beautiful that many came from Mobile to see them, and so they were opened to the public. This lovely brick house was built in 1935 and was the Bellingrath's home until Walter Bellingrath's death in 1955.

In the midst of the colorful gardens stands the brick and wrought iron mansion. The house's porches and railings are also covered with beautiful flowers, adding to the ornamentation. According to the architect, George B. Rogers, the house is a "mingling of the French, English and Mediterranean influences, while the interior represents a blend of decor embracing chiefly the English Renaissance and Colonial America." Inside, the house remains exactly as the Bellingraths left it with all of their furnishings intact. Both the home and the gardens are listed on the National Register of Historic Places.

The antique furnishings represent a wide variety of styles ranging from an English Chippendale dining room set to 18th and 19th-century Dresden china to a kitchen table made of Alabama marble.

Notable Collections on Exhibit

The home showcases a wonderful collection of furnishings and decorations including a French porcelain clock by Jacob Petit (c. 1790), a rare Versailles centerpiece of Meissen porcelain and ormolu, needlepoint portraits of George Washington and Robert E. Lee, and four different sets of twenty-two carat gold overlay service plates as well as nine complete dinner services. In addition, the gardens feature the most complete public display of the porcelain sculptures of Edward Boehm.

Florida

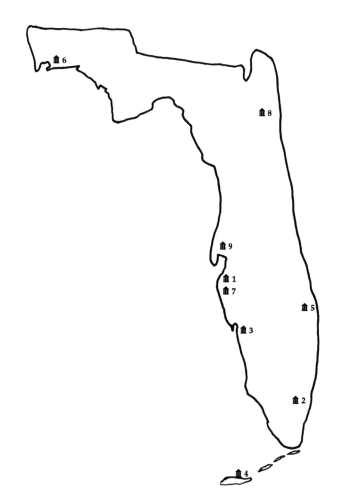

1. **Brandenton**
   Old Settler's House

2. **Fort Lauderdale**
   Bonnet House

3. **Fort Myers**
   The Henry Ford Home
   Thomas Edison Winter Home

4. **Key West**
   Ernest Hemingway Home and Museum
   Little White House
   Audubon House and Gardens
   The Wreckers Museum

5. **Palm Beach**
   Whitehall

6. **Pensacola**
   Historic Pensacola Village

7. **Sarasota**
   Ca' d'Zan

8. **St. Augustine**
   Gonzalez-Alvarez House
   Avero House

9. **Tampa**
   Tampa Bay Hotel
   Peter O. Knight House

Old Settler's House

604 15th Street East
Brandenton, FL 34208
(813) 749-7165

Contact: Manatee County Historical
Commission, Inc.

Open: Mon.-Fri. 9 a.m.–4:30 p.m.; Sun.
2–5 p.m.; closed Sun. in July and Aug.

Admission: Free. Guided tours.

Suggested Time to View House: 20 minutes

Facilities on Premises: Gift shop

Best Season to View House: All seasons

Number of Yearly Visitors: 35,000

Year House Built: 1912

Style of Architecture: "Cracker" Gothic

Number of Rooms: 6

On-Site Parking: Yes

Wheelchair Access: Yes

Description of House

This is an excellent example of a Florida rural farmhouse built between the 1870s and the first World War. The Old Settler's House was home to Will Stephens, a farmer who, with his wife, Roxie, and ten children, homesteaded in eastern Manatee County.

The house was built off the ground for cooling purposes, and is elevated two-and-a-half feet on wooden piers cut from heartpine. The board and batten walls make up the structure which is topped by a wood shingle roof. The house also features dog-trot construction with an attached kitchen, and porches on three sides. The house area also includes a smokehouse, a sugar cane mill and a syrup kettle. The interior maintains its primitive appearance with one fireplace, a wood stove, and no electricity or running water. Outside, an outhouse and a garden complete the complex. All furnishings displayed within the house have been collected and are appropriate to period.

Additional Information

The house forms part of Manatee Village Historical Park, an area which includes the county's first courthouse, built in 1860; a historic church, constructed in 1887; Wiggins Store, one of the region's first brick houses; and Bunker Hill School, a restored one-room schoolhouse.

Bonnet House

900 N. Birch Road
Fort Lauderdale, FL
(305) 563-5393

Contact: Bonnet House, Inc.

Open: May.-Nov., Tues.-Fri. Tours at 10, 11, 12, 1, 2; Sun. tours at 1 and 2 p.m.

Admission: Adults $7, seniors $5, groups (15 or more) **$5** House open by guided tour only, tram rides, nature tours

Suggested Time to View House: 60–90 minutes

Facilities on Premises: Small gift shop

Description of Grounds: 35 acres, half of which are mangrove swamp and not accessible for viewing

Best Season to View House: May-Nov.

Year House Built: 1920

Style of Architecture: Caribbean Plantation

Number of Rooms: 6 rooms open to the public

On-Site Parking: Yes **Wheelchair Access:** No

Description of House

Frederic Barlett, an artist from Chicago, studied art in Europe. In 1920, Frederic married Helen Birch, daughter of Hugh Taylor Birch. As a wedding gift, Mr. Birch gave Fredric and Helen thirty-five acres of beachfront property where Bonnet House is now located. After Helen's death in 1925, Fredric met and eventually married Evelyn Fortune from Indianapolis, who at 104 years old still resides at Bonnet House during the winter months.

This expansive subtropical estate located in the midst of condominiums and hotels along the Fort Lauderdale beach offers a glimpse into the past and displays delightful personal touches of its owners, Evelyn and Frederic Bartlett. The ironwork of the balcony's balustrades were made in New Orleans, and native materials were used in the construction of the house. Additional unique features include the Desert Garden, which opens onto a tropical courtyard, the north window in the artists studio, and paintings located on the ceilings of the loggia areas. The furnishings are a combination of original pieces collected by the owners Frederick and Evelyn Bartlett and period pieces. Many personal artistic accomplishments are also on display.

Notable Collections on Exhibit

Notable pieces of artwork on display include the Veiled Lady, a marble bust by Italian sculptor Giuseppe Croff; murals and artwork by Fredric Clay Bartlett; watercolors and oils done by Evelyn Fortune Bartlett; collections of Wedgeood and Spode china; as well as porcelains, religious figures, bottles, shells and steins. In addition, there are over 3,000 orchids on display in the orchid house.

The Henry Ford Home

2350 McGregor Blvd.
Fort Myers, FL 33901
(813) 334-7419

Contact: City of Fort Myers

Open: Mon.-Sat. 10 a.m.–4 p.m.; closed
Thanksgiving and Christmas Day.

Admission: Adult $5; children (6-12) $3;
children (under 6) free. Guided tours.

Suggested Time to View House: 45 minutes

Description of Grounds: The home is
situated on three and one-half acres on
the banks of the Calcosahatchee River.

Best Season to View House: Year round

Number of Yearly Visitors: 440,000

Year House Built: c. 1910

Number of Rooms: 14

On-Site Parking: Yes **Wheelchair Access:** Yes

Description of House

"Mangoes" was the winter home of Henry Ford, the world's first billionaire, and his wife, Clara. Ford was not a man of leisure; his work, his interests, and his creative ideas were all consuming. Whether engineering a new automobile or sighting an unusual tropical bird, he was an intense man of diverse talents. The Ford home allows visitors to experience the lifestyle of a small town bicycle mechanic and a farm girl who rose to world-wide fame and fortune, and offers a glimpse into the unusual friendship between Henry Ford, Thomas Edison, Charles Lindburgh, Harry Firestone, and Jim Newton. The Ford Home is an authentic restoration of "The Mangoes," the winter residence of Henry and Clara Ford from 1916 to 1931. This graceful fourteen-room home is furnished authentically to the historical period and taste of the Fords, and is located next door to the renowned Edison Winter Home. The beautiful grounds are planted with citrus bamboo and tropical foliage.

Notable Collections on Exhibit

Ford memorabilia on display include a melodeon, an Edison phonograph, and many photographs that have never before been on public display.

Additional Information

Henry Ford worked at many jobs before ending up at the Detroit Edison Illuminating Company, where he met Thomas Edison. They became such good friends that, in 1916, Ford bought the property next to Edison's winter home in Fort Myers, Florida. A combination tour of the Edison home and Ford home is available on Sundays from 12:30 p.m. to 4 p.m.

Thomas Edison Winter Home

2350 McGregor Blvd.
Fort Myers, FL 33901
(813) 334-7419

Contact: City of Fort Myers

Open: Mon.-Sat. 9 a.m.–4 p.m., Sun.
12–4 p.m.; closed Christmas and
Thanksgiving

Admission: Adults $7; children (6-12) $3;
children (under 6) free. Guided tours.

Suggested Time to View House: 90 minutes

Description of Grounds: The tour includes
botanical gardens, swimming pool,
laboratory and a four-room museum.

Best Season to View House: Year round

Number of Yearly Visitors: 440,000

Year House Built: 1886

Style of Architecture: Victorian

Number of Rooms: 7 in main house, 7 plus
servants quarters in guest house

On-Site Parking: Yes **Wheelchair Access:** Yes

Description of House

Thomas Edison, the famous inventor, spent his winters here from from
1886 to 1931. Edison gave us the light bulb, phonograph, and the motion
picture camera. He also maintained a chemical lab here, where he experi-
mented with plants to make rubber. Although Edison died in 1931, his
second wife, Mina, continued to come here until 1947.

Both the main house and guest house are constructed of clear spruce.
They were brought down in sections from Maine. The main house is two-
story building with a wing separated by a breezeway. The house also has
wrap around verandas. Mrs. Edison donated the house to the city in 1947
and left all the furnishings. The only rooms not open to the public at this
time are the bedrooms.

Additional Information

Soon after Thomas Edison built his winter home in Fort Meyers, he met
Henry Ford and was much impressed with the young man's ideas. A lasting
friendship developed between the two men, and Ford and his wife bought
the house next door. A combination tour of the Edison home and Ford home
is available on Sundays from 12:30 p.m. to 4 p.m.

Ernest Hemingway Home and Museum

907 Whitehead Street
Key West, FL 33040
(813) 294-1575

Contact: Ernest Hemingway Home and
Museum
Open: Daily 9 a.m.–5 p.m.
Admission: Adults $6; children $1.50.
Guided tours.

Description of Grounds: The grounds cover
one acre including a pool and guest
house. Many of the trees and shrubs on
the property were planted by Hemingway.
Year House Built: 1851
Style of Architecture: Spanish Colonial

Description of House

Hemingway, considered by many critics to be the greatest American author of all time and certainly one of the most popular, lived in the house with his second wife Pauline and their two sons. Here he penned most of his greatest novels and short stories including *A Farewell to Arms, Death in the Afternoon, Green Hills of Africa, The Short Happy Life of Francis Macomber, The Fifth Column, The Snows of Killmanjaro, For Whom the Bell Tolls,* and *To Have and Have Not.* He rose early and walked via a catwalk to his study in the loft of his poolhouse. Hemingway met writer Martha Gelhorn when she came to Key West to interview him. After his divorce, they were married. Hemingway owned the house from 1931 to 1961.

The spacious mansion was built in Spanish Colonial style of native rock hewn from the grounds. Furnishings, rugs, tile, and chandeliers were brought by the Hemingways from Spain, Africa and Cuba. Visitors can browse as long as they like through the museum and inspect the mementoes the Hemingways gathered on their worldly travels.

Luxuriant, exotic plants and trees decorate the property. Also, Hemmingway had the first swimming pool built in Key West. Constructed in the late 1930s, it is fed by two salt water wells eighteen-feet deep and drained by a dry well eight-feet deep. Having paid $20,000 for the pool, he took a penny from his pocket and pressed it into the wet cement of the surrounding patio. "Here, take the last penny I've got," he said jokingly. The penny is still there.

Additional Information

One living memorial to the late author has been preserved. Many cats and kittens still make their home here... descendants of the nearly fifty cats who lived here when "Papa" Hemingway—author, Nobel Prize winner, bullfight aficionado, big game hunter, deep-sea fisherman, world adventurer... and cat lover—called this his home.

Little White House

111 Front Street, P.O. Box 6443
Key West, FL 33041
(305) 294-9911

Contact: Little White House Company
Open: Daily 9 a.m.–5 p.m.
Activities: Guided tours

Description of Grounds: The house is located at the Navy Submarine Base in Key West.
Best Season to View House: Year round
Year House Built: 1890

Description of House

Historians rank Harry S Truman, thirty-third President of the United States, among America's ten best Presidents. This is particularly interesting because he was not popular during his Presidency (1945-52). This period is marked by many noteworthy events including the authorization of the first atomic bomb against Japan which brought about Japan's unconditional surrender, the creation of the Marshall plan which provided Europe with much-needed funds and assistance to rebuild after World War II, and the defense of South Korea after the invasion of North Korea. Truman also openly opposed Joseph McCarthy and his "red-scare" tactics.

The Little White House is located on land purchased by the Navy in 1854 for $10,400. In 1890, a New York contractor received $7,489 to build two frame dwellings, two stories high, without cellars, and surrounded with piazzas on both floors. In the early years of the 20th century, the two homes were converted into one and became the home of the base commandant. In June 1953, the house once again became two houses but returned to a single family dwelling in 1957. The restoration and interpretation of the house, which began in 1989, has been overseen by the Division of Archives, History and Records Management of the Department of State.

The Harry S Truman Little White House Museum captures the 175 halcyon days Truman spent in Key West during his Presidency. It allows the American public a unique opportunity to discover a very personal side of Harry Truman and how his down-to-earth, no-nonsense, feet-on-the-ground personality affected his governing style and the events of the day. The furniture and furnishings have been returned to their appearance during the Truman era.

Additional Information

The gardens have been restored according to Navy plans and archival records. Also, Thomas Edison lived here for six months during World War I when he was refining his depth charge invention.

Audubon House and Gardens

Contact: Mitchell Wolfson Family
Foundation

Open: 9:30 a.m.–5 p.m.

Admission: Adults $5; children $1. Birding
trips, lectures, and special programs are
scheduled regularly throughout the
year. Call for more information.

Suggested Time to View House: 1 hour

Facilities on Premises: Museum store,
Galleries

Description of Grounds: Visitors may walk
along brick pathways winding through
lovely tropical gardens with rare native
plantings, including many orchid trees

Best Season to View House: Summer-fall

Year House Built: 1830

Number of Rooms: 8

Style of Architecture: Frame

On-Site Parking: Yes **Wheelchair Access:** Yes

Description of House

The Audubon House was home to the large family of Captain John J. Geiger, a harbor pilot and master wrecker. The dwelling was built by ships' carpenters in the early 19th century and furnished with treasures from ships wrecked on the Florida reef. Captain Geiger and his heirs occupied the house for over 120 years. Neglected and slated for demolition in 1958, the deteriorating structure was saved when the concern of a local historian prompted Col. Mitchell Wolfson to purchase and restore the house. In 1832, John James Audubon lived here and used the surrounding natural resources as inspiration for his paintings. Today the house is operated by the Florida Audubon society in recognition of Audubon's contributions to the conservation movement.

This lovely two-story frame house has been restored to represent its original charm. One can almost picture Audubon seated on the second-story veranda sketching the spectacular water birds which became part of his masterwork, *Birds of America*. The house contain several exhibition galleries as well as furnished period rooms. The sitting room displays authentic pieces typical of 19th-century Key West including an exceptional pair of Chinese teakwood barrel arm chairs, a Queen Anne tea table, and a gold harp (c. 1740). The dining room contains many fine pieces of Chippendale furniture and Staffordshire pottery dating from 1820. Each room illustrates the elegance of a by-gone era.

Notable Collections on Exhibit

Special exhibitions dealing with Audubon, fine art, and the history and natural resources of the Florida Keys are shown in the second floor gallery. The gallery also houses a rare collection of porcelain birds and foliage made by Dorothy Doughty for the British Worcester Royal Porcelain Company.

The Wreckers Museum

322 Duval Street
Key West, FL 33040
(305) 294-9502

Contact: Old Island Restoration
Foundation, Inc.

Open: Year round, daily 10 a.m.–4 p.m.

Admission: Adults $2; children $.50; group
rates $1.50 each

Suggested Time to View House: 25 minutes

Description of Grounds: Spacious back
garden

Best Season to View House: Year round

Number of Yearly Visitors: 19,000-20,000

Year House Built: 1829

Style of Architecture: Key West "Conch"
style and Early Victorian

Number of Rooms: 7

On-Site Parking: No **Wheelchair Access:** No

Description of House

The oldest house in Key West, built in 1829, was the home of merchant seaman and "wrecker", Captain Francis B. Watlington. He oversaw the salvaging of wrecks on the reef. The dwelling's construction shows the influence of the early shipbuilders, and include a ship's hatch in the roof and interior wall boards running horizontally like a ship's hull.

The house is comfortably furnished in early Victorian style with a few pieces from earlier in the 18th century. Over one-third of the furnishings were original to the family whose lives spanned over eighty-five years in this house. The white clapboard house has dormer windows and an entrance porch; the back porch incorporates the cistern under a trap door. The house has the only original outside kitchen extant in the keys.

Notable Collections on Exhibit

The house exhibits five watercolors by contemporary New England marine painter Marshall Joyce showing Key West "Wreckers" at work. The captain's nine daughters inspired the display of antique toys and a miniature 1850 conch-style house, scaled one inch to one foot. This small house is furnished in Colonial through mid Victorian styles, with a tiny mural in the dining room.

Whitehall

P.O. Box 969
Palm Beach, FL 33480
(407) 655-2833

Contact: The Henry M. Flagler Museum
Open: Tues.-Sat. 10 a.m.–5 p.m.;
   Sun. 12–5 p.m.; closed Christmas
   and New Year's Day
Activities: Guided tours
Suggested Time to View House: 90 minutes
Facilities on Premises: Museum store
Description of Grounds: Four-acre
   grounds contain "Rambler" a
   restored railroad car
Best Season to View House: Year round
Number of Yearly Visitors: 120,000
Year House Built: 1901
Style of Architecture: Beaux Art Roman
Number of Rooms: 55
On-Site Parking: Yes **Wheelchair Access:** Yes

Description of House

Henry M. Flagler (1830-1913) was the founding partner with John D. Rockefeller of Standard Oil. He became interested in Florida during the 1850s, and by the time of his death in 1913, he had developed the entire east coast of the state, built a railroad from Jacksonville to Key West, and established St. Augustine, Daytona Beach, Palm Beach, and Miami as famous resorts.

This magnificent mansion was given by Henry M. Flagler as wedding present for his third wife Mary Lily Kenan in 1901. The style of the house is similar to the mansions found in that other notable resort—Newport, Rhode Island—and was designed by architects Carrere and Hastings. The floor plan is structured around a central courtyard in the Spanish Colonial style. Visitors can view this mansion much as it was when the Flaglers lived here. The interior decor was designed by the renowned decorators Pottier and Stymus and the furnishings on display are sixty percent original, twenty percent family donated, and twenty percent collected and representative of the period.

Notable Collections on Exhibit

Collections of costumes, lace, and fans, as well as paintings, sculpture, ceramics, silver and glass are just some of the special collections on display. Other exhibits show the local history of the area, and the building of the Florida east coast railway.

Historic Pensacola Village

120 East Church Street
Pensacola, FL 32501
(904) 444-8905

Contact: Historic Pensacola Preservation Board

Open: Mon.-Sat. 10 a.m.–4 p.m.

Admission: Adults $5; groups, seniors, military ID $4; children (4-16) $2. Guided tours, video presentation, craft demonstrations.

Suggested Time to View House: 1 hour

Description of Grounds: Open access to grounds, gardening projects at Lear and Dorr House

Best Season to View House: Feb.-April

Number of Yearly Visitors: 50,000

Year House Built: Varies, ranging from 1805 to 1888

Style of Architecture: Dorr-Greek Revival, Lavalle-Creole Cottage

Number of Rooms: Dorr-6, Lavalle-4

On-Site Parking: Yes **Wheelchair Access:** Yes

Description of House

Historic Pensacola Village is a unique museum complex which brings the romantic heritage of the Gulf Coast of Florida back to life. The village includes two of the finest coastal houses in Florida: the French Colonial Lavalle House, and the 1871 Dorr House. The Lavalle House contains hand-made provincial furniture and a fully equipped cooking hearth, while the Dorr House lets visitors glimpse the elegance of a late 19th-century lumber baron's lifestyle. Costumed guides provide the fascinating history of the area as well as give demonstrations of the lifestyle and crafts of the period.

Pensacola Village also features a Museum of of Industry, the Museum of Commerce, and the T.T. Wentworth, Jr. Florida State Museum. A streetscape is lined with buildings depicting turn-of-the-century businesses: a barber shop, a toy store, a print shop, a hardware store, and a pharmacy. For younger visitors, the Discovery Gallery, provides a wonderful "hands-on" experience that children will enjoy.

Notable Collections on Exhibit

Items on display include a Spanish helmet (16th century), an 1890s Eastlake-style barber chair, prehistoric American Indian pottery, a Union Army belt buckle, an English flintlock pocket pistol and an L&N railroad conductor's hat.

Ca' d'Zan

5401 Bay Shore Road
Sarasota, FL 34243
(813) 355-5101

Contact: John and Mable Ringling Museum of Art

Open: 10 a.m.–5:30 p.m., closed major holidays

Admission: Adults $8.50; seniors (55 and older) $7.50; children (under 12) free; also includes entry to museum and gallery. Guided tours.

Suggested Time to View House: 30–60 minutes

Facilities on Premises: Museum shop, restaurant, art galleries

Description of Grounds: The 66 acres of landscaped grounds are free to the public and open during museum hours.

Best Season to View House: Year-round

Number of Yearly Visitors: 250,000

Year House Built: 1924-26

Style of Architecture: Eclectic "palace"

Number of Rooms: 30

On-Site Parking: Yes

Wheelchair Access: Partial

Description of House

Ca' d'Zan, Venetian dialect for "House of John", is among the last of the grand eclectic "palaces" built by wealthy Americans in the late 19th and early 20th centuries. The mansion served as John Ringling's winter home where he lived while his circus was in between seasons. Ca d'Zan took over two years to complete at a cost of $1,500,000. Mable Ringling died in 1929, just two years after the mansion was completed. John Ringling died in 1936 at the age of seventy. Their impressive home has been restored to reflect the period of the 1920s when they resided here.

This imposing structure was originally intended to combine certain architectural features drawn from two of Mrs. Ringling's favorite buildings: the facade of the Doge's Palace in Venice, and the tower of the old Madison Square Garden where the circus regularly appeared. Bricks, terracotta blocks, and poured concrete were the primary construction materials, and terracotta was the main decorative material (interior and exterior) since the glazed finishes could best withstand the Florida sun. The interior plan of the house features a vast two-and-a-half story roofed court which served as the main living room. From Barcelona came thousands of old red barrel tiles for the roof, which is topped by a sixty-foot tower where a light shone when the Ringlings were in residence.

The furnishings also reflect the Ringlings' eclectic tastes. Most were acquired from estates—including those of the Astors and the Goulds—and reflect Italian and French Renaissance influence and the styles of Louis XIV, XV, and XVI of France.

Notable Collections on Exhibit
The house is filled with a collection of exquisite antique furnishings, works of art—including portraits of John and Mable Ringling by Russian American portraitist, Savely Sorine—and other fine decorations. There are notable 17th-century Flemish and English tapestries hanging on the walls, and a beautiful Steinway piano with a heavily ornamented rosewood case as well as an Aeolian organ.

Additional Information
Ca' d'Zan is part of the larger Ringling Museum of Art complex. The art galleries hold one of the premier collections of 17th-century Italian paintings as well as works by the Old Masters and other world-renowned pieces. In addition, the circus galleries display an extensive collection of circus memorabilia and artifacts including posters, prints, carved circus wagons, and props used by famous performers.

Gonzalez-Alvarez House

14 St. Francis Street
St. Augustine, FL 32084
(904) 824-2872

Contact: St. Augustine Historical Society

Open: Daily 9 a.m.–5 p.m.; closed
Christmas Day

Admission: Adults $5; seniors $4.50;
students $2.50; pre-schooler with parent
free. Guided tours.

Suggested Time to View House: 1 hour

Facilities on Premises: Museum store,
research library

Description of Grounds: Bricked pathways
and shaded benches offer a restful spot.

Best Season to View House: Late
spring-summer

Number of Yearly Visitors: 50,000

Year House Built: Documented from 1727

Style of Architecture: Downstairs Spanish,
2nd floor British

On-Site Parking: Yes **Wheelchair Access:** No

Description of House

Fourteen different families have lived in the house since it was first built. The first known family to live here was a Spanish soldier named Tomas Gonzalez. Gonzalez was an artilleryman at the fort. During the British occupancy of St. Augustine from 1763 to 1784, the house was occupied by Joseph Peavett and his wife Mary Evans Fenwick Peavitt. The historical novel *Maria* by Eugenia Price has been written about Mary Peavitt's life on St. Francis Street. The house was purchased by the Alvarez family in 1790 and stayed in that family for more than 100 years. The Alvarez family came to St. Augustine as bakers but became very active in politics. Geronimo Alvarez became the mayor of St. Augustine, and his son Antonio served frequent terms on the Board of Alderman as city treasurer and as mayor.

This Spanish *coquina* house was built not long after St. Augustine was burned by the British in 1702 and has been occupied by Spanish, British and American families. Visitors will see the unique evolution of a house, including the continuity and changes which can take place in one dwelling. The house is furnished to represent its different periods and artifacts found on the grounds are displayed. The Gonzalez Alvarez House (also known as the "Oldest House") is one of the most studied and best documented homes in the country.

Notable Collections on Exhibit

One of the most unusual items on display is a mahogany bed owned by General Joseph Hernandez, the commanding general at the Fort at the time the Indian leader Osceola was captured. The bed has unusually intricate carving and paintings representing the Biblical gospels.

Avero House

41 St. George Street
St. Augustine, FL 32084
(904) 829-8205

Contact: St. Photios Foundation, Inc.

Open: Daily 9 a.m.–5 p.m.; closed Christmas Day and Easter Sunday

Activities: Audiovisual program

Suggested Time to View House: 1 hour

Facilities on Premises: Book store/gift shop

Number of Yearly Visitors: 100,000

Year House Built: 1749

Style of Architecture: Spanish

Number of Rooms: 5

On-Site Parking: No **Wheelchair Access:** Yes

Description of House

The lot and Spanish house was owned by the Averos, a prominent *criollo* family from 1712 to 1763. In 1763, the Averos evacuated St. Augustine. In 1777, Patrick Tonym, the British Governor gave the house to the Minorcan priest, Father Pedro Campos, as a place of refuge for the remnant of the ill-fated New Smyrna Colony. This colony included 500 Greeks, the first colony of Greeks on the North American continent. In 1804, the heirs of the Averos sold the lot as well as the walls of an uninhabitable building. Walter Frazer acquired and remodeled the house from 1946 to 1952. The structure is presently owned by the National Greek Orthodox Church.

The walls are constructed of coquina (soft limestone) with stucco cover. The two-story Spanish-style home has an entrance through the courtyard. The interior is devoted to an exhibit on Greeks in America and a small Greek Orthodox shrine chapel.

Notable Collections on Exhibit

There are exquisite Byzantine-style frescoes on walls of the Shrine Chapel, with twenty-four karat gold highlights, and a small collection of fine Byzantine icons. The rooms also house changing special exhibits with themes related to Greek American history.

Additional Information

Visitors to St. Augustine should also plan to visit the Ximenez-Fatio House (20 Aviles Street). Built in 1798, the house features fine Spanish furniture and artifacts related to local history. It also has an unusual stone oven in the kitchen building.

Tampa Bay Hotel

401 W. Kennedy Blvd.
Tampa, FL 33606
(813) 254-1891

Contact: Henry B. Plant Museum
Open: Tues.-Sat. 10 a.m.–4 p.m.
Admission: Adults $2; children $.50.
Historical video, descriptive signage, audio tape introduction, interpreters available, Victorian Christmas Stroll (Dec. 1-21).
Suggested Time to View House: 1 hour
Facilities on Premises: Museum gift shop

Description of Grounds: Plant Park, tropical plantings, palm trees, fountains lead to the Hillsborough River
Best Season to View House: Year round
Number of Yearly Visitors: 45,000
Year House Built: 1891
Style of Architecture: Moorish Revival
Number of Rooms: Original hotel-511

Description of House

Built by Connecticut born Henry Plant and designed by John A. Wood, this magnificent hotel served as headquarters of Teddy Roosevelt and the Rough Riders during the embarkation period of the 1898 Spanish-American War. Clara Barton, Stephen Crane, and Richard Harding Davis occupied the building during this period. Other guests included Russian ballerina Anna Pavlova, Sarah Berhnardt, pianist Paderewski, Gloria Swanson, Babe Ruth, Winston Churchill, Thomas Edison and many others.

Built in 1891 by railroad and steamship magnate Henry B. Plant, the Tampa Bay Hotel served as the flagship of his hotel system. The magnificent architecture incorporates silver minarets, cupolas and domes as well as Victorian gingerbread verandas, the building is red brick. The structure was also notable as the first fully electrified building in the city. The 511-room hotel is now home to the University of Tampa and the Henry Plant Museum which showcases original furnishings and decorative arts from the hotel. The minarets are used as the symbol of Tampa, and the building and museum are a focal point of any visit to the city. Queen Elizabeth II was honored in the building during her 1991 visit.

Eighty percent of the museum's furnishings are original to the building. Many of the paintings have been gifts and are appropriate to the building and are of the period of the hotel's use from 1891 to 1930.

Notable Collections on Exhibit

Plant and his wife, Margaret, decorated the hotel in the grandest style, touring Europe and the Orient for art treasures and furniture. They bought primarily French and Oriental pieces and spectacular Venetian and Florentine mirrors. The building also has a fine display of hotel memorabilia including glassware, menus, postcards, stationery, and dining room pieces.

Peter O. Knight House

245 South Hyde Park Avenue
Tampa, FL 33606
(813) 259-1111

Contact: Tampa Historical Society
Open: Hours by appointment only
Admission: Free
Suggested Time to View House: 2 hours
Facilities on Premises: Book store
Description of Grounds: Small garden

Number of Yearly Visitors: 150
Year House Built: c. 1890
Style of Architecture: Queen Anne and
  Colonial Revival
Number of Rooms: 10
On-Site Parking: No **Wheelchair Access:** No

Description of House

The Knight family moved to Tampa from Fort Meyers in the 1880s and settled in this house after its construction in 1890. Peter Knight became one of Tampa's earliest prominent citizens, being instrumental in the formation of Tampa Gas, Tampa Electric, the Exchange Natural Bank and the development of Seddon Island. Knight also served in the state legislature and held numerous county and municipal positions.

The Knight House is one of the better late 19th-century houses in Hyde Park with its combination of many different period details and elements to create a rare example of a turn-of-the-century "rural cottage." The house has a delightful symmetry which is emphasized by the pyramidal section which breaks out of the porch at the entrance. This in turn is capped by a Gothic sort of gable with its untypical jerkin-head roof the plane of which "slides" down again to the entrance. The gable is further enhanced by the small quasi-Palladian window at its center which is sized to add interest to the gable but not overwhelm it. All of the furnishings have been collected and are appropriate to period.

Notable Collections on Exhibit

The house features a series of changing exhibits; past displays have been devoted to cigar manufacturing, maps, and aspects of local history.

Georgia

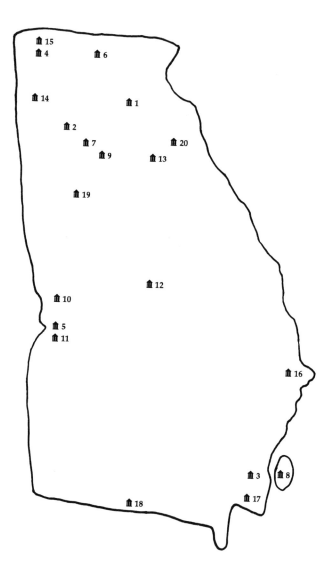

1. **Athens**
   Taylor-Grady House

2. **Atlanta**
   The Wren's Nest
   Swan House
   Tullie Smith Farm
   Rhodes Hall
   Williams-Payne House

3. **Brunswick**
   Hofwyl-Broadfield Plantation

4. **Chatsworth**
   Vann House

5. **Columbus**
   Pemberton House

6. **Dahlonega**
   Vickery House

7. **Indian Springs**
   Indian Springs Hotel

8. **Jekyll Island**
   *Jekyll Island Club Historic
      District*

9. **Juliette**
   1847 John Fitz Jarrell Residence
   1895 Dick Jarrell Residence

10. **LaGrange**
    Bellevue

11. **Lumpkin**
    Bedingfield Inn
    Westville

12. **Macon**
    Johnston-Felton-Hay House
    Sidney Lanier Cottage
    Old Cannon Ball House

13. **Milledgeville**
    The Old Governor's Mansion

14. **Rome**
    Chieftains
    Oak Hill

15. **Rossville**
    Chief John Ross House

16. **Savannah**
    Isaiah Davenport House Museum
    Owens-Thomas Museum
    Telfair Mansion and Art Museum

17. **St. Mary's**
    Plum Orchard Mansion

18. **Thomasville**
    Pebble Hill

19. **Warm Springs**
    Little White House Historic Site

20. **Washington**
    The Brick House

Taylor-Grady House

634 Prince Avenue
Athens, GA 30601
(706) 549-8688

Contact: Junior League of Athens
Open: Mon.-Fri. 10 a.m.–3:30 p.m.;
  preferably call for reservations
Admission: $2.50; $2 per person for groups
  (over 20 people). Guided tours.
Suggested Time to View House: 30 minutes
Best Season to View House: Spring

Description of Grounds: Small boxwood
  garden; large patio in rear for receptions
Number of Yearly Visitors: 10,000
Year House Built: 1840
Style of Architecture: Greek Revival
Number of Rooms: 10
On-Site Parking: Yes **Wheelchair Access:** No

Description of House

The home was built by General Robert Taylor, a planter and cotton merchant. General Taylor, whose military rank derived from the Georgia militia, moved from Savannah to Athens in order for his sons to attend the University of Georgia. In 1863, Major William S. Grady, father of Henry Woodfin Grady, bought the home from the Taylors while on furlough from the Confederate Army. Henry W. Grady, a native of Athens, lived here from 1865 to 1868 when he graduated from the university. As a managing editor of the *Atlanta Constitution*, Grady became the spokesman of the New South. An impressive orator, he stressed the importance of reconciliation between North and South after the Civil War.

As the only extant home of this influential Atlanta figure, the Taylor Grady home was designated a National Historic Landmark in 1976. This attractive Greek Revival structure's thirteen Doric columns are said to represent the thirteen original colonies. The furnishings are collected and appropriate for the period.

Additional Information

The Church-Waddell Brumley House, a Federal-style mansion at 280 East Dougherty Street, contains the Athens's visitor's center. Visitors to this historic city are advised to pick up the map for the walking tour which will take them by many impressive Greek Revival mansions and the unusual old double-barrel cannon which stands in front of the City Hall.

The Wren's Nest

1050 Ralph David Abernathy Blvd.
Atlanta, GA 30310
(404) 753-7735

Contact: The Joel Chandler Harris
Association, Inc.
Open: Tues.-Sat. 10 a.m.–4 p.m.; Sun.
1–4 p.m.; closed major holidays
Admission: Adults $3; seniors and teens $2;
children (4-12) $1. Guided tours, slide
presentation, story-telling programs.
Suggested Time to View House: 1 hour
Description of Grounds: 2½ acres of yard
and a "Briar Patch" for Br'er Rabbit
Best Season to View House: Spring
Number of Yearly Visitors: 21,000
Year House Built: 1872
Number of Rooms: 13

Style of Architecture: Queen Anne
Wheelchair Access: Yes

Description of House

Georgian author Joel Chandler Harris (1846-1908) lived in this attractive
Victorian home at the turn-of-the-century. He most famous for his recording
of the African-American folk tales known as the "Uncle Remus" tales. As a
journalist, he was one of the leading editorial writers of the *Atlanta Constitution*, the most influential Southern paper of the period. Joel wrote thirty
books, many reflecting life in rural Georgia; nine of his books contain 190
African-American folk tales he was trying to preserve. Joel was one of the
first members of the American Folklore Society. He lived in the house with
his wife, Esther LaRose Harris, six children, and his mother, Mary Harris. A
social man, Harris was visited by such notables as Andrew Carnegie and
James Whitcomb Riley.

The Wren's Nest is a good example of the Queen Anne-style architecture
which was popular during this period. The name of the house comes from
a family of birds that set up housekeeping in the family's mailbox. The
dwelling is being restored to its appearance circa 1900 with reproductions
of the original wallpapers, carpets and curtains. The Harris home is typical
of a middle class family of this period with ninety percent of the original
family furnishings, mainly Eastlake, on display. The rest of the furnishings
are of the same period; the museum is continuing to collect further period
pieces to complete the museum rooms.

Notable Collections on Exhibit

The reproduction wallpapers contain unique examples of early Art
Nouveau papers from around 1900. Joel Chandler Harris's bedroom con-
tains the original wallpaper, as well as some outstanding prints by artist
James Moser, who did the illustrations for Mr. Harris's first book.

Swan House

3101 Andrews Drive NW
Atlanta, GA 30305
(404) 261-1837

Contact: Atlanta History Center

Open: Nov. 1-March 1, Mon.
10:45 a.m.–4:45 p.m., Tues.-Sat.
9:45 a.m.–4:45 p.m., Sun. (and holidays)
12:45–4:45 p.m.

Admission: Adults $6; seniors and students (over 18 with ID) $4.50; students (6-17) $3; under 6 free. Guided tours, Atlanta Storytelling Festival (May), Garden Day (April), decorative arts lectures.

Suggested Time to View House: 30 minutes

Facilities on Premises: Museum shop

Description of Grounds: Gardens typical of the 1930s mansion; Victorian playhouse with display of period toys; trail through Swan Woods

Best Season to View House: Spring-fall

Number of Yearly Visitors: 66,000

Year House Built: 1928

Style of Architecture: Classical

Number of Rooms: 12

On-Site Parking: Yes **Wheelchair Access:** Yes

Description of House

Named for the swan motif found throughout the interior and exterior of the house, the classically designed Swan House was completed in 1928 for Mr. and Mrs. Edward Hamilton Inman, heirs to a cotton brokerage fortune. The house has been home to a number of notable figures in Atlanta society. The Inman family came to Atlanta immediately after the close of the Civil War and amassed a huge fortune as cotton brokers. The family was also involved in real estate, banking and transportation and at the turn of the century were key figures in all aspects of Atlanta's commercial life. Emily McDougald's grandfather was an Indian fighter from middle Georgia, owning large plantations in both states. Lizzie McDuffie, a black servant in the Inman household for thirty-two years worked for Franklin Roosevelt from 1933 until his death in 1945. She became his trusted advisor on "colored affairs," was instrumental in bringing black performers to the White House and played an important role in his three successful election campaigns.

The house was designed by Philip Trammell Shutze (1890-1982), a prominent Atlanta architect. The original formal gardens include terraced lawns, a cascading fountain, retaining walls with recessed ivy covered arches, and fountain statuary. The interior includes the original furnishings which range from 18th-century antiques to 20th-century decorative arts.

This well-known landmark contains much of the Inmans' original furniture and many of the original wall coverings and fabrics selected by famed New York interior decorator Ruby Ross Wood. The swan console tables are an outstanding example of the flamboyance of the English Rococo style.

Notable Collections on Exhibit

In 1982, Philip Trammell Shutze bequeathed his research library and his personal collection of decorative arts to the Atlanta Historical Society. Rotating selections from the Philip Trammell Shutze Collection of Decorative Arts are exhibited in three second floor rooms. Shutze's collection of antique Chinese export porcelain, English and European ceramics, as well as American, Chinese and English silver, rugs, paintings, furniture and other objects, provide insight into the taste of an individual whose architecture and distinctive style had a profound influence on the style of the city's affluent citizens.

Tullie Smith Farm

3101 Andrews Drive NW
Atlanta, GA 30305
(404) 261-1837

Contact: Atlanta History Center

Open: Nov. 1-March 1, Mon.
10:30 a.m.–4:30 p.m., Tues.-Sat.
9:30 a.m.–4:30 p.m., Sun. (and
holidays) 12:30–4:30 p.m.

Admission: Adults $6; seniors and students
(18 and over with ID) $4.50; students
(6-17) $3; under 6 free. Guided tours,
Folklife Festival (Oct.), Civil War
Encampment (July), Sheep to Shawl Day
(April).

Suggested Time to View House: 30 minutes

Facilities on Premises: Museum shop

Description of Grounds: Outbuildings
include a kitchen, barn, double corncrib,
blacksmith shop, log cabin. Appropriate
flowers and herbs.

Best Season to View House: Spring-fall

Year House Built: c. 1840

Number of Rooms: 7

Number of Yearly Visitors: 70,000

Style of Architecture: Plantation plain-style

On-Site Parking: Yes **Wheelchair Access:** No

Description of House

The Smith family built this attractive house in Dekalb County, about 1840 and occupied it until 1967, except for a brief period from 1877 to 1881. Miss Tullie Smith was the last owner and resident. The house was moved from suburban Atlanta to the Atlanta History Center and open to the public in 1972.

Architecturally, the Tullie Smith Farm is a plantation plain-style home. The two-story edifice evolved from an English farmhouse of similar style; this type of house was prevalent in colonial America until after the Civil War. The building features two main rooms upstairs and two main ones downstairs. At each end of the gabled roof stand twin brick chimneys. There are two low shed roofs, one of which covers the front porch and a parson's or traveller's room located at the end of the porch. The exterior siding is painted weatherboarding; the interior walls are horizontal boards with a simple door and window trim. An inventory of Robert Smith's possessions made when he died in 1846 is the basis for the collected furnishings. The furniture is typical of rural mid 19th-century Georgia: slat-back chairs, plain tables, and cupboards. There are also pieced quilts and woven coverlets decorating the beds.

Additional Information

Craftspeople demonstrate quilting, weaving, open-hearth cooking, blacksmithing, and other crafts at the house during the year. An exhibition about the history of the house and outbuildings, and about the Smith family, is open daily in the settlers' log cabin behind the house.

Rhodes Hall

1516 Peachtree Street, NW
Atlanta, GA 30309
(404) 881-9980

Contact: Georgia Trust for Historic
  Preservation
Open: Mon.-Fri. 11 a.m.–4 p.m.
Admission: Donation. Guided tours.
  Hall also available for meetings and
  receptions.
Suggested Time to View House: 1 hour
Year House Built: 1902-04
Style of Architecture: Romanesque
Number of Rooms: 15
On-Site Parking: Yes
Wheelchair Access: No

Description of House

This unusual castle is located in the midst of downtown Atlanta and provides a striking contrast to the modern office buildings surrounding it. Built as a residence in 1902 for the Amos G. Rhodes family, Rhodes Hall is an eclectic creation not easily defined by the architectural styles of the day. Rhodes asked architect Willis Denny to pattern his new home after the Rhineland castles Rhodes had admired on a trip to Europe during the late 1890s. Rhodes was a self-made man who began his career as a carpet tacker and ended up owning one of the country's largest chains of furniture stores.

The architect used elements of the Richardsonian Romanesque style in creating Rhodes's castle. This landmark's distinctive features include Syrian arches on the porte-cochere, a four-story corner tower, a steeply pitched roof of Vermont red slate topped with a copper fleur-de-lis, and battlements all around. The interior is equally distinctive in design and ornamentation. The first floor consists of a large reception hall based loosely on the Italian Renaissance style, a ladies parlor utilizing a sophisticated mix of 18th-century French styles, and a dining room that combines Romanesque with Art Nouveau styling. The floors are made of many fine woods including mahogany, maple, and oak parquet.

Additional Information

As a crowning touch for his impressive home, Rhodes commissioned the Von Gerichten Art Glass Company to create a series of painted and stained glass windows as a memorial to the Confederacy. The series, entitled "The Rise and Fall of the Confederacy", surrounds the carved mahogany staircase which winds from the first floor reception to the second floor hall. This monumental memorial to the Confederacy consists of over 1,250 pieces of German glass depicting fifteen Confederate generals and many battle scenes creates a lasting impression for all who view it.

Williams-Payne House

6075 Sandy Springs Circle
Atlanta, GA 30328
(404) 843-0860

Contact: Sandy Springs Historic Community Foundation

Open: Mon.-Fri. 10 a.m.–4 p.m.; closed New Years, 4th of July, Thanksgiving, Christmas

Admission: Adults $2; seniors and students $1; members and children (under 10) free. Guided tours, audiovisual presentation, school programs.

Suggested Time to View House: 45 minutes

Description of Grounds: Small park with historic springs, 1860 milk house, and gardens

Best Season to View House: Spring and summer

Number of Yearly Visitors: 1,300

Year House Built: 1869

Style of Architecture: Plain-style farmhouse

Number of Rooms: 4

On-Site Parking: Yes **Wheelchair Access:** Yes

Description of House

The Williams-Payne House offers visitors a fascinating view of life in a turn-of-the-century Georgian farm. The farmhouse was built by Walter Jerome Williams who lived here until his death in 1936. Williams had two wives and ten children who survived to adulthood. The property was sold by the Williams family about 1938 to Marie and Major Payne who reworked it extensively and lived in the house until the early 1980s.

This white clapboard house originally sat on 100 acres of land. The plain style architecture is typical of the area. The interior features some of the original wall paint and woodwork. This is one of a very few remaining houses built before 1900 which represents the area's rural agrarian society. The house is furnished to represent the period from 1870 to 1900.

Notable Collections on Exhibit

The collection of pottery, mainly jugs and churns is nearly all from the South and was purchased from Marie Payne's estate.

Hofwyl-Broadfield Plantation

Route 10, Box 83
Brunswick, GA 31520
(912) 264-9263

Contact: Georgia State Parks and Historic
Sites

Open: Tues.-Sat. 9 a.m.—5 p.m., Sun.
2—5:30 p.m., closed Mon., Thanksgiving
and Christmas Day

Admission: Donation, group rates available
with advance notice. Tours, audiovisual
program, plantation Christmas, Black
History activities in Feb.

Suggested Time to View House: 1 hour

Facilities on Premises: Visitor's center,
museum, sales desk

Description of Grounds: The plantation
grounds feature magnolias, camellias,
moss-laden oaks, and a wide marsh
where rice once grew.

Best Season to View House: Year round

Style of Architecture: Frame

Year House Built: c. 1850s

On-Site Parking: Yes **Wheelchair Access:** Yes

Description of House

Hofwyl-Broadfield Plantation offers visitors an illuminating glimpse of
19th and 20th-century plantation life in rural Georgia. Beginning in 1807,
William Brailsford of Charleston carved the future rice plantation from the
cypress swamps along the Altamaha River. Until the outbreak of the Civil
War, the plantation produced rice steadily. Thereafter, war, hurricanes, and
the lack of abundant labor led to the fall of the rice empire. Rice was last
planted here in 1915. Brailford's descendants, the Dent family, converted the
plantation to a successful dairy farm which produced high quality milk for
nearly thirty years.

The main plantation house is a modest structure built in the 1850s and
modified over the years. The house is furnished with fine antiques, many of
which belonged to the Dent family, owners of the dairy farm. In addition to
the main house, the plantation also features a number of interesting outbuildings including a commissary or plantation store, the pay shed which
shows the transition from slavery to freedom after the Civil War, servants'
quarters, and the milking barn and bottling house from the dairy farm days.

Additional Information

Visitors are encouraged to spend the entire day wandering through the
plantation, walking along the nature trail and through the garden. In addition, visitors may also want to visit the nearby Jekyll Island historic district
or the Fort King George historic site.

Vann House

Route 7, Box 7655
Chatsworth, GA 30705
(706) 695-2598

Contact: Georgia Department of Natural
Resources

Open: Tues.-Sat. 9 a.m.–5 p.m.,
Sun. 2–5 p.m.

Admission: Adults $1.50; children
(6-18) $.75

Description of Grounds: The house is
located on 3 acres of land.

Year House Built: 1804

Style of Architecture: Federal style, with
Georgian style modifications

On-Site Parking: Yes

Description of House

James Vann was the son of a Scot trader, who settled among the Cherokees in the 18th century and married a Cherokee woman. Vann's chief contribution to the Cherokees was his help in establishing the Moravian mission at Spring Place in 1801. While the brethren were interested primarily in bringing the gospel to the Indians, Vann's main concern was in educating the young people. In sponsoring the mission school, Vann contributed to the education of the men who were later leaders in the Nation—Elias Boudinot, Stand Watie, John Ridge and others. Vann's youngest son, Joseph, acquired the house and much of his father's property. In the 1830s the house and property was seized by the Georgia guard; eventually Joseph was compensated by the federal government.

The Vann house is a two-story house with solid brick walls that are crowned front and rear with a classic cornice. Each facade has two-story whitewashed plaster pilasters with two fanlighted doorways one above the other. Each door is framed by large painted wood paneling and opens off wide hallways onto covered porches. On each of the two main floors there are two rooms, with a wide hallway between. On the left of the main entrance, which faced the Federal Road, is an elaborately carved stairway, the oldest example of cantilevered construction in Georgia. The Vann House features outstanding handcarving , with the Cherokee rose predominating, on both the interior and exterior.

Pemberton House

Broadway and Seventh Streets
Columbus, GA 31906
(706) 323-7979

Contact: Historic Columbus Foundation

Open: Tours given Mon.-Fri. at 11 a.m. and 3 p.m., Sat. at 2 p.m., Sun. at 2 p.m.

Admission: $3. Guided tours of four historic houses in the heart of the Columbus Historic District

Suggested Time to View House: 1 hour

Facilities on Premises: Gift shop

Best Season to View House: Year round

Year House Built: c. 1850s

Style of Architecture: Victorian

Number of Rooms: 4

On-Site Parking: Yes

Description of House

This charming cottage on Seventh Street was home to Dr. John Stith Pemberton from 1855 to 1860. Pemberton worked as a druggist in Columbus, later in Atlanta, and was the originator of the formula for Coca Cola. Pemberton was an industrious druggist who manufactured many medicines, photographic chemicals, perfumes, and cosmetics. He was also known to have prepared and dispensed many of his own concoctions at the soda fount as a way of testing for flavor and public acceptance. One of these flavors, "the French Wine of Cocoa" is believed to have been the forerunner of the now famous Coca-Cola. Originally a headache cure, the formula did originally contain cocaine which was removed in 1903.

This simple four-room cottage was restored by a master craftsman after being donated to the historic foundation. The furnished rooms represent life during the Pembertons' residency, and many of their original possessions are on display. The Victorian parlor features many fine antiques including a brass woodbox, an Empire secretary holding early medicine texts, and a Victorian checkerboard (1859) with Shakespearean characters on the squares. Daguerrotypes and portraits of the Pembertons complete the decorations of this home listed on the National Register of Historic Places.

Notable Collections on Exhibit

To the rear of the building is the former kitchen which has been converted to a represent Pemberton's apothecary shop. The bottles range from earthenware and glass ones, found at the original site of the house, to the famous "Christmas" Coca-Cola bottle dated December 25, 1923.

Additional Information

The Pemberton House is a stop on the Historic Columbus Foundation's Heritage Corner walking tour. Other stops include the Walker-Peter-Langdon House, a Federal-style cottage considered the oldest in the city, and the Log Cabin (on Broadway) representing the lifestyle of early traders in the early 1800s prior to the settlement of Columbus.

Vickery House

Contact: The Dahlonega Club, Inc.

Open: Open by appointment

Admission: $1 donation. Guided tours, special programs, special Christmas open house

Suggested Time to View House: 45 minutes

Best Season to View House: All seasons

Number of Yearly Visitors: 1,000

Year House Built: 1860

Style of Architecture: Victorian

Number of Rooms: 14

On-Site Parking: Yes **Wheelchair Access:** Yes

Description of House

This attractive house was the home of Weir Boyd, a lawyer, legislator, drafter of a new state constitution in 1877, gold mine owner, colonel in the 52nd Georgia regiment and a member of the North Georgia College Board of Trustees. He also figured prominently in reconstruction of the college after the only college building was destroyed by fire on December 28, 1878. The daughter of Weir Boyd, Mattie, married Professor Benjamin Palmer Gaillard; they resided in the Vickery House until 1895 when they sold it to Professor E.B. Vickery.

The exterior is characterized by two-over-two windows framed by green shutters, weatherboards painted white, and a Victorian, one-story porch. The veranda has turned posts and turned uprights supporting the rail. Scroll design brackets with filigree appear in the angle formed by the veranda roof and posts. The veranda is on the northeast or front and southwest sides of the house, and the back section of the southwest side is enclosed in chimneys which have been rebuilt in restoration. The front door is half wood and half glass, the upper glass portion consisting of nine square panes. In typical Victorian fashion, there is a transom above the door. The house displays a lovely collection of period furnishings, many from the original residents.

Notable Collections on Exhibit

The house has a fine art gallery with some thirty paintings of local artists in addition to other artwork in the house. The original Vickery family furniture includes a Murphy bed (folding bed with springs), a bonnet dresser, a 200-year old oak dining table that was imported from England, two oak sideboards, two oak wash stands, and an oak library table.

Indian Springs Hotel

Highway 42, P.O. Box 215
Indian Springs, GA 30233
(706) 775-6734

Contact: Butts County Historical Society
Open: April-Nov., Tues.-Sun. 8 a.m.–5 p.m.
Admission: Adults $1; children (6-12) $.50;
under 6 free. Guided tours on request,
special events include Civil War Days in
Oct., Indian Days in Sept., and a Scottish
Festival in April, call for information.
Suggested Time to View House: 45 minutes
Best Season to View House: Spring and
summer
Number of Yearly Visitors: 2,000
Year House Built: 1823
Style of Architecture: Federal
Number of Rooms: 11
On-Site Parking: Yes **Wheelchair Access:** Yes

Description of House

The Indian Spring Hotel was built as a tavern and an inn by Chief
William McIntosh and Joel Bailey. The inn is unique in that it is the only
antebellum mineral springs hotel still standing in the state, and its history
reveals much of the culture and society of Georgia in the 19th century. Native
Americans had been coming to the area for many decades prior to the 1800s
for the benefits of the medicinal water. Chief McIntosh (half Creek and half
Scottish) built a cabin here which later became the hotel. In this building
McIntosh signed the Treaty of 1825 which turned the lands over to the
government; three months later this act ended up costing him his life. The
Varner family lived at the hotel the longest from 1850 to 1953. This was the
heyday of the hotel, when it gained a reputation as one of Georgia's finest
hotels as elegant as many found near springs in Virginia and New York.

This large hotel features a ballroom, a billiard room, bar, and all of the
other amenities associated with a resort. Restoration work continues to
decorate the building with the original paint, grained mantels and doors as
they were in 1823. The structure is currently furnished with collected period
furnishings and the rooms occasionally display temporary exhibits related
to local history.

Jekyll Island Club Historic District

375 Riverview Drive
Jekyll Island, GA 31527
(912) 635-2119

Contact: Jekyll Island Authority-Museum
Division

Open: Daily tours 10 a.m.–3 p.m.
on the hour

Activities: Guided tours; audiovisual
presentations; special programs

Suggested Time to View House: 2 hours
(entire site)

Facilities on Premises: Gift shop and
art gallery

Description of Grounds: The historic
district was the sight of a private club
from 1886 to 1942. The grounds are
attractively landscaped.

Year House Built: Structures in the Historic
District were built from 1886 to 1928

Best Season to View House: Spring

Number of Yearly Visitors: 50,000

Number of Rooms: Varies

Style of Architecture: Various

On-Site Parking: Yes

Description of House

Known as the "richest, the most exclusive, most inaccessible club in the world", Jekyll Island was once considered the idyllic private kingdom of the barons of American finance and industry from 1886 until 1942. The Rockefellers, Morgans, Goulds and Vanderbilts prized Jekyll's beauty and peace as the perfect winter retreat from the pressures of their hectic business and social schedules.

Today, the Jekyll Island Club Historic District is one of the largest restoration projects in the southeastern United States. Visitors to the district can step back in time while touring selected mansion-sized "cottages" restored and furnished as if their wealthy owners had just departed. Some of the more notable cottages include the DuBignon Cottage (c. 1884) with its unique wraparound porch, the Indian Mound Cottage (c. 1892) where Standard Oil director William Rockefeller used to spend his leisure time, and the Mistletoe Cottage (c. 1900), the location of many Jekyll Island socials. More than thirty buildings house a collection of period furnishings, decorative arts, historical photographs, and documents related to the club and its members.

1847 John Fitz Jarrell Residence

**Route 2, Box 220
Juliette, GA 31046
(912) 986-5172**

Contact: Jarrell Plantation State Historical Site

Open: Year-round, Tues.-Sat. 9 a.m.–5 p.m., Sun. 2–5:30 p.m.

Admission: Adults $1.50; children (6-18) $.75. Discounts for groups. Audiovisual programs; visitor center; guided tour of 1847 plantation house; self-guided tour of 14 original farm buildings; seasonal special events.

Suggested Time to View House: 15 minutes

Facilities on Premises: Visitor center

Best Season to View House: Spring and fall

Number of Yearly Visitors: 21,000

Year House Built: 1847

Number of Rooms: 8

Style of Architecture: Plantation plain style

On-Site Parking: Yes **Wheelchair Access:** Yes

Description of House

John Fitz Jarrell built the first dwelling on the land that holds this impressive plantation with more than twenty historic buildings. The site was a working plantation from the 1840s through the 1960s. Jarrell was a skilled carpenter, shoemaker, blacksmith, wheelwright, stone mason and farmer. Jarrell's plantation holdings grew to about 1000 acres, and by 1860 he had over forty five slaves working the land. During the Civil War, his livestock was taken and his cotton gin destroyed by a raiding party with Sherman's army. He was married twice and had fifteen children by both wives. John's daughter Mattie, lived in the house until 1957.

This one-and-a-half story plantation home has a shingle roof and a porch with a shed room, front room, bedroom, dining room and a store which served as grocery from 1900 to 1925. Only one interior room of this modest home was ever painted. The original 1847 flooring remains intact in much of the house.

Notable Collections on Exhibit

The Jarrell Plantation houses one of the largest collections of original family artifacts in the United States including farm equipment, hundreds of tools, furniture, clothing, and other handcrafted items. Most of the collection is on exhibit in the original buildings year-round.

Additional Information

This well-preserved plantation maintains many of the original gardens and outbuildings. Visitors can tour the 1847 plantation plain style house, the mill complex, the carpenter shop, the blacksmith shop and other buildings. The original garden where the Jarrell's grew their vegetables and flowers, is still planted each spring and fall.

1895 Dick Jarrell Residence

Route 2, Box 220
Juliette, GA 31046
(912) 986-5172

Contact: Jarrell Plantation State Historical Site

Open: Year-round, Tues.-Sat. 9 a.m.–5 p.m., Sun. 2–5:30 p.m.

Admission: Adults $1.50; children (6-18) $.75. Discounts for groups. Audiovisual programs; visitor center; guided tour of 1847 plantation house; self-guided tour of 14 original farm buildings; seasonal special events.

Suggested Time to View House: 10 minutes

Facilities on Premises: Visitor center

Best Season to View House: Spring and fall

Number of Yearly Visitors: 21,000

Year House Built: 1895

Style of Architecture: Farmhouse

Number of Rooms: 4

On-Site Parking: Yes **Wheelchair Access:** No

Description of House

Dick and Mamie Van Zandt Jarrell gave up school teaching and moved back to Dick's family plantation in 1895. Dick built the house with wood cut in his own sawmill. The couple had two children when they moved in and continued to have children until a total of twelve were born. Over the years, the industrious Jarrells added a sawmill, a gristmill, a cotton gin, a shingle mill, a syrup evaporator house and equipment, a farm implement shed, and a blacksmith/woodworking shop to the plantation. Many of these buildings are still visible today.

This small farm house was built in 1895 and featured two rooms with a kitchen and dining room separated from the main room by a narrow breezeway. The house served as a temporary home for the growing family until a new house was completed in 1920. Many of the furnishings are from the original family and include a handmade desk and bookcase and pieces of Eastlake and turn-or-the-century oak furniture.

Additional Information

The Jarrell Plantation hosts a number of annual events such as sheep-shearing, spinning and weaving, cane grinding and syrup making, and holiday celebrations. Call (404) 656-3530 for more information.

Bellevue

204 Ben Hill Street
LaGrange, GA 30240
(706) 884-1832

Contact: LaGrange Woman's Club
Open: Tues.-Sat. 10 a.m.–12 p.m., 2–5 p.m.;
closed on holidays
Admission: Adults $3; students $2.
Guided tours.
Suggested Time to View House:
30–60 minutes

Facilities on Premises: Sales desk
Number of Yearly Visitors: 400
Year House Built: 1850s
Style of Architecture: Greek Revival
Number of Rooms: 8
On-Site Parking: Yes **Wheelchair Access:** Yes

Description of House

This beautiful house was the home of an influential Georgian politician, Benjamin Harvey Hill. After graduating from the University of Georgia in 1844, Hill continued studying law in the office of William Dougherty in Heard County where he was admitted to the bar. He returned to Athens to marry Miss Caroline Holt, and the Hills moved to LaGrange, where Mr. Hill established a law practice. The Hills lived at Bellevue for twelve years and were known for their lavish hospitality. Leading statesmen of the Civil War years were frequent guests,including Jefferson Davis. As a U.S. Senator, Hill was known as "the Silver-tongued orator." A sad irony was the cancer of that famous tongue which resulted in his death at the age of fifty-nine.

The stately antebellum house known as Bellevue is regarded as one of the finest examples of Greek Revival architecture in all of Georgia. The house features magnificent Ionic columns across wide porticos as well as other interesting architectural details. Attractive interior features include handsomely carved cornices over doors and windows, black carrara marble mantels in the old double parlor, original floors, plaster ceiling medallions and custom-made wallpaper duplicating the original design in the entrance hall.

A piano is one of the few furnishings that remain from the Hill family. The rest has been collected by the club or donated by interested persons. Bellevue is listed on the National Register of Historic Places.

Notable Collections on Exhibit

Bellevue exhibits an extensive collection of Hill family memorabilia including papers, clothing, and photographs. A library of Civil War books comes from the collections of two area residents.

Bedingfield Inn

P.O. Box 1850
Lumpkin, GA 31815
(912) 838-6310

Contact: Westville Historic Handicrafts, Inc.

Open: Tues.-Sun. 1–5 p.m.; closed first full week in Jan., Thanksgiving, Christmas

Admission: Regular tour $1; deluxe tour $3.50 (includes refreshments), guided tours for groups by advance reservation

Suggested Time to View House: 2 hours

Facilities on Premises: Museum shop

Best Season to View House: Year round

Number of Yearly Visitors: 50,000

Year House Built: 1836

Style of Architecture: Federal vernacular

On-Site Parking: Yes **Wheelchair Access:** No

Description of House

Built by Dr. Bryan Bedingfield in 1836, the inn served as a family residence as well as a stopping place for stagecoaches and other travelers. Dr. Bedingfield was the first physician in Stewart County and his son also became a doctor. The inn provided a convenient stopping place for travelers between Americus and Eufaula, Alabama, to the west. During this period, Lumpkin was a busy frontier town and the inn provided a center for commercial and community activity.

The inn exhibits several period rooms typical for a 19th-century inn. The first floor contains the public room where men used to gather to exchange news and smoke and drink, and the ladies room where the women of the inn would gather for pleasant conversation. Two other rooms on the first floor served as family private rooms, but these too were often pressed into use as additional parlors for guests who desired privacy. The room over the public room was known as the common room. Here cheap accommodations were provided for those who lacked the means for private quarters. These guests often slept several to a bed or pallet on the floor without heat; it is the only room in the inn without a fireplace. All of the furniture and accessories date from the years prior to 1850. Some of the pieces were made by area cabinetmakers known for their fine woodworking ability.

Westville

P.O. Box 1850
Lumpkin, GA 31815
(912) 838-6310

Contact: Westville Historic Handicrafts Inc.

Open: Year-round, Mon.-Sat.
10 a.m.-5 p.m., Sun. 1–5 p.m.; closed
Thanksgiving, Christmas, and New
Year's Day

Admission: Adults $6; seniors $5; group
rates by prior arrangement only.
Reservations needed for specific tour
appointments; mule-drawn wagon ride.

Facilities on Premises: Gift shop; village
kitchens

Description of Grounds: Many gardens
and landscaped grounds

Best Season to View House: Year-round

Year House Built: c. 1850

On-Site Parking: Yes

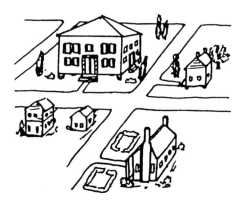

Description of House

Westville, on the outskirts of Lumpkin, is a living history village "where it is always 1850." Westville has assembled and restored a representative group of notable structures ranging from antebellum houses and shops to churches and public buildings all set in fifty-seven acres of rolling countryside in the Old Cotton Belt of the South.

The Greek Revival McDonald House was built for a local merchant. This attractive mansion features a front portico with two-story square columns and a cantilevered balcony on the second floor with latticework balustrade. The interior also contains many fine details such as the wood archways over the doors and light graining on the woodwork throughout the house. The house also boasts a formal garden with many period plantings.

The Wells House is one of the few remaining examples in the state of Lower Creek construction in a larger building. The original log structure is still visible on the west side of the first story. The house has two exterior chimneys and bird's beak notching in the log section. This modest home originally had a dirt floor in the cabin section with half-hewn logs forming the walls.

Other notable structures in the village include the Hagley Cotton Gin House, with a mule powered gin; the Climax Presbyterian Church, a Greek Revival church moved from a nearby town; a blacksmith shop and a pottery shop with a groundhog kiln built into the hill. A tour of the village provides visitors with an insightful view of 19th-century rural Georgia.

Additional Information

Within this setting, costumed citizens practice traditional trades such as blacksmithing and spinning. Visitors experience the daily life of a rural town just prior to the Industrial Revolution.

Johnston-Felton-Hay House

Contact: Georgia Trust for Historic
 Preservation
Open: Mon.-Sat. 10 a.m.–5 p.m.; Sun.
 1–5 p.m.; closed major holidays
Admission: Adults $4; students (12-college)
 $2; students (6-11) $1; school groups
 $.50; under 6 free. Guided tours.
Suggested Time to View House: 1 hour
Facilities on Premises: Museum store
Description of Grounds: Several acres of
 landscaped grounds with very old
 magnolias and ginkgo
Best Season to View House: Spring
 and fall
Number of Yearly Visitors: 41,000
Year House Built: 1855-59
Style of Architecture: Italian
 Renaissance Revival
Number of Rooms: 24
On-Site Parking: Yes
Wheelchair Access: Yes

Description of House

This impressive brick mansion was built by William Butler Johnston (1809-1887) and his bride after they returned from their honeymoon in Italy. Johnston began as a jeweler, and then expanded into railroads, banking, real estate, insurance, manufacturing, and public utilities. Later occupants included lawyer William Hamilton Felton (1860-1926) and his wife, Ellen Johnston, and Parks Lee Hay (1873-1957), founder of Bankers Health & Life Insurance Company. Hay's insurance company built Macon's first skyscraper.

The house, properly called Italian Renaissance Revival in styling, contains about 18,000 square feet of floor space in twenty-four main rooms. Built over a raised basement, it consists of a central block flanked by what were originally symmetrical wings. The central block, five bays wide in front, rises three full floors above the basement and is surmounted by a low-pitched, hipped roof and a two-story octagonal cupola with console buttresses. A two-story, semi-octagonal bay is located on the north side of the central block. A one story piazza stretches across the front of the house with a wooden balustrade between fluted wooden columns on pedestal bases.

The interior of the house has equally fine details. There are elaborate plaster ceilings, medallions, and cornices as well as ornate window and door frames. *Trompe l'oeil* marbleized walls embellish the front hallway on the main floor. A large variety of painted and stained glass windows decorate other areas of the house and include a memorial window to the poet Lord

Byron. Other features of the house reflect the occupant's wealth and status in the community such as an intercom system, central heating, and a ventilation system. The majority of the furnishings date from the Hay family's occupancy (1926-1962). Most of these pieces are 19th-century copies of 18th-century English and French styles. A few original Johnston pieces (1860-70) remain in the house such as the Eastlake-style dining room suite and sideboard.

Notable Collections on Exhibit

The house displays many fine pieces of artwork and period decorations. The most noticeable piece in the mansion's collection is the marble statue, "Ruth Gleaning" by the American sculptor, Randolph Rogers. The statue depicts the Biblical character, Ruth gleaning wheat in the field of Boaz.

Sidney Lanier Cottage

935 High Street
Macon, GA 31208-3358
(912) 743-3851

Contact: Middle Georgia Historical Society
Open: Mon.-Fri. 9 a.m.–1 p.m., 2–4 p.m.; Sat. 9:30 a.m.–12:30 p.m., closed major holidays
Admission: Adults $2.50; students $1; children $.50. Special group rates $2. Guided tours and special slide programs.
Suggested Time to View House: 45 minutes
Facilities on Premises: Museum shop

Description of Grounds: Formal garden in rear
Best Season to View House: Spring and summer
Number of Yearly Visitors: 20,000
Year House Built: 1840
Style of Architecture: Victorian Cottage
Number of Rooms: 7
On-Site Parking: Yes **Wheelchair Access:** Yes

Description of House

Sidney Clopton Lanier, noted Southern poet, was born in this house on February 3, 1842. Among Lanier's best known poems are "The Marshes of Glynn" and "Song of the Chattahoochee."

The simple, white clapboard cottage is an excellent example of the Victorian architectural period and is furnished in keeping with the period. The house maintains many of its original features including the original heart pine floors. An old-fashioned garden has been recreated in the rear of the house. In addition to serving as a house museum, the cottage is also the headquarters for the historical society.

Notable Collections on Exhibit

The Sidney Lanier memorabilia on display include a silver flute, a tea service, silver spoons, books and a chair, as well as hand delivered wedding invitations and family pictures.

Old Cannon Ball House

856 Mulberry Street
Macon, GA 31201
(912) 745-5982

Contact: Sidney Lanier Chapter

Open: Tues.-Fri. 10 a.m.–1 p.m., 2–4 p.m.;
  Sat.-Sun. 1:30–4:30 p.m.

Admission: Adults $3; children (over
  12) $1; children (under 12) $.50.
  Guided tours.

Suggested Time to View House:
  30–45 minutes

Facilities on Premises: Gift shop

Description of Grounds: Court yard in
  back, planted with shrubs and trees

Best Season to View House: Spring

Number of Yearly Visitors: 60,000 plus

Year House Built: 1853

Style of Architecture: Greek Revival

Number of Rooms: 13

On-Site Parking: Yes **Wheelchair Access:** No

Description of House

This beautiful mansion was the only house in Macon hit by Union forces during the Civil War. Judge Asa Holt, the builder of the house, was in the parlor when the house was struck by a cannon ball during an attack on the city by General Stoneman on July 30, 1864.

Handsome Ionic columns embellish the front of the house as well as the delicate drawn-wire railing on the porch and balcony. This perfectly proportioned white frame structure is considered an outstanding example of Greek Revival architecture. The rooms of the house are furnished with handsome antique pieces and ornaments, gold-leaf mirrors, beautiful crystal and china which are gifts from Macon homes dating as far back as the era in which the Cannon Ball House was built, creating an atmosphere of charm and elegance. The house is listed on the National Register of Historic Places and is the headquarters of the local chapter of the United Daughters of the Confederacy.

Notable Collections on Exhibit

In addition to the fine period furnishings, the house also contains a Confederate Museum in the old servants' headquarters with an exhibit of artifacts related to Macon and the Confederacy.

Old Governor's Mansion

120 South Clark Street
Milledgeville, GA 31061
(912) 453-4545

Contact: Georgia College
Open: Tues.-Sat. 10 a.m.–4 p.m., Sun.
  2–4 p.m.; closed on holidays
Admission: Adults $3; students $1. Guided
  tours.
Suggested Time to View House: 45 minutes
Description of Grounds: The mansion is
  located on a one-acre lot with large trees,
  boxwoods and camellias
Best Season to View House: Spring and fall
Number of Yearly Visitors: 5,000
Year House Built: 1835 to 1838
Style of Architecture: Greek Revival

On-Site Parking: Yes **Wheelchair Access:** Yes

Description of House

Patterned after the Palladio's Villa Rotonda and Villa Foscari, this home for Georgia's governors from 1838 to 1868 is considered to be one of the most perfect and imposing examples of Greek Revival architecture in America. Symbolic of the "New Republic", it was the fourth house built as an Executive Mansion after the Revolution. The exterior appearance is distinguished by its Ionic-columned portico topped by a classic impediment. The column caps and bases are made of New England granite as are the window and door sills. The most commanding feature of the mansion is the central rotunda which rises fifty feet high to a domed ceiling of recessed plaster panels with gold decoration on the ornamental moldings.

The predominating style of the furniture is English Regency. In addition, there are many examples from the French Empire and American Federal periods which cover the same period, as well as a collection of Georgia-made pieces. During this period in American history, trade with China was carried on, and many objects of art were imported and decorated the fine houses of the day. The Governor's Mansion is no exception to this display of the Oriental influence in decoration.

Notable Collections on Exhibit

Items on exhibit include a desk and an overmantel mirror, both are Chippendale in design, but carry the same date as the house. Rugs, with the exception of one in the entrance hall, were woven in France, and each was specially designed for the room in which it was placed.

Chieftains

501 Riverside Parkway
Rome, GA 30162-0373
(706) 291-9494

Contact: Chieftains Museum, Inc.

Open: Tues.-Fri. 11 a.m.–4 p.m.;
Sun. 2–5 p.m.

Admission: Adults $1; children free.
Guided tours, audiovisual presentations,
special lectures.

Suggested Time to View House:
45–60 minutes

Facilities on Premises: Gift shop with book
store

Description of Grounds: Herb
gardens—wild flowers on river bank

Best Season to View House: March-May

Style of Architecture: Piedmont
Plantation-style

Number of Yearly Visitors: 20,000

Number of Rooms: 10

Year House Built: 1794

On-Site Parking: Yes **Wheelchair Access:** Yes

Description of House

This attractive house was home to a Cherokee leader known as Major Ridge, a man who walked the delicate line between maintaining his native heritage and adapting to the white man's culture in late 18th and early 19th-century Georgia. Major Ridge was born in 1771 in a small village on the Hiwassee River in south Tennessee. There the Ani-Yunwiyah—Real People as the Cherokee called themselves—found one of the last havens for their traditional lifestyle. While still in his teens, he fought in the last series of border wars against the Unakas, or white settlers, in the Carolinas and Georgia. During the 1800s, Ridge was active in the formation of the Cherokee nation. He earned the rank of major fighting alongside Andrew Jackson against the Creek in the War of 1812. During this time, he formed the opinion that the best tactic for the preservation of the Cherokee people was to adapt to the white man's ways while retaining their traditional culture.

At the core of the house is a log cabin, built about 200 years ago. In 1828, it was expanded into a typical Piedmont style plantation house; the expansion was possible because of the prosperity of Ridge's holdings. Unfortunately, Ridge was forced to leave his lovely home in 1835 and moved West with other Native Americans. Over the years, rooms were rebuilt and the kitchen was attached. In the 1920s, two wings with elegant Palladian windows were added. In 1969, the home became a museum.

Notable Collections on Exhibit

The museum offers a permanent historic exhibit with paintings of family members who owned or living in house, lithographs of early Cherokees, and 18th and 19th-century furnishings. There are also changing special exhibits featuring local artists or historic themes.

Oak Hill

189 Mount Berry Station
Rome, GA 30149-0189
(706) 291-1883

Contact: Oak Hill and The Martha Berry
Museum

Open: Tues.-Sat. 10 a.m.–5 p.m.; Sun.
1–5 p.m.; closed all national holidays;
groups by reservation

Admission: Adults $3; children, $1.50;
groups, $1.50 adult, $.75 children.
Guided tours, filmed presentation

Suggested Time to View House: 2 hours

Facilities on Premises: Gift shop, weaving
studio

Description of Grounds: Nature trails and
formal gardens

Best Season to View House: April-Oct.

Number of Yearly Visitors: 20,000 plus

Year House Built: 1847

Style of Architecture: Georgian

Number of Rooms: 12

On-Site Parking: Yes

Wheelchair Access: Yes

Description of House

Oak Hill was the family home of Martha Berry (1866-1942), the founder
of Berry College. This unique institution was founded to serve children of
lower Appalachia, it is now among the leading small liberal arts colleges in
America. Martha's father, Captain Thomas Berry, was a distinguished
veteran of the Mexican-American and Civil Wars. He was also a cotton
grower and broker. Her sister later became Princess Eugenia Ruspoli of
Rome, Italy.

This classic antebellum mansion uses Georgian style architecture. The
home once functioned as a cotton plantation. Oak Hill is distinguished by
identically columned facades on the front and back.

Notable Collections on Exhibit

The house is maintained as it was in 1942 with the entire family collection intact. All furnishings, china, silver, books and paintings are displayed
as they were used in home. Outstanding furniture includes Chinese Chippendale and Federal mirrors, an Aubusson rug, and a Waterford chandelier.
The extensive art collection housed in museum includes the Ruspoli collection of European paintings, furnishings and statuary.

Chief John Ross House

P.O. Box 863
Rossville, GA 30741
(706) 861-3954

Contact: Chief John Ross House Association
Open: May 1-Sept. 1, Mon.-Sun., 1–5 p.m.; closed Wed.
Admission: Free, donations accepted. Guided tours
Suggested Time to View House: 25 minutes
Facilities on Premises: Sales desk
Best Season to View House: Spring and fall
Number of Yearly Visitors: 2,000
Year House Built: 1797
Style of Architecture: Log cabin
Number of Rooms: 5

On-Site Parking: Yes **Wheelchair Access:** No

Description of House

This simple log cabin is a memorial to John Ross, one of the great chiefs of the Cherokee nation. Ross struggled unsuccessfully against Andrew Jackson's plan to drive the Cherokees west of the Mississippi, after the discovery of gold in north Georgia. He witnessed, in despair, the horrible scene of U.S. soldiers herding, as cattle, Indian men, women, and children for the journey West. Indescribable was the suffering, heartbreak and death of so many on the journey known as the Trail of Tears. Quatie, Ross's first wife, died of pneumonia, on route to Oklahoma, due to cold and exposure, after she gave her blanket to a sick child.

The cabin was built in 1797 by John McDonald, the maternal grandfather of John Ross. He was a Scotch trader who established a trading post on the Tennessee River at what is now known as Chattanooga. The two-story log cabin has plank flooring and rock chimneys, assembled with wooden pegs. Today, it maintains ninety percent of its original construction. The cabin was probably the first school in north Georgia and later served as Ross's headquarters before his forced move to Oklahoma.

Notable Collections on Exhibit

Furniture and decorative objects on display include a kitchen table (a replica of the one used by the John Ross household), ironstone dishes and pressed glassware, an ornate bedstead from a later Ross home, a handwoven bedspread and a piece of embroidery in an upstairs bedroom.

Isaiah Davenport House Museum

324 East State Street
Savannah, GA
(912) 236-8097

Contact: Historic Savannah Foundation

Open: Mon.-Sat. 10 a.m.—4:30 p.m., Sun.
1:30 p.m.—4:30 p.m., closed Thur. and
major holidays

Admission: Donation.. Tours given on hour
and half hour, last tour begins at 4 p.m.

Suggested Time to View House: 1 hour

Facilities on Premises: Museum shop

Description of Grounds: A beautiful
garden is accessible to the public

Best Season to View House: Summer-fall

Year House Built: 1820

Style of Architecture: Federal

Number of Rooms: 10

On-Site Parking: Yes

Description of House

The Isaiah Davenport House was completed in 1820 by a Rhode Island master builder who was trained as a ship builder. Isaiah Davenport came to Savannah in 1807 and married Sarah Rosamond Clark in 1809. Using the knowledge he gained in his New England home and copying what he could find in current architectural texts, Davenport created this fine example of traditional Federal architecture. During his years in Savannah, Davenport prospered as a master builder, became a city alderman, and later died of yellow fever in 1827.

The Davenport House nearly met the fate of many historic houses. By the 1950s, the structure had deteriorated and developers wanted to raze the building to make room for a parking lot. Concerned citizens rallied round and raised funds to save the house and create the Historic Savannah Foundation. Today the interior has been restored and features a lovely elliptical double stairway and a fanlight over the door. The house is furnished with 19th-century furnishings and features several pieces belonging to the Davenports.

Owens-Thomas Museum

124 Abercorn Street
Savannah, GA
(912) 233-9743

Contact: Owens-Thomas House and
Museum
Open: Oct.-Aug.: Tues.-Sat. 10 a.m.-5 p.m.,
Sun.-Mon. 2-5 p.m. Closed Sept. and
major holidays
Admission: Adults $3; students $2;
children (6-12) $1.
Description of Grounds: A beautiful
formal parterre garden
Year House Built: 1817 to 1819
Style of Architecture: English Regency

Description of House

The stylish residence was built for Richard Richardson, a cotton merchant and banker from New Orleans, and his Savannah born wife, Francis Bolton, the sister-in-law of William Jay. The Richardsons were doomed to lose their splendid house soon after completion. For a short time, the house was rented to Mrs. Mary Maxwell. In 1830, George W. Owens, Congressman, lawyer, and at one time mayor of Savannah, purchased the house from the bank of the United States. It remained in the Owens family until 1951 when George Owens's granddaughter bequeathed it to the Telfair Academy.

The Owens-Thomas House is considered by architectural historians to be the finest example of an English Regency house in America. The house was designed in England by William Jay, a young architect from Bath. Because it was designed in London, before Jay had ever come to Savannah, it has a subtlety and sophistication not found in other Southern homes of the period. The floors are Georgia pine and many of the walls are made of "tabby," a local mixture of burnt shells, sand, and water. The interior of the house is an outstanding interpretation of the Regency style with its columned foyer and unique bridge spanning the stairwell at the second story. The house is furnished with a number of original pieces, including some that belonged to the original owner of the house, Richard Richardson.

Notable Collections on Exhibit

Among the important objects displayed in the home are a Philadelphia mahogany dining table with twelve chairs, a marble-topped console table, two rare New York carved giltwood looking glasses. There are examples of Duncan Phyfe's work in the Sheraton style, a mahogany caned back settee, a five legged mahogany card table and also an upholstered mahogany sofa. Further complementing the highly refined setting are rare selections of China Trade porcelains, blue and white Canton porcelains (c. 1750-1840), and a prized wine pitcher made by Samuel Kirk Baltimore (c. 1815).

Additional Information

General Lafayette, the celebrated Revolutionary War hero, stayed in the house and delivered his famous balcony speech to a crowd of Savannahians.

Telfair Mansion and Art Museum

121 Barnard Street
Savannah, GA
(912) 232-1177

Contact: Telfair Mansion and
  Art Museum
Open: Year-round, Tues.-Sat.
  10 a.m.–5 p.m., Sun. 2–5 p.m.,
  closed major holidays
Admission: Adults $2.50; students $1;
  children (6-12) $.50; children
  (under 6) free; also free on Sun.
  Tours; guided tours available in
  French, Italian and Spanish
  by special arrangement
Year House Built: 1818
Style of Architecture: Regency

Description of House

The mansion was built for Alexander Telfair, son of Edward Telfair the governor of Georgia and a Revolutionary patriot. The residence occupies the site of Government House, home of the Royal Governors of Georgia from 1760 to the end of the Revolutionary War. In 1875, Mary Telfair, sister of Alexander and the last member of the Telfair family, bequeathed the home and its furnishings to the Georgia Historical Society to be opened as a museum.

The Telfair Mansion, considered one of the most important buildings in Georgia, was built in 1818. The building was designed by William Jay, a young English architect noted for introducing Regency architecture to America. The exterior is characterized by several distinctive features of the Regency style, including major emphasis on the columned porch with stairs extending from both sides. The interior space is marked by the accurately restored period rooms, particularly the octagon and dining rooms. The Telfair Mansion was dedicated as a National Historic Landmark in 1977 and is the oldest public art museum in the Southeast.

Notable Collections on Exhibit

The mansion exhibits a distinguished collection of fine and decorative arts. Such important objects as the Telfair family's Duncan Phyfe sideboard, Savannah-made silver, and an ensemble of Boston regency furniture are displayed in the opulent rooms. The museum displays an unsurpassed collection of American, French, and German Impressionist paintings including the brilliant palettes of Willard Metcalf, Childe Hassam, Frederick Frieseke, and George Bellows.

Plum Orchard Mansion

P.O. Box 806
St. Mary's, GA 31558
(912) 882-4335

Contact: Cumberland Island National
Seashore

Open: April-Sept., Sun.; Oct.-March, the
first Sun. of the month. Reservations
recommended.

Admission: $6 plus tax per person for the
ferry trip to Plum Orchard in addition to
the customary ferry rate to the island..
Ferry ride to the island and interpretive
tour of Plum Orchard mansion's
interior; camping permitted.

Description of Grounds: The house is
located on Cumberland Island.

Year House Built: 1898

Number of Rooms: 30

Style of Architecture: Georgian Revival

Description of House

The house was built as a wedding present by Lucy Carnegie to her son George Lauder Carnegie and his wife Margaret Thaw. Lucy was the wife of Thomas Carnegie, brother and business partner of steel magnate, Andrew Carnegie. Later, in 1971 the mansion was donated to the National Park Foundation and the Carnegie's were instrumental in helping win Congressional support for the establishment of Cumberland Island as a National Seashore.

Their lovely mansion was built on the foundations of an earlier mansion known as Dungeness. The earlier mansion had been the home to Revolutionary War hero Nathaniel Greene and his wife, Catherine. Plum Orchard Mansion is a thirty-room Georgian Revival style mansion constructed in 1898. The interior of the house is restored to the appropriate period of the house.

Additional Information

As a complement to a visit to Plum Orchard Mansion, visitors should take the time to visit the Ice House Museum, located next to Dungeness Dock. Here, within a restored 19th-century ice house, you will discover the fascinating, often turbulent history of Cumberland Island. This history includes not only thriving Native American towns, Colonial Spanish missions, English forts and villages, but also the likes of James Oglethorpe (the founder of Georgia), General Nathaniel Greene, and inventor Eli Whitney.

Pebble Hill

P.O. Box 830
Thomasville, GA 31799
(912) 226-23441

Contact: Pebble Hill Foundation

Open: Tues.-Sat. 10 a.m.–5 p.m., Sun. 1–5 p.m., closed Labor Day-Oct. 1, Thanksgiving snd Christmas

Admission: Adults $5, children (6-12) $2.50. Guided tours, last tour begins at 4 p.m.

Suggested Time to View House: 2 hours

Facilities on Premises: Visitor's center, gift shop

Description of Grounds: The gardens in front of the main house are filled with dogwoods, azaleas, and camellias

Best Season to View House: Spring- summer

Year House Built: c. 1820

On-Site Parking: Yes **Wheelchair Access:** Yes

Description of House

Pebble Hill is an outstanding example of an antebellum plantation with numerous outbuildings complementing the beautiful main house. The history of Pebble Hill Plantation and that of Thomas County are inseparable. Thomas Jefferson Johnson, author of the bill creating Thomas County, was also the founder of Thomasville. He built the first house on Pebble Hill about 1827. Julia Ann, his daughter, married a local planter named John W.H. Mitchell and inherited the plantation after her parents died. In 1850, the Mitchells replaced the original structure with a house designed by the young English architect, John Wind. In 1896, the plantation was sold to Howard Melville Hanna, an industrialist from Cleveland, who used the home as a winter retreat. His daughter, Kate, worked to restore the mansion to its former glory and built gatehouses, a Jersey barn, and a country store. Some of the more notable people to have visited the plantation include Presidents Dwight Eisenhower and Jimmy Carter, and the Duke and Duchess of Windsor. Pebble Hill is filled with furnishings and decorations collected by the families over the years; all have been remarkably well preserved.

Notable Collections on Exhibit

The house reflects the avid collecting interests its former residents and items on display range from an outstanding collection of porcelain, silver, crystal and glassware to an unusual arrangement of arrowheads and Indian memorabilia. Many fine paintings hang on the walls such as notable Audubon prints, as well as works by British and American artists. Of special interest are the many horse and hound paintings.

Additional Information

Visitors to Pebble Hill will enjoy a walk through the landscaped grounds with its many outbuildings including horse stables, a dog kennel, which once sheltered nearly 100 dogs, a dog hospital, a log cabin school, a garage with a 1934 Packard and a 1948 Lincoln, and a working carpenter's shop.

Little White House Historic Site

Route 1, Box 10
Warm Springs, GA 31830
(706) 655-3511

Contact: Georgia Department of Natural
Resources

Open: Daily, 9 a.m.–5 p.m.; closed
Thanksgiving and Christmas day

Admission: Adults $4; children (6-18) $2;
under 6, free. Introductory film, special
programs

Suggested Time to View House: 1 hour

Facilities on Premises: Gift shop/snack bar

Description of Grounds: Walkways to
building

Style of Architecture: Modified Greek
Revival

Best Season to View House: Spring-fall

Number of Yearly Visitors: 115,000-130,000

Number of Rooms: 6

Year House Built: 1932

On-Site Parking: Yes **Wheelchair Access:** Yes

Description of House

Franklin Delano Roosevelt first came to Warm Springs while governor
of New York state in 1924, searching for relief from polio. In this small
western Georgia community, Roosevelt found the rejuvenating spring
waters and soon after built this country mountain home. His stays at Warm
Springs renewed his spirit and gave him the strength to meet the challenges
of four Presidential elections, an economic depression, and World War II.
He died here on April 12, 1945.

Roosevelt chose a beautiful site on the north slope of Pine Mountain
overlooking a deep wooded ravine for his Little White House. The small
frame dwelling was completed in the spring of 1932. The house and original
furnishings represent Roosevelt's desire for simple comfort and restful
enjoyment.

Notable Collections on Exhibit

The most historically significant object on display is the unfinished b
watercolor portrait being painted of President Roosevelt when he suffered
the fatal seizure on the morning of April 12, 1945. Some items of furniture
are from the Val-Kil Industries that were sponsored as a result of Eleanor
Roosevelt's interest in helping the common people during the Great Depression.

The Brick House

P.O. Box 661
Washington, GA 30673
(706) 678-2013

Contact: Callaway Plantation
Open: March 1-Dec. 15, Tues.-Sat.
10 a.m.–5 p.m., Sun. 2–5 p.m.
Admission: Adults $2; children (12 and under) $1; adult groups $1.50; school groups $.50. Guided tours, craft demonstrations, "Mule Day" (early Oct.), "Christmas at Callaway" (first weekend in Dec.)

Suggested Time to View House:
60–90 minutes
Facilities on Premises: Country store
Best Season to View House: April-Oct.
Number of Yearly Visitors: 8,000
Year House Built: 1869
Style of Architecture: Greek Revival
Number of Rooms: 10
On-Site Parking: Yes **Wheelchair Access:** Yes

Description of House

This working plantation brings history alive for visitors to this rural Georgian community. The land was originally part of a land grant given after the American Revolution. The Callaway family arrived in 1783 and have held this land to the present time.

The great manor house, built of red brick made at the site and designed in Greek Revival style, was constructed in 1869. The home remains virtually unaltered; the doors, mantels and most of the plaster are original and have survived in remarkably good condition. Connected to the rear of the mansion by a breezeway is the self-contained brick kitchen. Each room is furnished with excellent examples of period furniture; some belonged to the Callaway family.

Additional Information

The oldest building in the complex, the hand-hewn log cabin, was probably an early settler's first home constructed around 1785. The house exhibits many early domestic and agricultural tools as well as primitive furniture. The grounds also feature a smokehouse, pigeon house, a barn and a cemetery. Adjacent to the plantation stands the Gilmer House, the boyhood home of George Gilmer who served two terms as Georgia's governor in the early 19th century.

Kentucky

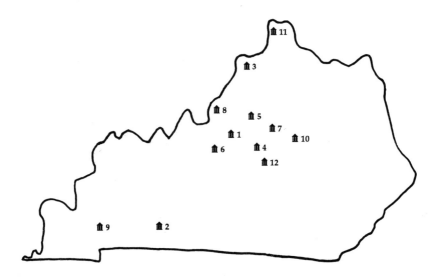

1. **Bardstown**
   My Old Kentucky Home

2. **Bowling Green**
   Historic Riverview at Hobson Grove

3. **Carrollton**
   Butler-Turpin House

4. **Danville**
   McDowell House and Apothecary Shop

5. **Frankfort**
   Berry Hill Mansion
   Executive Mansion
   Liberty Hall & The Orlando Brown House
   Old Governor's Mansion
   Vest-Lindsey House

6. **Hodgenville**
   Lincoln's Boyhood Home

7. **Lexington**
   Ashland
   Waveland State Historic Site

8. **Louisville**
   Farmington
   Locust Grove
   Thomas Edison House
   Ferguson Mansion

9. **Princeton**
   Adsmore Museum

10. **Richmond**
    White Hall

11. **South Union**
    1824 Centre Family Dwelling

12. **Stanford**
    William Whitley House

My Old Kentucky Home

U.S. 150, P.O. Box 323
Bardstown, KY 40004
(502) 348-3502

Contact: Kentucky Department of Parks

Open: June-Labor Day, 8 a.m.–7:15 p.m.;
May and Labor Day-Oct. 8 a.m.–4:45 p.m.;
Nov.-April, 9 a.m.–4:45 p.m., closed major
holidays

Admission: Adults $4; seniors $3.50;
children (6-12) $2. Guided tours by
costumed docents, outdoor musical
drama in summer months, Christmas
candlelight tour, call for more information
and schedule.

Suggested Time to View House: 1 hour

Facilities on Premises: Gift shop,
recreational facilities

Description of Grounds: Rolling blue grass
hills surround the mansion; a
campground is available nearby.

Best Season to View House: Summer

Year House Built: 1818

Style of Architecture: early Georgian

Number of Rooms: 7

On-Site Parking: Yes **Wheelchair Access:** Yes

Description of House

Considered the most recognized historic site in Kentucky, My Old Kentucky Home achieved immortality through the song of the same name by Stephen Foster. Judge John Rowan, a cousin of Stephen Foster's father, completed the house in 1818 and named it "Federal Hill". While visiting in 1852, Foster was inspired to write his world-famous song. During his brief lifetime of thirty-seven years, Foster wrote more than 200 songs including "Oh Susannah" but none of his works are as well-known as the song played before the Kentucky Derby each year. The house's owner, Judge Rowan, was famous in his own right having achieved distinction as a U.S. Senator. At Federal Hill, Rowan was known for lavish entertainment and received such celebrated guests such as Henry Clay and Aaron Burr.

The Rowans originally lived in a basic log house on the property before building this fine Georgian-style home. The design was based on houses Rowan had seen traveling between Maryland and Washington, D.C. and combines Georgian proportions with a Federal-style entry. The imposing brick structure has seven large rooms with fifteen-foot ceilings and yellow poplar floors. The hall, a copy of Independence Hall in Philadelphia, has twelve stairs on each side of the arch. In 1840, a fire caused by lightening nearly destroyed the home and when it was rebuilt Rowan created a ballroom, a large hallway, and a workroom on the third floor. The home's decor, including rare and beautiful period furnishings, is much as it was when Foster was a guest here.

Additional Information

For summer visitors, My Old Kentucky Home offers a special attraction of a musical performed in an outdoor amphitheater celebrating Stephen Foster's music. Contact (800) 626-1563 for information.

Historic Riverview at Hobson Grove

P.O. Box 10059
1100 West Main Avenue
Bowling Green, KY 42102-4859
(502) 843-5565

Contact: Hobson House Association, Inc.

Open: Tues.-Sat. 10 a.m.–noon, 1–4 p.m.; Sun. 1–4 p.m.; hours extended to 5 p.m. from May-Oct.

Admission: Adults $3.50; students $1.50; 6 and under free; group discounts on request. Guided tours, special events and programs throughout the year.

Suggested Time to View House: 50 minutes

Facilities on Premises: Museum shop

Description of Grounds: 13 acres of the estate which once included 400 acres

Best Season to View House: Spring-fall

Number of Yearly Visitors: 5,000 plus

Year House Built: Started 1857, completed 1872

Style of Architecture: Italianate

Number of Rooms: 17

On-Site Parking: Yes   **Wheelchair Access:** No

Description of House

Riverview at Hobson Grove is a handsome Italianate structure begun in 1857 by Atwood and Julia Van Meter Hobson. Construction halted when Confederate forces occupied the town and used the partially built home to store ammunition though the Hobsons were Union sympathizers. Completed in 1872 and used as Hobson residence until 1952, the house consists of two floors plus a full basement and an observatory.

Noted as one of the finest examples of Italianate architecture in Kentucky, the home is on the National Register of Historic Places.

The house maintains a number of notable features including elaborately painted ceilings in the double parlors, done by Fritz Leiber (c. 1873) and a unique ventilation system utilizing the cupola of the Italianate structure. There is also an unusual water system in the attic of the home by which water was supplied to the second floor bathing area. The furnishings are appropriate for a south-central Kentucky family home of the 1860 to 1890 period, and feature several original family-owned pieces.

Notable Collections on Exhibit

There is an outstanding collection of 19th-century furniture (pre 1891), ranging from Sheraton county pieces to Eastlake inspired pieces. In addition, an impressive collection of pre 1891 silver, silverplate and a wide variety of items used in dining and entertaining are on display.

Butler-Turpin House

P.O. Box 325
Carrollton, KY 41008
(502) 732-4384

Contact: Kentucky State Parks

Open: Memorial Day-Labor Day,
9 a.m.–5 p.m.

Admission: Adults $1.50; children $.75;
children (under 6) free. Guided tours.

Suggested Time to View House: 30 minutes

Description of Grounds: The house is
located in General Butler State Resort
park, an area filled with many
recreational facilities, nature trails and
wooded areas.

Best Season to View House: Summer

Year House Built: 1859

Style of Architecture: Kentucky vernacular

Number of Rooms: 8

On-Site Parking: Yes

Description of House

Philip Turpin, member of a prominent Kentucky family, built this fine home in 1859 along with a carriage house, stables, and other necessary buildings. Turpin lived here with his wife, Mary Eleanor Butler, the niece of General William Butler for whom the park is named. The Butler family was also well-known in Kentucky having distinguished themselves militarily in the Revolutionary War and other conflicts. The Turpins and their children moved into their new home in 1859. However, Mary was not able to enjoy her new home for long; she died in 1860. Philip sold the house in 1880 to H.J. Whitehead, and moved to Louisville, where he died two years later.

The Butler-Turpin House is a three-bay, two-story brick structure of the Kentucky vernacular style with Italianate and Greek Revival influences. The residence was typical for a well-to-do Kentucky landowner of the period. This fine example of a mid 19th-century farmhouse has a one-and-a-half story stone kitchen located south of the main house and connected by a roofed porch. The interior features the original staircase with cherry balusters and handrails on the north side of the central hall. In order to make the scrollwork trim on the end of the steps curve at the turn of the stairway, a clever carpenter used leather instead of wood. The door and window moldings on the first floor are of Greek "ear" design. The mantelpieces in all the rooms are simple Greek Revival. The original high baseboards remain intact throughout the house.

The house today contains an excellent collection of Empire, Regency, and early Victorian furniture (c. 1819-1850) which represents the type and style that the Turpins would have used.

McDowell House and Apothecary Shop

125 South Second Street
Danville, KY 40422
(606) 236-2804

Contact: Ephraim McDowell
Cambus-Kennith Foundation

Open: Mon.-Sat. 10 a.m.–noon, 1–4 p.m.;
Sun. 2–4 p.m.; closed Mon. from
Dec.-Mar.

Admission: Adults $3; seniors and students
$2; children $.50; groups (10 or more) $2
(reservation in advance). Guided tours,
special activities.

Suggested Time to View House: 1 hour

Facilities on Premises: Gift shop

Description of Grounds: Formal garden
and herb garden

Year House Built: 1795 to 1820

Number of Yearly Visitors: 2,500-3,500

Number of Rooms: 7

Best Season to View House: May-Sept.

Style of Architecture: Georgian

On-Site Parking: No **Wheelchair Access:** No

Description of House

This modest, brick house was home to one of the country's most notable pioneer doctors, Epraim McDowell. McDowell came to Danville from Virginia with his father, Samuel, at the age of twelve. Later, he studied at the University of Edinburg, and began to practice medicine in 1795. McDowell married Sarah Shelby, daughter of Governor Isaac Shelby in 1802, and together they had nine children. In this house McDowell made some of his first medical breakthroughs in surgery. On Christmas day in 1809, he performed the first surgery for the removal of a large ovarian tumor. Dr. McDowell's success thus paved the way for modern abdominal surgery and earned him the name the "Father of Abdominal Surgery." Dr. McDowell practiced here and also went to surrounding states to perform surgery; his successful operations brought him considerable fame. Ironically, he died in 1830 of an ailment which surgery could have saved—appendicitis.

The house has several distinct elements, each built during a different period. The white, frame front section was constructed in 1804 using a town house-style with two rooms upstairs and two downstairs divided by a hall. The earlier back section (c. 1790) originally served as a kitchen and later as an apothecary shop for Dr. McDowell's patients. This shop was the first in Kentucky and the first used west of the Allegheny mountains. A second apothecary was built in 1785 and now houses the offices and gift shop.

The furniture represents the period of Dr. McDowell's practice and most has been carefully collected. There are also some original family pieces and portraits on display.

Notable Collections on Exhibit

The house exhibits a fine collection of antique chairs, coins, old English silver, quilts, and samplers. The collection in the apothecary features delft drug jars, Queensware, many early bottles, scales, and mortars and pestles.

Berry Hill Mansion

700 Louisville Road
Frankfort, KY 40601
(502) 564-3000

Contact: Office of Historic Properties
Open: Mon.-Fri. 8 a.m.–4:30 p.m.; closed
weekends and holidays
Description of Grounds: Available for
picnics and hikes

Year House Built: Main block 1900, Gothic
music room 1910-1912
Best Season to View House: Year round
Style of Architecture: Georgian Revival
Number of Rooms: 22
On-Site Parking: Yes **Wheelchair Access:** Yes

Description of House

Situated on a prominent western bluff overlooking the state capitol and Frankfort, the George Franklin Berry estate was originally called Juniper Hill because of the many red cedar trees on the property. Berry was a prosperous distiller in the area whose wealth is evident in this fine mansion.

Constructed in 1900, the original stone mansion was designed by the eminent Louisville architectural firm of McDonald and Dodd. The structure's design is a notable example of mansions erected between 1865 and 1917 in the Georgian Revival style. Stones which were used to build the twenty-two room structure at Jupiter Hill came from the property and the mansion rests on a full stone cellar blasted from solid rock. The site's most outstanding feature, however, is an elaborate music room built in the Gothic Revival style. With pipes rising behind an intricately carved oak grill, a massive cathedral organ dominates the north wall of the music room. Two European wood carvers, one a native of Nuremburg, spent two years carving ornamentation for the room. Large bay windows, stained glass, and a library balcony once used to seat string ensembles further attest to the room's prominence. Completed in 1912, the music room still remains the mansion's architectural and focal point.

Additional Information

Berry Hill currently houses offices for state government agencies but is open for public viewing during regular office hours.

Executive Mansion

Capitol Avenue
Frankfort, KY 40601
(502) 564-8004

Contact: Office of Historic Properties
Open: Tues. and Thur. 9–11 a.m.; closed on
major holidays
Admission: Free. Guided tours, hands-on
student activities, teacher materials for
pre and post-site visits.
Suggested Time to View House: 30 minutes

Description of Grounds: Formal French
gardens at the front of the mansion
Best Season to View House: Spring,
especially at Derby (May)
Number of Yearly Visitors: 100,000 plus
Year House Built: 1914
Style of Architecture: Beaux Art
Number of Rooms: 25
On-Site Parking: No **Wheelchair Access:** No

Description of House

This beautiful Beaux Art-style mansion has been home to twenty-one Kentucky governors including the current governor. The mansion sits on the east lawn of the Capitol grounds on a bluff overlooking the Kentucky River. The design and appearance of the building was modeled after the Petit Trianon, Marie Antoinette's villa near the Palace of Versaille in France.

Designed by C.C. and E.A. Weber of Fort Thomas, Kentucky, historians credit much of the ultimate design to its first resident, Governor James McCreary. The twenty-five room, three-story mansion was finally completed for the aging governor's second term. Nearly eighty-feet tall and 200-feet long, the mansion has walls of solid brick, faced with Bowling Green limestone. The front portico is supported by four pairs of Ionic columns. A sonte balustrade and terrace create an impressive entrance. The formal reception room, salon, and ballroom all open off cross hallways, and the state dining room, a large semi-circular bay, has tall windows framing a clear view of rolling hillsides in the distance. The interior features many exquisite details and decorative features including hallo lighting in the state dining room with rows of light bulbs mounted in rosettes. Double stairways wind gracefully upward to the private living quarters. The mansion was added to the National Register of Historic Places in 1972.

Notable Collections on Exhibit

In addition to the fine architectural details, the Executive Mansion houses many notable items belonging to former governors. There is a collection of battleship silver crafted in Philadelphia in sterling silver, and paid for by the contributions of Kentucky citizens; the cost was $30,000 in 1889. A pair of silver demi-tasse cups which belonged to Governor and Mrs. A.O. Stanley (1915-1919) are on display as well as a pair of silver candleabras owned by Kentucky's first governor, Isaac Shelby (1792 to 1796 and 1812 to 1816).

Additional Information

Visitors to the Executive Mansion should also take the time to stop by at the State Capitol, another notable Beaux Art-style building just a few minutes away. Following in the French style, the Capitol Building has a state reception room modeled after Marie Antionette's drawing room at the Palace of Versaille and a rotunda dome patterned after the dome over Napoleon's tomb in the Hotel des Invalides in Paris. In addition, there is a unique collection of French-fashioned miniature replicas of Kentucky's first ladies on display.

Liberty Hall &
The Orlando Brown House

218 Wilkinson Street
Frankfort, KY 40601
(502) 227-2560

Contact: Society of Colonial Dames

Open: March-Dec., Tues.-Sat.
10 a.m.–4 p.m., Sun. 2–4 p.m.; closed
major holidays

Admission: Adults $4.50, students $2
(combined admission to both houses).
Guided tours.

Suggested Time to View House:
30 minutes for each house

Description of Grounds: An 18th-century
garden extends from the houses to the
Kentucky River.

Best Season to View House: Spring and
summer

Year House Built: Liberty Hall-c. 1796,
Orlando Brown House-1835

Style of Architecture: Liberty
Hall-Georgian, Orlando Brown
House-Greek Revival

On-Site Parking: No

Description of House

These two fine historic houses stand side by side in Frankfort's oldest residential neighborhood. Liberty Hall was the home to John Brown, one of the first Senators from Kentucky. According to history, Brown named the lovely Georgian mansion after his grammar school in Virginia. The house features a distinctive L shape and a large Palladian window which overlooks the street. Liberty Hall is furnished with an excellent collection of period furnishings, including many heirlooms and artifacts which belonged to the Brown family. One of the most impressive features of the house is the two-acre garden filled with boxwoods which extends down to the banks of the Kentucky River.

The society's other property, the Orlando Brown House, was a gift from Senator Brown to his son. Designed by noted architect Gideon Schryoth, the designer of the old Kentucky Capitol, the house represents one of the first examples of Greek Revival architecture in the city. Like Liberty Hall, the Orlando Brown House also exhibits many fine period furnishings, family portraits, and an outstanding collection of silver and china.

Together, the two houses's collections represent the lifestyle and achievements of several generations of one of the most prominent families in the state.

Old Governor's Mansion

420 High Street
Frankfort, KY 40601
(502) 564-5500

Contact: Office of Historic Properties
Open: Tues. and Thur. 1:30–3:30 p.m.;
  closed holidays
Admission: Free. Guided tours.
Suggested Time to View House:
  20–30 minutes
Description of Grounds: Enclosed side
  garden and small herb garden
Best Season to View House: All year
Number of Yearly Visitors: 40,000 plus
Year House Built: 1798
Style of Architecture: Federal style with
  Georgian features
Number of Rooms: 14

On-Site Parking: No **Wheelchair Access:** Yes

Description of House

Kentucky's Old Governor's Mansion is said to be the oldest official residence still in use in the United States. This stately brick mansion has been home to thirty-three Kentucky governors, and nine lieutenant governors. Two former governors, Robert P. Letcher and Thomas Metcalfe, assisted with the construction of the building although the architect remains unknown.

Situated in historic downtown Frankfort, this two-story structure features Flemish bond brickwork on all four sides. Often referred to as "the Palace" in its early days, the mansion has always been distinguished by the hospitality of its occupants. The parlor and formal dining room have welcomed many notable Presidents, officials of state, and dignitaries such as Theodore Roosevelt, Andrew Jackson, Louis Philippe of France, the Marquis de Lafayette, and Henry Clay. The mansion is listed on the National Register of Historic Places.

The furnishings are a combination of collected period and reproduction pieces together with pieces owned by former residents. Some of the notable furnishings include a Sheraton sideboard, a Hepplewhite banquet table and chairs, and several vernacular furnishings crafted by local artisans.

Notable Collections on Exhibit

Several pieces of historical memorabilia are on display including a clock given to Governor J.C.W Beckham after leaving office by the citizens of Frankfort (1900-1907) and a tea set given to the mansion by Eleanor Beckham in memory of her father.

Vest-Lindsey House

401 Wapping Street
Frankfort, KY 40601
(502) 564-6980

Contact: Office of Historic Properties
Open: Weekdays 8 a.m.–4 p.m.;
 closed on holidays
Admission: Free. Guided tours.
Suggested Time to View House: 20 minutes
Description of Grounds: Small garden
 and courtyard
Best Season to View House: Spring-fall
Number of Yearly Visitors: 1,100
Year House Built: 1820
Style of Architecture: Federal
Number of Rooms: 12

On-Site Parking: No **Wheelchair Access:** Yes

Description of House

The house was the boyhood home of George Graham Vest, U.S. Senator for twenty-five years. Vest is best remembered for his closing trial arguments in the 1870 suit over a man's killing of his neighbor's dog. From his famed "tribute to a dog" speech, Vest coined the immortal line "Dog is man's best friend." Daniel Weisiger Lindsey also lived in the house. He was a Union Army major general, adjutant general and Inspector General of the Kentucky military forces.

The Vest-Lindsey House is a small Federal-style home built with red brick in a Flemish bond pattern. From 1965 to 1976 the building served as the headquarters for the Kentucky Heritage Commission. It was then refurnished with antiques and reproductions to reflect its original 19th-century decor and opened to the public.

Additional Information

The Vest-Lindsey House is located in a four-block area known as "A Corner in Celebrites" which has been designated a National Register District. A walking tour through this oldest residential neighborhood in Frankfort will take you past twenty-eight historic homes and churches. The Vest-Lindsey house now serves as the official state meeting house, but remains open to the public for tours.

Lincoln's Boyhood Home

Route 31E
Hodgenville, KY 42748
(502) 549-3741

Contact: National Park Service

Open: Memorial Day-Labor Day, 9 a.m.–7
p.m., other times 9 a.m.–5 p.m., closed
on holidays

Admission: Adults $1, children $.50. Tours.

Suggested Time to View House: 30 minutes

Description of Grounds: Located in a
national park with nature trails and
picnic facilities

Best Season to View House: Spring-fall

Number of Yearly Visitors: 1,100

Year House Built: 1808

Number of Rooms: 1

Style of Architecture: Log cabin

On-Site Parking: Yes **Wheelchair Access:** Yes

Description of House

This national historic site houses the simple, log cabin where one of our nation's greatest Presidents was born. The cabin is now housed in a memorial building designed by John Russell Pope and built between 1909 and 1910. Abraham Lincoln's family moved to the Sinking Creek Farm in 1808. The original cabin was probably a typical frontier dwelling, about eighteen by sixteen feet, with a dirt floor, a window covered with greased paper, a single door, a low chimney made of clay, straw, and hard wood. Lincoln was born on February 12, 1809 in this humble setting. Two years later, the family moved ten miles east to a farm on Knob Creek where the soil was richer and farming better. In 1816, while Lincoln was still a young man, the family crossed the Ohio to Indiana where he would grow into manhood and continue his education. Visitors to the birthplace and park will receive insight into the austere and poor beginnings of the man who would shape so much of our history.

Additional Information

The cabin and memorial are located in a large park with nature trails and an environmental study area. A walk along the forest trail will give visitors a good idea of the natural resources the Lincoln family had to work with and just how resourceful these early Kentucky settlers were.

Ashland

120 Sycamore Road
Lexington, KY 40502
(606) 266-8581

Contact: Henry Clay Memorial Foundation
Open: May 1-Oct. 31, Mon.-Sat.
9:30 a.m.–4:30 p.m., Sun. 1–4:30 p.m.;
Nov. 1-April 30, Mon.-Sat. 10 a.m.–4 p.m.,
Sun. 1–4 p.m.
Admission: Adults $4; children $1.50; group
rates available. Guided tours.
Suggested Time to View House: 45 minutes

Facilities on Premises: Gift shop
Description of Grounds: 18 acres
surrounding the house, garden
Number of Yearly Visitors: 15,000
Year House Built: 1855
Style of Architecture: Italianate
On-Site Parking: Yes **Wheelchair Access:** No

Description of House

Born in Virginia in 1777, the American statesman Henry Clay ventured
to Lexington when he was twenty, after studying under the brilliant attorney
George Wythe. Here he began the practice of law and an illustrious political
career that was to span fifty years. Clay not only served in the Senate for
fifteen years, but also as Speaker of the House, a post he was elected to the
very first day he took his seat with that body. He further distinguished
himself as a negotiator of the Treaty of Ghent, which ended the War of 1812,
and as Secretary of State under John Quincy Adams. Clay ran unsuccessfully
for the U.S Presidency three times, in 1824, 1832 and 1844. Though bitterly
disappointed by these defeats, he consoled himself with his now famous
statement, "I would rather be right than be President."

Utilizing the same foundation and Henry Clay's original Federal floor
plan, Ashland incorporates handsome decorative elements in the Italianate
style. The house has elaborate cast-iron hoodmolds and stone quoins on its
exterior, marble mantels in every room, and is considered an outstanding
example of Italianate architecture. The interior of Ashland has natural finish
ash woodwork, cut from trees on the estate, as well as pieces of furniture
made from the same wood. The major portion of the furnishings belonged
to the Clay family and dates from the 1850s through the 1890s.

In addition to the main house, the outbuildings include two ice houses, dairy cellar, smoke house, carriage house, keeper's cottage and privy house.

Notable Collections on Exhibit

There are many fine paintings on the walls of Ashland including a portrait of Henry Clay by Jouett and other family portraits, with two by well-known Kentucky artist Frazier. A fine set of Belter furnishings is included in the collection. Also on display is a collection of Henry Clay memorabilia including a campaign banner used in the 1844 election and a copy of a very large Inman portrait of George Washington and his family.

Additional Information

Visitors to Waveland will enjoy the twenty acres of lawn, woodlands, and a charming formal garden. The wide variety of trees, several more than 200 years old, includes a gingko tree, a species that Clay himself imported to central Kentucky.

Waveland State Historic Site

225 Higbee Mill Road
Lexington, KY 40514
(606) 272-3611

Contact: Kentucky Department of Parks
Open: March 1-mid Dec., Tues.-Sat.
 10 a.m.–4 p.m., Sun. 2–5 p.m.; closed
 Thanksgiving
Admission: Adults $2.50; students $1;
 seniors $2. Guided tours.
Suggested Time to View House: 45 minutes
Description of Grounds: Picnic area,
 playground
Best Season to View House: Spring-fall
Number of Yearly Visitors: 12,000
Year House Built: 1847
Number of Rooms: 12

Style of Architecture: Greek Revival
On-Site Parking: Yes **Wheelchair Access:** Yes

Description of House

This distinguished mansion was built for Joseph Bryan Sr., a relative of state hero Daniel Boone. A skillful entrepreneur, Bryan employed artisans such as ironworkers, carpenters, brick masons and stone masons to build his family's home. His son, Joseph Henry Bryan, inherited the estate and became famous for his love of horse racing. Bryan's fascination with horses led to the establishment of a large race course with an amphitheater across Higbee Mill from the mansion, and another track to its right. The world famous trotter, "Wild Rake," won every heat he entered, and was sold in the 1880s to William Rockefeller for $7,800. His most notable victory was "The Kentucky Oaks" in 1886. 1894 ended the Bryan family inhabitation of Waveland as it was sold that year to Sallie A. Scott. She in turn sold it to James A. Hulett, Sr. in 1899, who sold it to the Commonwealth of Kentucky for the University of Kentucky's use as an experimental farm in 1956.

Waveland is a large L-shaped country house with several notable dependencies connected by walks to the brick terrace surrounding the residence. The mansion's entrance features a large tetrastyle portico; and two-storied pilasters and full entablature on the south, west and east sides of the building. The last features a four-bayed recessed double gallery. The entrance doorway contains small fluted Ionic columns in antis, and it has a frieze of anthemions adapted from the north frontispiece of the Erechtheum on the Acropolis at Athens. Although not a high-style house designed by a sophisticated architect, Waveland is a noble example of its type. This attractive house was the ideal home setting for an affluent Kentucky planter of the mid 19th century. The majority of furnishings are collected and are appropriate for the period.

Additional Information

Complementing the main house are three original outbuildings: the slave quarters, a smoke house and an ice house. The grounds also feature lovely herb and flower gardens for visitors's enjoyment.

Farmington

3033 Bardstown Road
Louisville, KY 40205
(502) 452-9920

Contact: Historic Homes Foundation, Inc.

Open: Mon.-Sat. 10 a.m.–4:30 p.m., closed major holidays

Admission: Adults $3; seniors $2.50; students (6-18) $1; group rates available, please inquire. Guided tours (last tour begins at 3:45 p.m.), special events.

Suggested Time to View House: 1 hour

Facilities on Premises: Gift shop

Description of Grounds: A 19th-century garden and apple orchard are accessible to the public.

Best Season to View House: Spring-fall

Style of Architecture: Federal

On-Site Parking: Yes

Year House Built: 1810

Number of Rooms: 14

Wheelchair Access: Partial

Description of House

This stately home was built in 1810 by John and Lucy Fry Speed,using a plan designed by Thomas Jefferson. The original 552-acre farm was occupied by members of the Speed family from 1808 until 1865, and then lived in by a series of owners until purchased by the foundation. The Speeds were a prominent Louisville family and entertained many notable guests. In 1841, Abraham Lincoln, a close friend of the Speeds's sons, Joshua and James, enjoyed an extended visit at Farmington. The house also holds the distinction of being the first house museum in Louisville.

Farmington is a graceful embodiment of the Federal style of architecture. Striking Jeffersonian features of its perfectly proportioned fourteen rooms include two octagonal rooms, the adventurously steep and narrow "hidden stairway", and the fanlights between the front and rear halls. Exquisite reeded doorways, carved mantels and marbleized baseboards add elegance to the interior. Most of the structure, including the woodwork, brass, and glass, is original and in excellent condition. The 18-acre site also includes an elaborate 19th-century garden, stone springhouse and barn, blacksmith shop, apple orchard, and a remodeled carriage house where receptions are held.

The furnishings on display represent the period prior to 1820 and range from elegant pieces decorating the formal parlor to more primitive pieces in the winter kitchen. There are also several family-owned pieces on exhibit.

Notable Collections on Exhibit

The period furnishings contain many notable items including a Duncan Phyfe mahogany table, a Speed family silver bridal service, and a Georgian silver cruet set (c. 1813).

Locust Grove

561 Blankenbaker Lane
Louisville, KY 40207
(502) 897-9845

Contact: Historic Homes Foundation, Inc.

Open: Mon.-Sat. 10 a.m.–4:30 p.m., Sun.
1:30–4:30 p.m., closed major holidays

Admission: Adults $3; seniors $2.50;
students (6-18) $1; group rates available,
please inquire. Guided tours (last tour
begins at 3:30 p.m.), audiovisual
presentation.

Suggested Time to View House: 1 hour

Facilities on Premises: Gift shop

Description of Grounds: The house has a
beautiful quadrant shrub garden and
flowering cutting garden.

Best Season to View House: Spring-fall

Year House Built: 1790

Number of Rooms: 15

Style of Architecture: Georgian

On-Site Parking: Yes **Wheelchair Access:** Yes

Description of House

Major William Croghan and his wife, Lucy Clark, began developing this country seat above the falls of the Ohio River in 1790. Croghan had come to Louisville following Revolutionary War Service to survey lands with his future brother in law, George Rogers Clark. By the time General Clark came to live with the Croghans at Locust Grove in 1809, his expeditions in the old Northwest Territory were legendary. Other notable guests to the home include three U.S. Presidents: James Monroe, Andrew Jackson, and Zachary Taylor, as well as John James Audubon and Aaron Burr. General Clark's younger brother, William Clark (of Lewis and Clark fame), came to the house to tell of his adventures in the Pacific Northwest.

Locust Grove represents frontier Georgian architecture at its finest. The interior features elegant wood paneling and fireplaces in nearly every room. The second floor ballroom with its well-preserved French wallpaper was the home's social center and still exhibits a harp which must have been used to entertain the many notable guests. The period furnishings have been collected for display and include many fine Kentucky-made pieces such as cabinets and tables as well as a Pembroke tea table and a Dumoutet coffee and tea service made in Philadelphia for Lucy Croghan in 1810. Locust Grove has been designated a National Historic Landmark.

Additional Information

The extensive grounds include a variety of outbuildings as well as the period gardens. Varieties of trees and plants known to have grown in Kentucky before 1818 are planted throughout the grounds. In addition, visitors are encouraged to visit the foundation's other properties, Farmington and the Thomas Edison House, also located in Louisville.

Thomas Edison House

729-31 East Washington Street
Louisville, KY 40202
(502) 585-5247

Contact: Historic Homes Foundation, Inc.

Open: Tues.-Thur. and Sat. 10 a.m.–2 p.m.; closed New Year's Day, Easter, Derby Day, Thanksgiving, Christmas Eve and Day

Admission: Adults $1.50; seniors $1; children under 6 free. Guided tours, audiovisual presentation.

Suggested Time to View House: 20 minutes

Facilities on Premises: Small gift shop/book store

Description of Grounds: A patio surrounded by perennial garden is currently being installed.

Best Season to View House: Spring and summer

Number of Yearly Visitors: 1,400

Style of Architecture: Double shotgun

Year House Built: 1850s

Number of Rooms: 4

Description of House

Thomas Alva Edison (1847-1931), born in Milan, Ohio, came to Louisville in 1866. He managed to find work with the Western Union Company. His stay in Louisville ended when he spilled sulphuric acid damaging his employer's desk which promptly caused him to be fired. Edison's only return to Louisville was in 1883 when he came to supervise the installation of generators which were to supply electricity to the 4,600 incandescent lamps used to light the Southern Exposition. This important fair was the first to be illuminated by the lamps invented by Edison. He not only established the first industrial research laboratory to make "inventions on order", he also developed over 1,000 patents during his lifetime, the greatest number held by an American inventor, and was the one of the founders of General Electric.

The house is a small, simple cottage where Thomas Edison rented a single room during part of the one-and-a-half years he worked in Louisville as a telegrapher after the Civil War. Built in the 1850s, the cottage is one of the few remaining shotgun duplexes in Louisville. Many artifacts of Edison's era can be viewed, some with "hands-on" experience. All of the furnishings have been collected and are appropriate to period.

Notable Collections on Exhibit

There is a great collection of early light bulbs as well as various other Edison inventions and memorabilia.

Ferguson Mansion

1310 South Third Street
Louisville, KY 40208
(502) 635-5083

Contact: The Filson Club Historical Society
Open: Mon.-Fri. 9 a.m.–5 p.m.; Sat.
9 a.m.–12 p.m.; closed national holidays
and Kentucky Derby
Admission: $3. Guided tours for groups
(with reservation), special interest
seminars and speakers.

Suggested Time to View House: 20 minutes
Facilities on Premises: Museum
Number of Yearly Visitors: 6,000 plus
Year House Built: 1905
Style of Architecture: Beaux-Arts
Number of Rooms: 20
On-Site Parking: Yes **Wheelchair Access:** Yes

Description of House

Edwin Hite Ferguson was born in Newport, Rhode Island in 1815. By the age of twenty-four, the young man was already in business as a member of the firm of Reed & Ferguson, wholesalers of food products. He made his mark and fortune, however, in cotton-seed oil, used principally in food-processing and soap making. He formed the Kentucky Refining Company in 1885 to refine the oil, setting up a manufacturing plant at Shelby and Goss. This became the second largest such operation in the world. In 1898 he married Sonia Fullerton Marfield of a prominent Chilicothe, Ohio family and in 1899 purchased the property where he built the mansion. Their only child, Margret, later married Army captain Earl Major, who was engaged in the bond business in Louisville in the 1920s.

The Ferguson Mansion, built between 1901 and 1903 by Edwin Hite Ferguson shortly after his marriage, is one of the most memorable and most palatial of the homes lining Third Street in Old Louisville. Designed by the local architectural firm of Dodd & Cobb, the house is in the then-fashionable style of Beaux-Arts Classicism, derived from French architectural practice. Architectural historian Walter Langsam has noted that "The house would not look out of place in the Bois de Boulogne" or on a Parisian boulevard. Beaux Arts has been called a style "with plenty to look at."

Some pieces are original to the house; most rooms are adapted to be used by the Filson Club (i.e. offices, reading and work rooms).

Notable Collections on Exhibit

There are over 200 portraits and landscapes by Kentucky artists on display as well as a mural in the dining room based on a German hunting legend. The carriage house features a museum of Kentucky history with displays related to pioneer leaders, an 1850 fire engine, the Shakers in Kentucky, moonshine still, model steamboat, and a collection of Kentucky silver.

Additional Information

The Filson Club is primarily used for genealogical research.

Adsmore Museum

304 North Jefferson Street
Princeton, KY 42445
(502) 365-3114

Contact: Board of Trustees of George Coon Public Library

Open: Tues.-Sat. 11 a.m.–4 p.m., Sun. 1:30–4 p.m.; closed New Year's Day, Easter Sunday, July 4th, Thanksgiving Day, Christmas Eve and Day

Admission: Adults $3; children (under 12) and students touring with school groups free. Guided tours with costumed docents.

Suggested Time to View House: 1 hour

Facilities on Premises: Gift shop, log house which houses a gunsmith shop

Description of Grounds: Located on 4 acres in downtown Princeton

Best Season to View House: Spring and summer

Number of Yearly Visitors: 16,000

Year House Built: 1857

Style of Architecture: Greek Revival

Number of Rooms: 9

On-Site Parking: Yes **Wheelchair Access:** Yes

Description of House

This beautiful mansion has built in 1857 by John Higgins, but has been home to two prominent families, the Garretts and the Smiths. Governor Osborne, the third governor of Wyoming, married Selena Smith in this home in 1907. He was the first assistant secretary of state under Woodrow Wilson. The Smiths were parents to Mayme Garrett, the wife of Robert Garrett. Garret served as director of insolvent banks under Andrew Mellon until his death in 1930. His daughter, Katherine, lived here until she died and left the house to be opened as a museum.

This impressive home has solid brick walls, some close to eighteen inches thick. When the Garretts acquired the home in 1900, they completely overhauled the house. They installed steam heat and running water and made major structural and decorative changes. These included new Corinthian columns, a gambrel roof to replace the old, and hand-carved Federal mantels added to the downstairs rooms. A Colonial Revival stairway was also added as well as a full attic and basement. The brick kitchen, breakfast room and pantry were added in 1920 and the house was painted a creamy yellow.

All of the furnishings were owned by the Garretts and the overriding influence is Victorian, however, there are pieces which predate the Victorian era. The presentation of the costumed docents changes with the seasons or when the house is decorated for special events which represent the lives of the people who lived here.

Notable Collections on Exhibit

The brass cornices and chandeliers are outstanding; one chandelier being a Sevre handpainted porcelain chandelier. The collection of china, linens, crystal, porcelains, lamps and furniture as well as mirrors and old clocks are all considered to be fine collections.

Additional Information

The home is called Adsmore because an old aunt who came to visit soon after the home was bought by this family in 1900 said "You should call this place 'Addsmore' because you are always adding to it." At one point, one "d" was dropped and the current spelling , "Adsmore", was made at Miss Garrett's request in her will.

White Hall

500 White Hall Shrine Road
Richmond, KY 40475
(606) 623-9178

Contact: Kentucky Department of Parks

Open: April-Oct. 9 a.m.–4:30 p.m.,
closed Mon.

Admission: Adults $3; children (6-12) $2.
Guided tours with costumed docents,
Christmas celebration, special events,
call for more information.

Suggested Time to View House: 1 hour

Facilities on Premises: Gift shop

Description of Grounds: 13 acres of
landscaped grounds surround the house

Best Season to View House: Spring-fall

Year House Built: 1798 (original structure)

Style of Architecture: Georgian with
Gothic Revival additions

Number of Rooms: 15

On-Site Parking: Yes

Wheelchair Access: Partial

Description of House

White Hall is really a house within a house. The original Georgian-style structure known as Clermont was built by General Green Clay in 1798. General Clay was the father of noted abolitionist, politician, and friend of Abraham Lincoln, Cassius Clay. The new building, White Hall, was built above and around Clermont in the 1860s. Most of the construction took place while Clay was serving as ambassador to Russia. The prominent architect Thomas Lewinski and builder architect John McMurty designed and built this addition to the original structure which more than doubled the size of the home. Clay and his wife, Mary Jane, entertained many guests at their new home when he returned from abroad in 1870, but unfortunately the marriage was troubled and they divorced in 1878.

The original two-story brick structure was simple in design and consisted of seven rooms with fireplaces in each. The first floor of the new White Hall was made level with the older section of the house. Clermont's old stairways were removed; however, despite the addition of front and rear staircases, circulation through the house was difficult. Noteworthy features of the house include high ceilings, a sweeping staircase, and a forerunner of a central heating system fueled by two fireboxes in the basement leading to fireplaces in several rooms of the new section of the home. In addition, the house contains a unique indoor bathroom with a washbasin, a commode, and a bathtub made of hollowed out poplar log lined with copper. Many of the beautiful period furnishings on display are original to the Clay family.

1824 Centre Family Dwelling

P.O. Box 30, US 68-80
South Union, KY 42283
(502) 542-4167

Contact: Shakertown at South Union
Open: March 15-Nov. 15, daily 9 a.m.–5 p.m., Sun. 1–5 p.m.
Admission: Adults $2.50; children (ages 6-12) $1; groups $2 each. Orientation by guide, educational events.
Suggested Time to View House: 30–60 minutes
Facilities on Premises: Museum shop

Description of Grounds: One outbuilding accessible
Best Season to View House: Spring and fall
Number of Yearly Visitors: 14,000
Year House Built: 1822-1833
Style of Architecture: Georgian with Shaker influence
Number of Rooms: 42
On-Site Parking: Yes **Wheelchair Access:** Yes

Description of House

The house was occupied by the Centre family at South Union, a communal group who were the most dedicated in the village. The house was first occupied in 1833 and continued to be the home of the Centre family until 1922. The house's inhabitants numbered as many as ninety before the Civil War and as few as nine in the early 1920s. The South Union Shakers were an industrial group who marketed many of their products throughout the South and lived a celibate, religious, progressive lifestyle within the confines of their communal settlement.

The Centre Family Dwelling was one of four dormitories located in the Shaker village of South Union, active from 1807 to 1922. It is one of the finest buildings built by the Shakers in the U.S. and houses one of the country's largest collections of western Shaker furniture. The structure features beautiful supportive arches in the interior hallways and original paint on the woodwork. There is exceptionally fine craftsmanship in all aspects of the architecture. All furnishings and personal artifacts are original "Shaker" but approximately 75 percent of collection is original to South Union.

Notable Collections on Exhibit

A fine collection of South Union furniture is exhibited in the Centre house museum but there are also rare collections of Shaker-made silk and other textiles, basketry, woodenware, tools and other examples of the South Union Shakers' material culture.

Additional Information

The house is supported by an 1835 smoke and milk house, which occupies a nearby outbuilding. Four other Shaker buildings are visible but not currently owned by Shakertown at South Union, a non-profit organization dedicated to the preservation of South Union's folklife and material culture. The organization also owns the 1917 Shaker post office building, still in operation today, and the 1869 Shaker Tavern, a hotel built by the Shakers used today as a tea room and bed and breakfast.

William Whitley House

Route 1, Box 232
Stanford, KY 40484
(606) 355-2881

Contact: Kentucky Department of Parks

Open: June-Aug., 9 a.m.–5 p.m., Sept.-May. closed Mon.

Admission: Adults $4; seniors $3.50; children (6-12) $2. Tours.

Suggested Time to View House: 1 hour

Facilities on Premises: Gift shop

Description of Grounds: 10 acres of park land with picnic tables and a playground

Best Season to View House: Summer-fall

Year House Built: 1785

Style of Architecture: Georgian

Number of Rooms: 10

On-Site Parking: Yes

Wheelchair Access: Partial

Description of House

William Whitley was one of the courageous frontiersman who helped to shape early Kentucky history. He achieved the rank of captain in the Kentucky Militia for his actions against the Indians in the late 18th century. His house, located on Wilderness Road, was a popular stop for travelers going to Kentucky through the Cumberland Gap. The Whitley estate was known as Sportsman's Hill because of the racetrack Whitley built near his home in 1788. His unusual circular trackway ran races in a counter-clockwise direction in opposition to the traditional British style of racing. Many notable Kentuckians attended Whitley's racetrack including George Rogers Clark, James Harrod, and Samuel McDowell.

This attractive brick house was constructed using a Flemish bond pattern (with one brick laid lengthwise, the next endwise) which was more expensive than other methods of the time. Usually houses were built with the Flemish bond pattern on the front wall; in Whitley's case the style was used on all four. Inside the house, the walnut and pine fielded paneling, the S-shaped carvings over the fireplace, the crown molding, and chair railings throughout the house, are evidence that Whitley must have been able to find skilled craftsmen to complete the structure. Today, visitors to the Whitley House will see a fine example of a frontier house with period furnishings and extraordinary architectural and decorative details.

Louisiana

1. **Arabi**
    Beauregard House

2. **Baton Rouge**
    Magnolia Mound Plantation

3. **Cloutierville**
    Bayou Folk Museum–
    Kate Chopin Home

4. **Darrow**
    Tezcuco Plantation
    Houmas House Plantation

5. **Destrehan**
    Destrehan Plantation

6. **Franklin**
    Arlington Plantation
    Oaklawn Manor
    Grevemberg House

7. **Napoleanville**
    Madewood Plantation House

8. **New Iberia**
    Shadows-on-the-Teche

9. **New Orleans**
    The 1850 House
    Hermann-Grima House
    Gallier House Museum
    Beauregard-Keyes House
    Pitot House Museum
    Williams Residence

10. **Port Allen**
    Aillet House
    Allendale Plantation Slave Cabin

11. **White Castle**
    Nottoway

Beauregard House

Chalmette National Historical Park
Arabi, LA
(504)589-4430

Contact: Jean Lafitte National
  Historical Park
Open: 8 a.m.–5 p.m.
Admission: Free

Description of Grounds: Located in the
Chalmette section of Jean Lafitte National
Park
Year House Built: 1833
Style of Architecture: French-Louisiana

Description of House

The Chalmette National Historical park pays tribute to the Battle of New Orleans, the last major battle between the United States and Great Britain during the War of 1812. Although the battle had little military value because the Treaty of Ghent had already been signed, it did secure America's right to the Louisiana territory. The battle also made a hero of a future President, Andrew Jackson, and he would forever be known as the "hero of New Orleans".

Visitors can learn more about this historic site by stopping at the Beauregard House which now serves as a visitor's center for the park. This beautiful example of French-Louisiana architecture was built some eighteen years after the Battle of New Orleans and is named for its last private owner, Judge Rene Beauregard, the son of the famous Confederate general. Originally built by Alexander Baron, the house features Doric columns and impressive double galleries. Never associated with a plantation, the house served as a country residence for a succession of wealthy people in the 19th century.

Today, the house contains exhibits related to the War of 1812 and the famous battle which lives in history.

Magnolia Mound Plantation

2161 Nicholson Drive
Baton Rouge, LA 70802
(504) 343-4955

Contact: Magnolia Mound Plantation
Open: Tues.-Sat. 10 a.m.–4 p.m., Sun.
1–4 p.m.; closed major holidays
Admission: Adults $3.50; seniors $2.50; 13
and over $1.50; ages 6-12 $.75; under 6
free. Open-hearth cooking, lectures,
workshops, children programs.
Suggested Time to View House: 1 hour
Facilities on Premises: Gift shop
Description of Grounds: 16 acres with a
herb and vegetable garden, crop garden,
and a grove of oaks (some over 200 years)
Best Season to View House: Spring and fall
Style of Architecture: French Creole with
West Indies influence
Number of Yearly Visitors: 18,000
Number of Rooms: 6

Year House Built: c. 1791
Wheelchair Access: No

Description of House

Magnolia Mound is the oldest structure in Baton Rouge and is typical of the houses built by French settlers on early Mississippi River plantations. The house has been restored to represent the period of residency of Armand Duplantier from 1800 to 1830. Duplantier was an *aide-de-camp* to Lafayette in the American Revolution. Later he became a prominent figure in the Spanish colony around Baton Rouge, was a captain of the militia, held various posts in government and corresponded with President Jefferson.

The West Indies influence can be seen in the house's wide doorways designed to catch cross breezes, the Paris green shuttered windows and broad shaded galleries overlooking grove of ancient live oaks. Built of Cypress grown on the property, the building features *bousillage* (mud and moss) construction. The parlor exhibits classically detailed moldings and hand carved Adam-style mantel and rare wooden cove ceiling. Wallpaper is reproduced from scrap found during restoration and dated 1810. Magnolia Mound displays a documented collection of furniture and decorative arts from the early 19th century, and is considered the largest public collection of early Louisiana and Federal style furniture. The house is listed on the National Register of Historic Places.

Notable Collections on Exhibit

There is a permanent exhibit devoted to the origins and influences of French Creole architecture. Changing exhibits feature Acadian textiles, English mochaware pottery, and early lighting devices.

Additional Information

An overseer's house, a carriage house, an open-hearth kitchen and pigeonnier are the extant outbuildings found on the property.

Bayou Folk Museum– Kate Chopin Home

P.O. Box 411
Cloutierville, LA 71416
(318) 379-2233

Contact: Assoc. for the Pres. of Hist. Natchitoches

Open: Mon.-Sat. 10 a.m.–5 p.m., Sun. 1–5 p.m. Closed on Thanksgiving and Christmas Day

Activities: Tours

Description of Grounds: The restored home is framed by beautiful magnolias and graceful wrought-iron and brick fence.

Year House Built: 1806

Style of Architecture: Early 19th-century home

Description of House

Author Kate Chopin, moved into the house in 1879, with her husband Oscar and five children. In 1899, she published what is considered her finest work—*The Awakening*. This controversial novel describing a woman's sexuality and desire for self-fulfillment was met with shock and outrage. The reaction prompted Kate's gradual withdrawal from writing and contributed to her much delayed entry into the halls of literary fame. A master storyteller, she was seventy-five years ahead of her time.

This gracious home was already old when Chopin arrived to live here. Built by slaves between 1806 and 1813, the structure typifies early 19th-century homes of the area. The original house was built of handmade brick, heart cypress and heart pine, square wooden pegs, and a mixture of mud and Spanish moss. Some of the original contents remain: glass panes, the upstairs wainscotting, and the double French doors opening onto the balcony. The present furnishings were found in the Cane River area and restored locally.

Additional Information

Although the original outbuildings no longer remain, two small buildings have been added to the grounds. Behind the main house is a structure that was used for years as a doctor's office. Moved to the property in 1938, and now restored with the belongings of several plantation doctors, the office is dedicated to Dr. Eleanor Worsley, the first woman doctor in Natchitoches Parish. Adjacent to the office stands a 100-year-old blacksmith shop, complete with farm tools and equipment dating from the 1800s.

Houmas House Plantation

40136 Highway 942 Burnside
Darrow, LA 70725-2302
(504) 473-7841

Contact: Houmas House Plantation

Open: Feb.-Oct., 10 a.m.–5 p.m.; Nov.-Jan.,
10 a.m.–4 p.m.; closed Thanksgiving,
Christmas and New Year's Day

Admission: Group rates by prior
arrangement. Guided tours every hour
and half hour; catered meals with
advance notice.

Facilities on Premises: Gift shop

Description of Grounds: Lovely formal
gardens beneath majestic, moss-laden
live oaks.

Year House Built: 1840

Style of Architecture: Greek Revival

Description of House

The 20,000 acres of the Houmas Plantation made fortunes for men like John Burnside, who bought Houmas and 12,000 acres for one million dollars in 1858. And it was Burnside who saved Houmas from the ravages of the Civil War. A native of Ireland, Burnside declared immunity as a British subject and thus avoided occupation by Union forces. Houmas flourished as the greatest sugar domain in the state under Colonel William Porcher Miles in the late 1800s, producing twenty million pounds of sugar per year. The home fell into disrepair during the Great Depression, but in 1940 the house and remaining grounds were bought by Dr. George B. Crozat for his country home. He lovingly restored the house to its pristine magnificence. Today the heirs of Dr. Crozat still live at Houmas House.

Houmas Plantation was a tract of land along the Mississippi River purchased from the Houmas Indians in Colonial times by Maurice Conway and Alexandre Latil. It was Latil who built the rear house in the late 1700s, with characteristics of both Spanish and rural French architecture. The magnificent Greek Revival mansion was built in 1840 John Smith Preston and his wife, Caroline. Her father, Revolutionary War hero Wade Hampton, had bought the property in 1812. The original four-room dwelling at the rear was preserved. Later, it was attached to the great house by an arched carriage way. Houmas House is furnished with 1840s period museum pieces of early Louisiana craftsmanship.

Additional Information

The impressive architecture of Houmas House has also been captured for film and television. The mansion was the setting for the movie, *Hush, Hush, Sweet Charlotte*, starring Bette Davis as well as several television programs.

Tezcuco Plantation

3138 Highway 44
Darrow, LA 70725
(504) 562-3929

Contact: Tezcuco Plantation, Inc.

Open: Daily 10 a.m.–5 p.m.

Admission: Adults $5.50; senior citizen and children (13-17) $4.50; and children (4-12) $2.75. Grounds tours $3.50. Guided tours and Bed and Breakfast accommodations are available in the original restored slave cottages.

Facilities on Premises: Restaurant, antique and gift shop

Description of Grounds: Formal gardens, life-size dollhouse, chapel, commissary, blacksmith shop, gazebo's and Civil War museum

Suggested Time to View House: 1 hour

Number of Yearly Visitors: 50,000

Style of Architecture: Greek Revival

Best Season to View House: Spring

Year House Built: 1855

Number of Rooms: 10

Description of House

The land which comprises the Tezcuco plantation has had a long and interesting history. The area is known as White Hall after a home built by Marius Pons Bringier, who left Provence, France and settled on the "Acadian Coast" on the banks of the Mississippi River. Marius's daughter, Elizabeth, married Judge Augustine Dominique Tureaud and built their home on Union Plantation. Their son, Benjamin, married his cousin, Algea, the daughter of Michael Doradou Bringier of L'Hermitage Plantation. Benjamin built Tezcuco, adjoining the Union Plantation. Tezcuco means "Resting Place." and is named after a lake in Mexico where Benjamin Tureaud did a tour of duty.

This raised cottage was constructed over a five year period with cypress from the plantation's own swamps and bricks from its kilns. The ceiling cornices and center rosettes in the house have intricate plaster details and all the interior doors and windows sashes still have the original false graining (called *faux bois*) which was painstakingly painted by hand. The galleries are adorned with wrought iron in the traditional grapevine pattern. All fireplaces are coal burning and made of cast iron. All windows are triple sashed so they could be used as doors to walk into the galleries. Each of the rooms is furnished in exquisite detail with collected and original furnishings ranging from a Victorian gold-leaf mirror (c. 1880) to a Louis XIV-style carved rosewood table (c. 1850) to a hand-carved bed made of chestnut.

Notable Collections on Exhibit

Tezcuco showcases an outstanding collection of period furnishings, an unusual assortment of antique dolls, American art pottery, and Civil War memorabilia which includes a Civil War Spar torpedo boat used to ram ships on the river.

Destrehan Plantation

9999 River Road
Destrehan, LA 70047
(504) 764-9315

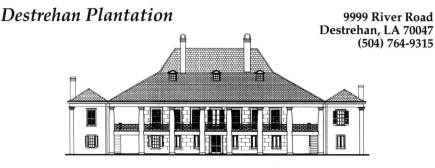

Contact: River Road Historical Society
Open: Daily 9:30 a.m.–4 p.m. Closed major holidays
Admission: Adults $5; teens $4; children $3; 5 and under free. Costumed guides; fall festival; special occasions.
Suggested Time to View House: 35–40 minutes
Facilities on Premises: Gift shop

Description of Grounds: Plantation with four ancient moss-draped live oaks.
Best Season to View House: Spring
Number of Yearly Visitors: 54,000
Year House Built: 1787
Number of Rooms: 22
Style of Architecture: Louisiana Colonial style

Description of House

In 1792, statesman Jean Noel Destrehan, the son of a French aristocrat statesman, acquired the estate from his father-in-law, Robin de Logny. He and his brother-in-law, Etienne de Bore, first mayor of New Orleans, perfected the granulation of sugar, thereby starting an industry that proved to be most profitable to Louisiana planters.

Built in 1787, Destrehan is the oldest documented plantation house left intact in the lower Mississippi Valley. In 1810, twin wings on either side were added. Around 1830 to 1840 a major renovation was undertaken changing the facade and interior to the Greek Revival style. The house's most important architectural features are its West Indies hip roof, brick between post lower level and *bousilage entre poteaux* (mud, moss, and horse hair between posts) and the blending of French Colonial and Greek Revival architectural styles. Several pieces of the collection are from the original residents and the furnishings plan is to interpret the early to mid 19th century.

Notable Collections on Exhibit

The collection displays several notable Louisiana-made pieces including the secretary desk of Judge Pierre Rost and a bed made by Dutriel Barjon, a free man of color from Haiti whose shop was on Royal Street in New Orleans. Several oil portraits decorate the walls including one of Jean Noel Destrehan and his daughter, Zelia (c. 1818). The other known painting of Jean Noel is on exhibit at the Museum of Art in New Orleans.

Additional Information

Destrehan has four live oaks that are members of the Live Oak Society surrounding the house.

Arlington Plantation

P.O. Box 1143
Franklin, LA 70538
(318) 828-2644

Contact: Arlington Plantation
Open: Tues.-Sat. 10 a.m.–4 p.m.;
  Jan.-Feb. by appointment
Activities: Tours
Year House Built: c. 1830s
Style of Architecture: Greek Revival

Description of House

The house was built by the Carlin family, original settlers in Franklin. Arlington is now privately owned, but graciously opened to the public on a regular basis. Arlington Plantation stands on the banks of the Bayou Teche. Elaborate restoration of the Greek Revival-style home recaptures the grandeur of plantation life. The original porticos are supported by fluted composite order capital columns at the front of the bayou side of the house, while smaller, identical porticos adorn the sides of the structure. The interior design is of cruciform style with crossing hallways dividing the main floor. This impressive mansion is listed on the National Register of Historic Places. Period antiques, many of which are original to Arlington, grace the interior.

Oaklawn Manor

P.O. Box 1143
Franklin, LA 70538
(318) 828-0434

Contact: Oaklawn Manor
Open: Daily 10 a.m.–4 p.m.
Activities: Tours
Year House Built: 1837
Style of Architecture: Greek Revival

Description of House

This grand Greek Revival mansion built by Alexander Porter, an Irishman, who became an important Louisiana statesman. After the Civil War the manor saw troubled times, until it was rescued by Captain Clyde Barbour, who restored the manor and furnished it with European antiques. In 1963 Oaklawn was again restored by owners Mr. and Mrs. George Thompson. It is currently privately owned.

This antebellum mansion was built in 1837. The three-story Greek Revival house is constructed of handmade brick with walls almost twenty-inches thick and a massive foundation. Oaklawn is aptly named as it is surrounded by the largest oak grove in the South. This lovely home also features beautiful gardens modeled after the Gardens of Versailles.

Grevemberg House

P.O. Box 1143
Franklin, LA 70538
(318) 828-5608

Contact: St. Mary Chapter of the
Louisiana Landmarks Society
Open: Thurs.-Sun. 10 a.m.–4 p.m.

Activities: Tours
Year House Built: c. 1851
Style of Architecture: Greek Revival

Description of House

Although named after a later occupant, this large Greek Revival mansion was built by Henry C. Wilson on a site which is now Franklin Park. The house was acquired by the Grevemberg family in 1857.

Like many antebellum mansions, the structure is built of cypress and maintains the original cypress floor. Four magnificent columns support the pediment. The Grevemberg House is typical of residences built in the Franklin area during the 1850s.

Additional Information

The Franklin Historic District contains was listed on the National Register of Historic Places and contains over 400 noteworthy structures. Since much of the original town was built over again when the railroad came, many of the surviving mid 19th-century structures, like the historic houses, are grand monuments in an essentially turn-of-the-century townscape. Visitors will not want to miss discovering this experience for themselves.

Madewood Plantation House

4250 Hwy. 308
Napoleanville, LA 70390
(504) 369-7151

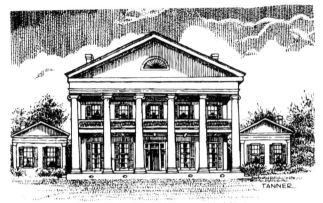

Contact: Madewood Plantation House
Open: Daily 10 a.m.–5 p.m. Closed Thanksgiving and Christmas Day.
Activities: Daily tours; overnight accommodations; annual Christmas Heritage Banquet in early Dec.; and arts events throughout the year

Description of Grounds: The plantation house faces Bayou Lafourche.
Year House Built: 1846
Style of Architecture: Greek Revival Mansion
Number of Rooms: 21

Description of House

This gracious mansion was built for Colonel Thomas Pugh, whose family is buried in Madewood's picturesque cemetery. Purchased in 1964 by Mr. and Mrs. Harold K. Marshall, Madewood was restored to its former splendor and furnished with elegant period antiques, many collected when their son Keith Marshall, the present owner, studied as a Rhodes Scholar in Oxford, England.

Built in 1846, the twenty room white-columned Greek Revival mansion truly resembles a Greek Temple. This impressive structure was designed by Henry Howard, a noted architect form Cork, Ireland. Massive Ionic columns grace the front facade which invite visitors to enter the full-length entrance hall finished in the *faux bois* style signed by the artist Cornelieus Hennessey. The interior features an unsupported curved staircase which rises to the second floor. The mansion also contains a vast ballroom which hosts the Madewood Arts Festival. Madewood has been meticulously restored and decorated with an outstanding collection of furnishings gathered to complement the elegance of the rooms.

Notable Collections on exhibit

Madewood's fine period furnishings include a 17th-century Italian altarpiece, a Renaissance Revival oak desk, a Napoleon couch, and a rosewood chaise with original velvet upholstery which is part of a set designed by noted furniture maker John Belter.

Shadows-On-The-Teche

317 East Main Street
New Iberia, LA 70560
(318) 369-6446

Contact: National Trust for Historic Preservation

Open: Daily 9 a.m.–5 p.m.; closed Thanksgiving, Christmas and New Year's Day

Admission: Adults $5; senior citizens $4; children (12 and up) $3; discounts available for groups. Guided tours and special events.

Suggested Time to View House: 60 minutes

Facilities on Premises: Gift shop and meeting place

Description of Grounds: Three acres of gardens with azaleas, camellias, and live oaks

Year House Built: 1834

Style of Architecture: Greek Revival facade with French Colonial floor plan

Description of House

The house was built by wealthy sugarcane planter David Weeks to serve as the center of his extensive plantation system. In the 1920s, the Shadows became one of the South's first private restorations when the builder's great-grandson, William Weeks Hall, returned the house to its former beauty and revived the tradition of southern hospitality. Four successive generations of the Weeks family lived here, each leaving its own imprint on the house. This is literally the house that sugar built, since sugar was the source of the family's wealth before the Civil War.

Set in the lush, semi-tropical region of southern Louisiana, known as Acadiana, the Shadows is situated underneath Spanish-moss draped live oaks. The mansion is a unique building reflecting local interpretation of the Classical Revival style with Tuscan columns and French and English influences. These culminate in the distinctive architectural style typical of many southern Louisiana country houses. The exterior staircase, the lower floor, flush the with ground and paved with brick and marble, and the deep galleries on the first and second floors are typical features of such antebellum houses. The house is significant because of its architecture, the amount of documentation on the property (17,000 documents in the Weeks family papers at Louisiana State University) and because of the high standard of interpretation and preservation which the mansion receives. Most of the furnishings are from the period prior to 1865; eighty percent were original to the Weeks family.

Notable Collections on Exhibit

In addition to its fine architectural features, Shadows-on-the-Teche displays an outstanding collection of period furnishings. The family-owned items include portraits of Mary C. Weeks Moore, William Frederick Weeks, Frances Weeks, and Alfred Weeks by John Beale Bordley. Noted artist Adrien Persac is represented with watercolors of the plantation property in 1861. The furnishings represent two periods: the ground floor of the house is in the early 1840s style while the second floor is in the late 1840s and early 1850s. The house depicts everyday life on a sugar plantation during the antebellum era. Typical items include four-post beds with mosquito netting, armories, chairs and sofas upholstered with haircloth, needlework pictures, and a whale-oil burning lamps.

Additional Information

Celebrities such as Cecil B. De Mille, Walt Disney, D.W. Griffith, H.L. Mencken and Henry Miller enjoyed the lush gardens and subtle beauty of this historic setting.

The 1850 House

523 St. Ann Street, Jackson Square
New Orleans, LA
(504) 568-6968

Contact: 1850 House, Louisiana State Museum

Open: Tues.-Sun. 10 a.m.–5 p.m.; closed major holidays

Admission: Adults $3; seniors and teens $1.50; children (under 12) free. Guided tours.

Suggested Time to View House: 1 hour

Facilities on Premises: Gift/book shop

Description of Grounds: A historic park in the heart of New Orleans' French Quarter

Best Season to View House: Spring and fall

Number of Yearly Visitors: 20,000

Year House Built: 1850

Number of Rooms: 10

On-Site Parking: No **Wheelchair Access:** No

Description of House

Baroness Micaela Almonester de Pontalba constructed the two rows of town houses that flank Jackson Square on St. Ann and St. Peter Streets from 1849 to 1851. This was land she had inherited from her father, Don Andres Almonester y Roxas. Micaela had been married some years before to Joseph Xavier Celestin de Pontalba, her cousin, and they lived in France. Although their union produced several children, the marriage was unhappy and turbulent and it ended in separation.

Over the years, since the Louisiana State Museum opened the 1850 House as a period house museum, it has grown in sophistication and historical accuracy thanks to many donations of furniture and decorative arts of the 1850s and also as a result of continuing research by the museum curatorial staff on decorative arts, household technology and domestic life in the country and particularly in New Orleans in the mid 19th century. The interior has been restored with the original paint colors, flagstone paving in the entrance hall and stairhall, and accurate reproductions of the carpet and window hangings. The furnishing plan is not based upon any person or family who lived here, but it does reflect mid 19th-century prosperity, taste and daily life in New Orleans.

Notable Collections on Exhibit

The 1850 House exhibits historical and religious objects, figurines, musical instruments, flowers, and decorative objects. The dining room features a seventy-five piece "Old Paris" tableware set as well as alabaster plates, a brass candelabra, and other fine period furnishings.

Hermann-Grima House

818-820 St. Louis
New Orleans, LA 70112
525-5661

Contact: Christian Woman's Exchange
Open: Mon.-Sat. 10 a.m.–4 p.m.
Admission: Group discounts available.
Guided tours, decorated for Christmas.
Suggested Time to View House: 1 hour
Facilities on Premises: Exchange shop
Description of Grounds: A large courtyard
with parterre beds and period plantings
including old roses and citrus trees
Best Season to View House: Year round
Number of Yearly Visitors: 20,000 plus
Year House Built: 1831
Style of Architecture: Georgian English
with Louisiana French or Creole kitchen
On-Site Parking: No **Wheelchair Access:** Yes

Description of House

Samuel Hermann, a German immigrant arrived in Louisiana the year after the Louisiana Purchase. Initially settling in a small town up-river from New Orleans, he arrived in the city with his new wife Emeranthe Becnel around 1815 during what many call the Golden Age of New Orleans. By 1831 he had amassed a tremendous fortune as an entrepreneur, banker and broker with wide-ranging interests. Unfortunately, Hermann's successes were not immune from the financial panic of 1837; in 1844 he was forced to sell his luxurious house to Felix Grima, a criminal court judge and notary. The house remained in the Grima family until 1921 and was purchased by the Christian Woman's Exchange in 1924.

This handsome two-story brick residence built by Samuel Hermann in 1831 is generally considered to be the best extant example in the Vieux Carre (French Quarter) of American influence on New Orleans architecture. Constructed by Virginia architect-builder William Brand, it was one of the most elegant houses in the city, boasting an impressive courtyard, wineroom, cast-iron cistern, and stable buildings. The interior features marble mantels, *faux bois* doors, a hand-carved wood frieze embellishing the pocket doors separating the parlor from the dining room, and an impressive kitchen complete with oven, *potagers* (large pots), and an open hearth.

Notable Collections on Exhibit

The collection includes family portraits from the period from 1830 to 1860, and some of the original decorative arts. Much of the furniture and decorative arts have been collected and are appropriate to the period.

Gallier House Museum

1118-1132 Royal Street
New Orleans, LA 70116
(504) 523-6722

Contact: Gallier House Museum

Open: Mon.-Sat. 10 a.m.–4:30 p.m., Sun.
12–4:30 p.m.; closed major holidays

Admission: Adults $4; seniors and students
$3; children (6-12) $2.25; groups (10 or
more) $2.50 per person. Guided tours,
films, interpretation of special Victorian
housekeeping techniques (Memorial
Day-Labor Day), Christmas decorations.

Suggested Time to View House: 45 minutes

Facilities on Premises: Gift and book shop

Number of Yearly Visitors: 25,000

Year House Built: 1857-1860

Style of Architecture: French Quarter
townhouse

Number of Rooms: 14

On-Site Parking: Yes **Wheelchair Access:** Yes

Description of House

Gallier was born in England in 1827, the son of an Irish architect-builder who brought his family to America in 1832. The father, James Gallier, Sr., became a successful architect in New Orleans. He was well-known for designing the St. Charles Exchange Hotel (1835) and Municipality Hall (1845), now known as Gallier Hall in his honor. He turned his practice over to his son James Gallier, Jr. in 1849, and in 1857 the younger Gallier began working on an elegant new townhouse which would be home for himself, his Creole wife, Aglae, and their four small daughters.

This beautiful Victorian home reflects the young architects innovative ideas about residential comfort and convenience. These include a cast-iron cooking range which supplied hot water to the plumbing system and a modern bathroom. Because ventilation was important for comfort during the hot, humid summers, Gallier incorporated a skylight and ceiling vents into his design. The house has been meticulously restored to represent the mid 19th-century period with colorful wool carpets woven on antique looms in England, period French wallpaper, and hand-painted window shades. The collected furnishings are based on an extensive inventory of Gallier's estate taken at his death in 1868. Gallier House is listed as a National Historic Landmark accredited by the American Association of Museums.

Notable Collections on Exhibit

Fine mahogany and rosewood furniture made or used in New Orleans predominates, but utilitarian items such as a cypress ice box, ironing equipment, and a flycatcher appear in their proper places. The kitchen collection is extremely varied and includes some original mid 19th-century pieces.

Beauregard-Keyes House

1113 Chartres Street
New Orleans, LA 70116
(504) 523-7257

Contact: Romantic Beauregard-Keyes
House
Open: Mon.-Sat. 10 a.m.–3 p.m.
Admission: Donation. Guided tours by
docents in period costumes.
Facilities on Premises: Gift shop
Description of Grounds: Reconstructed
formal gardens
Year House Built: 1826

Description of House

The house was built in 1826 by Joseph Le Carpentier, a well-to-do auctioneer. Seven years later, it came into the possession of John A. Merle, the consul of Switzerland. Through the years of its checkered history, the house had many owners and in 1865, when General Pierre G.T. Beauregard, the noted Confederate leader who hailed from Louisiana returned to New Orleans, he lodged here for 18 months. The house slowly sank into dilapidation and by 1925, it changed hands and the owner wanted to demolish it. A group of patriotic ladies raised funds and saved the house. In 1944, Francis Parkinson Keyes, well-known novelist, came to Louisiana and eventually took over the house. She transformed the house into the stately edifice that it had been once before. In 1948, the Keyes Foundation was formed and the house entrusted to its care. Mrs. Keyes made the cottage her winter residence for a quarter of a century and wrote several of her books here, among them *Dinner at Antoine's, Chess Player (Paul Morphy)*, and *Blue Camellia*.

The Beauregard-Keyes house is one of the most romantic and fascinating old houses in a city which boasts of many interesting landmarks. This Louisiana raised cottage is the only mansion in the French Quarter with a large ballroom. The Beauregard Chamber features heirloom pieces which belonged to the General and his family.

Additional Information

This impressive house maintains three of the original outbuildings: slave quarters, which have been renovated to form a study; and two side buildings which house a library and gift shop.

Pitot House Museum

1440 Moss Street
New Orleans, LA 70119
(504) 482-0312

Contact: Louisiana Landmarks Society
Open: Wed.-Sat. 10 a.m.–3 p.m.
Admission: Adult $3; children
(under 12) $1. Guided tours.
Description of Grounds: On Bayou St. John
Year House Built: c. 1775
Style of Architecture: 18th-century
Plantation House

Description of House

James Pitot bought the typical colonial Louisiana plantation house in 1818 as a country home for his family. Mr. Pitot served as the first mayor of the incorporated city of New Orleans from 1804 to 1805 and later was appointed by Louisiana's governor to the position of parish court judge.

The Pitot House, built in the last quarter of the 18th century, is one of the few West Indies style houses which lined the Bayou St. John in the 1700s. The house, with its stucco-covered, brick-between-post construction and double-pitched hipped roof, was painstakingly restored to its original 18th-century condition by the Louisiana Landmarks Society in the 1960s. The building also serves as headquarters for the society which works vigorously to preserve the old neighborhoods and landmarks of this historic city.

The house has been furnished with Louisiana and American antiques from the early 1800s in keeping with the style and period of James Pitot.

Additional Information

There are a number of historic houses outside the French Quarter which visitors should take the time to visit while in New Orleans. The Longue Vue House and Gardens (Metairie Road) is a lovely Greek Revival mansion surrounded by eight acres of beautiful gardens. The interior boasts a fine collection of 18th and 19th-century antiques. Call (504) 488-5488 for more information and directions.

Williams Residence

533 Royal Street
New Orleans, LA 70130
(504) 523-4662

Contact: The Historic New Orleans Collection

Open: Tues.-Sat. 10 a.m.–3 p.m.; closed major holidays

Admission: $2 per person; no one under 12 admitted. Guided tours.

Suggested Time to View House: 45 minutes

Description of Grounds: French Quarter patio

Best Season to View House: Spring

Number of Yearly Visitors: 2,500

Year House Built: 1889

Style of Architecture: Townhouse

Number of Rooms: 8

On-Site Parking: No

Wheelchair Access: Yes

Description of House

Located behind the Historic New Orleans Collection, the Williams House represents the elegance of mid 20th-century New Orleans. Leila Moore Williams and Lewis Kemper Williams, New Orleans civic and social leaders, are the co-founders of the foundation that administers the Historic New Orleans Collection, a museum and research center for state and local history. The couple has since died but their legacy lives on in this fine house and its collections.

The house was built in 1889 as a "shot-gun" style structure and was remodeled in the 1940s to conform to the elegant life-style if its mid 20th-century owners. The furnishings displayed are those of the Williams family, the owners of the house since 1939. The house is decorated with an eclectic collection of antiques, Chinese export porcelains, and pieces of Louisiana origin.

Additional Information

The Historic New Orleans Collection is actually a complex of buildings with galleries of changing exhibits related to cultural and historical topics. The 1792 Merieult House exhibits maps of the old city, documents related to the Louisiana purchase, and a portrait of Bienville, the founder of the city.

Aillet House

845 North Jefferson Avenue
Port Allen, LA 70767
(504) 336-2422

Contact: West Baton Rouge Historical
Association
Open: Tues.-Sat. 10 a.m.–4:30 p.m.;
Sun. 2-5 p.m.; closed major holidays
Admission: Free. Guided tours.
Suggested Time to View House: 20 minutes
Description of Grounds: Grounds feature
slave quarters cabin
Best Season to View House: Spring-fall
Style of Architecture: French Creole with
Anglo influence
Number of Yearly Visitors: 4,000
Number of Rooms: 7

Year House Built: c. 1830
On-Site Parking: Yes **Wheelchair Access:** No

Description of House

Jean Dorville Landry was the original owner of this modest house which has been faithfully restored to its original appearance by the historical association. It is believed that he built the home for his bride Aureline Daigle whom he married in 1828. Jean was a successful planter and, at the time of his death in 1864, still owned and resided in this cottage. The house is named after a later occupant, Anatole Aillet, a descendant of Thomas Aillet, an Acadian who had arrived in Louisiana in 1785. The building remained in the Aillet family for over 100 years until it was purchased by the society.

The Aillet House is a fine example of French Creole architecture with important regional characteristics as mud and moss construction *(bousillage)*, and wrap-around mantels. The house is raised on high brick piers and is constructed of pegged heavy timber. The exterior is painted white with black trim, based on the results of a paint analysis. The interior still retains some original treatments, such as *faux bois*, which uses paint to resemble wood. The roof has a very high steep pitch with side gables enclosing two chimneys. A wide front gallery is supported by six large turned columns. The two front doors are French in style and the facade is symmetrical. The two front rooms are also symmetrical and nearly identical in size. The two small back rooms or *cabinet* are separated by an enclosed hall with a stairway leading to the attic, which was probably used as a bedroom for the young men.

Currently, the interior of the Aillet House is unfurnished while the restoration continues. Even without furniture, the house conveys the spirit of the 19th-century lifestyle and is of architectural interest for visitors to the area.

Allendale Plantation Slave Cabin

845 N. Jefferson
Port Allen, LA
(504) 336-2422

Contact: West Baton Rouge Museum
Open: 10 a.m.–5 p.m.
Activities: Plantation lifestyle
demonstrations
Description of Grounds: Located on the
grounds of the Aillet House
Year House Built: c. 1800
Style of Architecture: Frame

Description of House

The pre-Civil War cabin was moved from the Allendale Plantation in West Baton Rouge Parish to the Museum grounds in 1976. The cabin is believed to be one of the oldest left standing in the parish, and to have been built by Henry Watkins Allen who owned and lived on the Allendale plantation. The restoration of this cabin has preserved a part of the property built by General Allen, a man of many talents. Allen was a soldier, orator, author, sugar planter, chemist, and iron importer. He also served as Louisiana's last Confederate governor in 1863. The city of Port Allen is named for him.

The restoration emphasizes early rural Louisiana architecture and shows a part of the way of life the craftsman and laborers knew as they tackled the problems of survival. The structure gives insight as to the durable all-cypress Creole type cabin in the South in the 1800s. The cabin serves as a focal point for plantation lifestyle demonstrations which include cooking in the kitchen fireplace.

Nottoway

P.O. Box 160
White Castle, LA 70788
(504) 545-2730

Contact: Nottoway Plantation

Open: Daily 9 a.m.–5 p.m.; closed Christmas Day

Admission: Adults $8; children $3. Guided tours, overnight accommodations, restaurant; wheelchair access is limited to the ground floor.

Suggested Time to View House: 45 minutes

Facilities on Premises: Gift shop

Description of Grounds: Park like setting of century old oaks.

Best Season to View House: Spring and fall

Number of Yearly Visitors: 100,000

Year House Built: 1859

Number of Rooms: 64, 11 open to public

Style of Architecture: Greek and Italian

On-Site Parking: Yes **Wheelchair Access:** Yes

Description of House

In 1849, John Hampden Randolph, an extremely prosperous sugar planter, commissioned one of the largest and finest homes in the South to be built. Ten years later, Nottoway was completed to accommodate Mr. Randolph's eleven children and to afford all the wants and needs of a 7,000 acre sugar plantation. The palatial residence was designed by New Orleans architect Henry Howard. The completed sixty-four room mansion when completed was the largest house in the state. Nottoway was saved from total destruction during the Civil War by a Northern gunboat officer, a former guest of the Randolphs. Luckily, the house survived and has been carefully restored to its former splendor by the current owners.

Nottoway is an American castle, a gem of Italianate and Greek Revival style, the epitome of luxury and magnificence. Boasting 53,000 square feet, Nottoway brought innovative and unique features to the South. Indoor plumbing, gas lighting and coal fireplaces marked the historical importance of this home. In addition, the intricate lacy plaster friezework, hand-painted Dresden porcelain doorknobs, hand-carved marble mantels, Corinthian columns and a 654-foot ballroom are all part of this monument to a bygone era. Most of the furnishings are collected and appropriate to the period, while some are original to the house.

Additional Information

Nottoway's grandeur is accentuated by the more than 200 windows which provide an outstanding view of the river, landscaped lawns, and live oaks. The upper floors of the mansion also serve as a bed and breakfast inn.

Mississippi

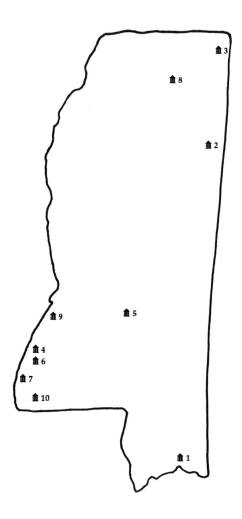

1. **Biloxi**
   Beauvoir –The Jefferson
   Davis Shrine

2. **Columbus**
   Blewett-Harrison-Lee House
   Liberty Hall
   Rosewood Manor
   Temple Heights
   Waverly
   White Arches

3. **Corinth**
   Curlee House

4. **Fayette**
   Springfield Plantation

5. **Jackson**
   Fortenberry-Parkman Farm
   Manship House
   Governor's Mansion

6. **Lorman**
   Rosswood Plantation

7. **Natchez**
   Dunleith
   Rosalie
   The House on Ellicot Hill
   Lansdowne
   The Burn
   Auburn
   Stanton Hall
   Longwood
   Magnolia Hall
   Monmouth

8. **Oxford**
   Rowan Oak

9. **Vicksburg**
   Cedar Grove Mansion
   Duff Green Mansion
   McRaven
   Anchuca
   Martha Vick House

10. **Woodville**
    Rosemont Plantation

Beauvoir—The Jefferson Davis Shrine

2244 Beach Blvd.
Biloxi, MS 39531
(601) 388-1313

Contact: United Sons of Confederate Veterans, Inc.

Open: Daily 9 a.m.–5 p.m.; closed Christmas

Admission: Adults $4.75; seniors and active military $4.25; children (6-15) $2.50; under 6 free; group rates available. Guided tours for groups, orientation film, special programs (Spring Pilgrimage-March, Confederate Memorial Day-April)

Suggested Time to View House: 2 hours

Description of Grounds: The 84-acre estate includes cemetery, lair, picnic area, nature trail

Best Season to View House: April-Oct.

Number of Yearly Visitors: 85,000

Year House Built: c. 1848-1851

Style of Architecture: Greek Revival

Number of Rooms: 9

On-Site Parking: Yes **Wheelchair Access:** Yes

Description of House

Although this gracious antebellum mansion has had many residents in its time, none is more famous than the former President of the Confederacy, Jefferson Davis. For ten years after his release from Fortress Monroe, Davis sought a permanent place of peace. Finally in 1877, at the age of sixty-nine, he accepted an invitation from a lifelong friend, Mrs. Sarah Dorsey, to visit her home on the Gulf Coast known as Beauvoir (beautiful view). Davis enjoyed his stay so much that he arranged to purchase the mansion, and here with his wife and child he lived quietly and wrote major historical works on the history of the Confederacy until his death in 1889.

Beauvoir is constructed in the style of a Louisiana raised cottage flanked by two pavilions. From the front, visitors will see an impressive view of the Gulf of Mexico. The interior features Rococo-style frescoed walls and rounded corners in the reception hall and both parlors. The house has been completely restored to represent the period of Davis's occupancy and the period furnishings include many fine Victorian pieces and family-owned items.

Notable Collections on Exhibit

The ground floor of the house contains the Davis Family Museum with eleven rooms of Victorian furnishings and decorative arts, family portraits and personal effects. The Confederate Museum located on the property exhibits a large collection of Civil War military artifacts.

Blewett-Harrison-Lee Home

7th Street North
Columbus, MS 39703
(601) 327-8888

Contact: S.D. Lee Foundation
Open: Tues. and Thurs. 1–4 p.m.,
   and by appointment
Facilities: Historical museum
Best Season to View House: Year-round
Year House Built: 1844
Style of Architecture: Italianate

Description of House

The popular historic site in downtown Columbus was built in 1844 by Major Thomas Blewett. His daughter, Regina, married the distinguished lawyer, James T. Harrison, who had the honor of defending Jefferson Davis after the Civil War. The case involving the former President of the Confederacy never came to trial. The Harrisons' daughter married Stephen D. Lee, a soldier famous for giving the order to "fire the shot heard round the world" which signalled the start of the Civil War. After the war, the Lees occupied the home for the rest of their lives.

This stately building is furnished in part as a historic home while several other rooms contain the collections of the local historical society. The museum features Civil War artifacts and memorabilia, and an outstanding collection of bridal gowns dating back 100 years. Period furnishings, some of which were donated by General Lee's daughter, decorate the upstairs bedroom.

Additional Information

The city of Columbus and the surrounding area has a wealth of beautiful historic homes. Most of them are privately owned and only open to the public during the annual Columbus Pilgrimage in April. Homes such as Twelve Gables, a former Civil War hospital; Shadowlawn, a stately Greek Revival structure with Gothic influences; and The Cedars, the oldest house in Columbus, open their doors to visitors during this traditional event. Contact the Chamber of Commerce for more information (601) 328-4491.

Liberty Hall

Open: By appointment only, contact Visitor's Bureau at (800)-327-2686 for information

Description of Grounds: The grounds feature the family burial plot

Best Season to View House: Spring-summer

Year House Built: 1832

Style of Architecture: Greek Revival

Description of House

Liberty Hall was built by the ancestors of the current owners, the family of a former Senator from South Carolina family who moved to the area seeking new and fertile soil. Members of the same family have lived in the house for five generations.

Located on the outskirts of Columbus, Liberty Hall overlooks tall evergreens surrounded by a split-rail fence. The entranceway is graced by two pairs of white columns in typical Greek Revival fashion. The interior displays a unique series of painted panels of French country scenes lining the dining room. Apparently, they were painted by a South Carolina artist who traveled to Liberty Hall and lived there for nearly a year. Unfortunately, he had to leave before his work was finished due to the start of the Civil War. The panels remain unfinished to this day. The house also features a group of magnificent paintings of French Hugenot ancestors as well as other fine pieces of artwork. Many of the furnishings are original to the house, others have been collected to complement the style and decor.

Rosewood Manor

719 7th Street North
Columbus, MS 39703
(601) 329-1191

Open: By appointment only, contact
Visitor's Bureau at (800)-327-2686 for
information

Description of Grounds: A rose garden
and a gazebo

Best Season to View House:
Spring-summer

Year House Built: 1835

Style of Architecture: Greek Revival

Description of House

Rosewood Manor, now privately owned and occupied, was originally built as the city home of planter Richard Sykes. He built this beautiful home for his new bride, a "Yankee" girl, who was, unfortunately, extremely superstitious. The mansion was built on a hill near a ravine, and the young bride refused to live in the house because she feared that vapors from the ravine would cause illness. She eventually returned to the North and Sykes married a Southern girl who appreciated the beauty of the home.

One of the oldest houses in Columbus, Rosewood uses the popular Greek Revival-style of architecture. The walls are close to three-feet thick and are constructed from bricks made at the site. The original heart pine flooring has remained intact for over 150 years. Rosewood is listed on the National Register of Historic Places and is furnished with an excellent collection of period antiques, selected and displayed by the current owners and occupants.

Additional Information

The manor takes its name from the exquisite rose gardens which surround the house. The landscaped grounds also feature huge native trees, boxwood plants, and a recently constructed gazebo.

Temple Heights

515 9th Street North
Columbus, MS 39703
(601) 329-1191

Open: By appointment only, contact
Visitor's Bureau at (800)-327-2686 for
information

Description of Grounds: Landscaped
grounds and a garden

Best Season to View House:
Spring-summer

Year House Built: 1837

Style of Architecture: Federal and
Greek Revival

Description of House

This distinguished mansion has a rich architectural history which the current owners will recount to interested visitors on tours arranged in advance. Built in 1837, Temple Heights combines Federal and Greek Revival styles to create an impressive facade. The house has a classic entablature supported by fourteen Doric columns. The four columns on the garden facade are each carved from a single tree trunk and were part of the original construction. Temple Hall has four stories with a hall and two rooms on each floor; the fourth floor is called a "habitable" attic.

The house contains many notable features including locks on the hall doors manufactured from 1830 to 1837 by a British firm and which bear the symbol of King William IV. One of the locks shows the scratched name of Anne Fontaine, etched there during the Reconstruction period. In addition, the house features distinctive woodwork in the drawing and dining room and random-width flooring of quarter-sawn pine. The attractive rooms feature the first marble mantels in Columbus. In addition, Temple Heights is furnished with Empire and Restoration pieces appropriate to the 1837 to 1844 period of occupancy by the original builder of the house, Richard T. Brownrigg.

Waverly

Highway 50
Columbus, MS 39703
(601) 329-1191

Open: By appointment only, contact Visitor's Bureau at (800)-327-2686 for information

Description of Grounds: Beautiful grounds with the state's largest magnolia tree

Best Season to View House: Spring-summer

Year House Built: 1852

Style of Architecture: Modified Greek Revival

Description of House

In an area filled with splendid antebellum mansions, Waverly represents one of the finest. Built in 1852, the house was once the center of thousands of acres and had its own lumber mill, leather tannery, brick kiln, and even a brick and marble swimming pool. The National Fox Hunters Association was founded at Waverly in 1893, evidence of its social standing in the community. This attractive mansion has been carefully restored by the current owners who purchased it in 1962 after nearly fifty years of vacancy.

The front and rear facades of this elegant mansion feature Ionic columns on the two-story recessed galleries and Doric columns at the doors. One the most distinctive features of the house is an octagonal observatory with sixteen windows and a paneled ceiling. Apparently this served as a natural cooling system for the house by drawing warm air up and out of the house through the open windows. Further evidence of the sophisticated taste of the former occupants can be seen in the twin circular cantilever staircases (with 718 hand-turned spindles) which rise three floors to the observatory. Waverly is listed on the National Register of Historic Places and has been declared a National Historic Landmark.

White Arches

122 7th Avenue South
Columbus, MS 39703
(601) 329-1191

Open: By appointment only, contact Visitor's Bureau at (800)-327-2686 for information
Best Season to View House: Spring-summer

Year House Built: 1857
Style of Architecture: Combined Gothic, Italianate, and Greek Revival elements

Description of House

This graceful mansion has witnessed some tragic events in its former residents' lives. Local legend says that a beautiful young girl, Mary Oliver, was despondent at her boyfriend's leaving for war. Her parents gave a party to lift her spirits, and Mary went out on the balcony for air, caught a cold, then pneumonia, and died. It was said that her brokenhearted parents left the house and never returned.

Despite its morbid history, White Arches offers a rich architectural experience for visitors to Columbus. The structure combines Gothic, Greek Revival, and Italianate details in a style unique to the city known as "Columbus Eclectic". The delicate Gothic arches have a cloverleaf design and help support sloping metal roofs over the galleries. The Italianate element is evident in the octagonal tower with an observatory on the top floor. Four double doors lead from the second floor of the tower onto a balcony with a cast iron railing with solid brass balls atop each corner post.

The interior of the home is equally striking with its elegant floor-to-ceiling bookcases in the library and a handsome mahogany staircase leading to the second floor. Visitors will be intrigued be the early use of closets in the upstairs bedrooms as well as the children's bedroom on the first floor which once served as an ante-room for the storing of hoop skirts. White Arches truly represents an era of sophistication and charm through its fine architectural and decorative details, including the silver doorknobs found throughout the house.

Curlee House

301 Childs Street
Corinth, MS
(601) 287 5269

Contact: City of Corinth
Open: Thurs.-Mon. 1–4 p.m.
Admission: Adults $1.50; children
(under 12) $.50. Guided tours.
Suggested Time to View House: 1 hour
Description of Grounds: Landscaped
grounds with English boxwood trees
Best Season to View House:
Spring-summer
Year House Built: 1857
Number of Rooms: 10

Style of Architecture: Greek Revival
On-Site Parking: Yes

Description of House

Now owned by the city of Corinth, Curlee House has had a number of owners over the years since it was built in 1857. During the Civil War, the house was owned by William Simonton and served as headquarters for the Confederate Generals Braxton Bragg and Earl Van Dorn and was later occupied by Union General Henry W. Halleck. The house takes its name from Mary Elizabeth Curlee who lived here from 1875 to 1883. For several months during 1875 the house served as the Corinth Female Seminary while a college building was being completed. After 1883, the house had various owners until Shelby Hammond Curlee purchased the property and brought the house back into the Curlee family.

This charming house has also been called the "Veranda House" because of its light, airy rooms and the verandas which surround the exterior. The architect is believed to have been from New Orleans and local tradition points to Martin Siegrist of Corinth as the contractor. He was a master builder and a native of Switzerland. The house has the original tall windows and high ceilings with iron moldings. All of the rooms are decorated with fine 19th-century furnishings including several gold-framed mirrors.

Additional Information

Curlee House has beautifully landscaped grounds designed by Charles Gillette of Richmond, Virginia during the 1930s. The grounds are surrounded by large square bricks from an earlier period laid during this period.

Springfield Plantation

Route 1, Box 201
Fayette, MS 39069
(601) 786-3802

Contact: Historic Springfield Foundation
Open: March-Nov. 15, 9:30 a.m.–dusk; Sun. 10:30 a.m.–dusk; hours may vary rest of year, call to verify
Admission: Adults $5.50; seniors $5; children (4-11) $2.50; group rates, please inquire. Guided tours.
Suggested Time to View House: 1 hour
Description of Grounds: Landscaped grounds with English boxwood trees
Best Season to View House: Spring-summer
Year House Built: 1857
Number of Rooms: 10

Style of Architecture: Greek Revival
On-Site Parking: Yes

Description of House

This beautiful mansion has witnessed a number of historic events over the years. The house was constructed by Thomas Marsten Green, Jr., a wealthy planter from Virginia. Here in 1791, Green's father married future President Andrew Jackson to Rachel Robards, a friend of the Green family. The marriage ran into difficulties for several reasons. As a former judge, Colonel Green's ceremony was illegal under the Spanish law of the territory of the time. Even worse, it later turned out that Rachel was not completely divorced from her first husband, Captain Robards, and she and Jackson had to be remarried in Nashville in January of 1794, causing the slander that in Jackson's view finally ruined her health and caused her death just before he took office as the seventh President of the United States. Rachel was his one great love, and he never remarried, spending both terms in the White House as a widower.

Springfield is one of the most significant buildings in American architectural development. Built from 1786 to 1791 during the Spanish domination of west Florida (Mississippi), it is the first structure in the entire Mississippi Valley to show English Colonial architectural influence, which includes the full colonnade across the entire facade and the only English Crown glass. In addition, Springfield remains almost entirely original, including magnificent Georgian-Adams-Federal woodwork and mantels hand-carved in Virginia in the 18th century. The house is furnished with a collection of 18th-century period furniture.

Additional Information

Springfield, still a working plantation after more than two centuries, offers the beauty, elegance, and romance of the Colonial South during the colorful days of Spanish rule. Springfield's oldest remaining slave quarters has been restored and a visit down the old "quarter road" is most interesting, and also a beautiful walk.

Fortenberry-Parkman Farm

1150 Lakeland Drive
Jackson, MS
(601) 354-6113

Contact: Mississippi Agriculture and
Forestry Museum

Open: Mon.-Sat. 9–5 p.m.; Sun. 1–5 p.m.,
closed Thanksgiving and Christmas

Admission: Adults $3; seniors $2.75;
children (6-18) $1. Tours, exhibits,
demonstrations, many special events
including country fair, jazz festival,
harvest celebrations, and Christmas
open house, call for information and
schedule.

Description of Grounds: The grounds
contain a complete rural town and
feature a nature trail and a swinging
bridge

Suggested Time to View House:
30 minutes for house

Best Season to View House: Spring-fall

Style of Architecture: Farmhouse

Facilities on Premises: Heritage center, gift
shop, cafe, country store

Year House Built: 1860

On-Site Parking: Yes **Wheelchair Access:** Yes

Description of House

This living history museum presents a slice of country life from
Mississippi's recent past. The Fortenberry-Parkman Farm was built in Jefferson Davis County in 1860 and restored as it was in 1920. The main house
and nine other buildings have been preserved exactly as they were before
being donated to the museum. Below the farm is a working cane mill where,
in season, visitors may see syrup being made. In addition to the farm
buildings, the town also features the offices and shops that made up small
town life including a general store, a doctor's office, a schoolhouse, and a
Masonic lodge. The Bisband Cotton Gin stands of the far edge of town. Here
visitors are able to see hand-picked cotton ginned and baled.

Notable Collections on Exhibit

The Fitzgerald Collection is housed in a building behind the Heritage
Center. The collection features a wide variety of antiquities ranging from
butter molds to muzzle loaders. The main attraction is an extensive exhibit
of Indian artifacts considered one of the finest collections in the South.

Additional Information

In addition to the historic sites and living history demonstrations,
visitors will also enjoy a pleasant stroll along the nature trail line with a large
variety of trees native to the area. There is also an unusual swinging bridge
and an outdoor pavilion at the end of the trail.

Manship House

420 East Fortification Street
Jackson, MS 39202
(601) 961-4724

Contact: Mississippi Department of
Archives & History

Open: Tues.-Fri. 9 a.m.–4 p.m.; Sat.-Sun.
1-4 p.m.; closed state holidays

Admission: Free. Guided tours, orientation
video, special events, summer
workshops for children, Christmas and
Halloween activities, slide lectures.

Suggested Time to View House:
30–45 minutes

Facilities on Premises: Visitor's center

Description of Grounds: Trees and
plantings appropriate for the period

Best Season to View House: Year round

Year House Built: 1857

Number of Rooms: 9

Number of Yearly Visitors: 5,000

Style of Architecture: Gothic Revival

On-Site Parking: Yes **Wheelchair Access:** Yes

Description of House

This charming Gothic Revival house has been home to one of Mississippi's leading families. Charles Henry Manship (born 1812) was a native of Talbot County, Maryland. He apprenticed in his youth to a chair-maker in Baltimore and learned the trade of ornamental painting. In 1838, after settling in Jackson, he married Adalinde Daley. The couple had fifteen children, ten of whom lived to adulthood. Manship was active in all phases of city government, serving as clerk, alderman, and mayor. He was mayor of Jackson during the Civil War and surrendered the town to Union forces during the occupation by General Sherman in 1862. One son, Luther Manship, was lieutenant governor of Mississippi from 1908-12. The American sculptor, Paul Manship, is a grandson of Charles Henry Manship.

This Gothic Revival-style cottage was built at a time when that style was more popular in this area. The interior plan features three bedrooms, a parlor, a sitting room, a dining room, a bathing room, a side hall, and a center hall. Examples of Manship's original woodgraining and marbling still survive. Wallpapers are reproductions of the original designs which could have come from Manship's own shop in Jackson. The house was in family hands until 1975 when it was purchased by the state for the purpose of restoration.

The historic house is restored to December 1888, the date of a significant event in the life of the family—the golden wedding anniversary of Charles Henry and Adalinde Manship. Many furnishings are original and the collected pieces are appropriate for a middle-class family home of the period.

Notable Collections on Exhibit

Among the notable furnishings on display are a wardrobe, a framed decorative sign with a family inscription and a keepsake box with "Kate Manship" lettered on it made by Manship. Two other items, a child's high chair and a bookcase-on-stand, may have also been made by him.

Governor's Mansion

300 E. Capitol Street
Jackson, MS 39201-0000
(601) 359-3175

Contact: Mississippi Department of
Archives and History
Open: Tues.-Fri. 9:30–11 a.m.; closed for
holidays during Christmas
Admission: Free. Guided tours.
Suggested Time to View House: 30 minutes
Best Season to View House: Spring
Number of Yearly Visitors: 20,000
Year House Built: 1839-42
Style of Architecture: Greek Revival
Number of Rooms: 11
On-Site Parking: No
Wheelchair Access: Yes

Description of House

This impressive mansion has been home to forty-two Mississippi governors since it was first built in 1839. Designed by state architect William Nichols, the Greek Revival structure soon became on of Jackson's best known landmarks. Every governor has lived here since that time, and it holds the distinction of being one of the oldest houses built by the state to be an official residence. During the Civil War the mansion also served as headquarters for General William T. Sherman.

The exterior features a semi-circular, two-story front portico supported by four fluted Corinthian columns with delicately carved capitals. The design strongly resembles the south portico of the White House. The interior is decorated with hand-crafted cornices, lintels, and ceiling friezes. There are many other original details such as the carvings over doorways and sliding doors on the first floor, heart of pine floors, and carved reset mantel in one bedroom. Most of the furnishings were purchased during the last restoration (1972-75); some pieces belonged to former Governors.

Notable Collections on Exhibit

The mansion displays an exquisite collection of 19th-century furnishings, a mahogany card table attributed to Duncan Phyfe, a Philadelphia work table (c. 1820) with gilded dolphin supports, an Empire Argand chandelier, and many fine sets of china and glassware.

Rosswood Plantation

Lorman, MS 39096
(800) 533-5889

Open: March-Dec. 8:30 a.m.–5 p.m., Sun.
12:30–5 p.m.; Jan.-Feb. by appointment

Admission: Adults $6; children
(5-12) $2.50. Tours.

Suggested Time to View House: 30 minutes

Facilities on Premises: Gift shop, mansion
also serves as a bed and breakfast inn

Description of Grounds: Mansion is
located on a 100 acre estate with
landscaped grounds and gardens

Best Season to View House: Summer-fall

Year House Built: 1857

Style of Architecture: Greek Revival

On-Site Parking: Yes

Number of Rooms: 14

Wheelchair Access: partial

Description of House

The mansion at Rosswood was built by David Schroder for Dr. Walter Ross Wade. Schroder also designed the nearby mansion at Windsor, considered the grandest mansion in the area, which now lies in ruins due to a fire. Rosswood was named for Isaac Ross, the grandfather of Dr. Wade and one of the first settlers to the area after the Revolutionary War. Rosswood was the site of a battle during the Civil War. When the fighting had ended, Mrs. Wade gathered up the wounded and turned the house into a hospital for both Union and Confederate soldiers.

The mansion is constructed entirely of cypress from the sills under the floors to the shingles on the roof. The only exceptions are the heart pine floor and the stairway railings made of walnut. The scale of the house is evident in the hallways; some of the floorboards are thirty-six feet long. The workmanship throughout the house is exceptional from the unusually detailed moldings to the "shadow" columns found beside the front and back doors. The dining room ceiling features an unusual medallion of carved wood in the form of grape and icanthus leaves. The mansion is listed on the National Register of Historic Places.

The mansion houses an excellent collection of furnishings belonging to many of the original owners. Some of the exceptional items on display are a crystal chandelier, an oak liquor cabinet known as a "tantulus" because it tantalized the servants in the house, a hand-carved mahogany bed, and a Queen Anne display cabinet with a display of Dresden angels and figurines.

Notable Collections on Exhibit

In addition to the many notable furnishings the dining room features an outstanding collection of crystal, china, and silver collected over many years. One silver water pitcher is American coin silver, and a pair of silver candelabra are English in origin. There is also a seventy-two piece German crystal goblet set and a complete set of heirloom Limoges china on display.

Dunleith

84 Homochitto Street
Natchez, MS 39121
(601) 446-3500

Contact: Natchez Pilgrimage Tours

Open: Tues.-Sat. 9:30 a.m.–5 p.m.,
Sun. 12:30–5 p.m.

Admission: Adults $4; youths (6-17) $2;
three house package: adults $10; youths
$5; four house package, adults $13;
youths $6.50.

Suggested Time to View House: 1 hour

Facilities on Premises: Gift shop

Description of Grounds: This antebellum
mansion stands on a beautifully
landscaped forty-acre park complete
with outbuildings.

Year House Built: 1855

On-Site Parking: Yes

Style of Architecture: Greek Revival Temple

Description of House

This spectacular Greek Revival mansion rises majestically over a forty-acre landscaped park right in the heart of Natchez. Dunleith has been called the most photographed house in America and is the only house in Mississippi with wide double galleries and twenty-six massive Tuscan columns completely surrounding it. This striking exterior is matched by the regal interior with its French Zubor wallpaper and imported carpets. The period rooms are furnished with splendid examples of 18th and 19th-century English and French antiques. Dunleith is listed on the National Register of Historic Places and has been the backdrop for several films set in the South.

In addition, a three-story service wing attached to the rear of the house contains a kitchen and an antebellum bathroom. Dunleith has a complete series of outbuildings which complement the elegant mansion. The grounds of the estate contain a two-story hen-house, a Gothic house-stable building, and a matching Gothic hot-house.

Additional Information

Each year the city of Natchez hosts an annual pilgrimage which takes visitors through many privately-owned antebellum mansions. The tour includes close to twenty homes in this beautiful city such as Elms Court, a superb example of a suburban villa; and Linden, home to the first Senator from Mississippi. Contact Natchez Pilgrimage Tours at (800) 647-6742 for information and schedule.

Rosalie

South Broadway at Canal Street
Natchez, MS 39121
(601) 445-4555

Contact: Mississippi State DAR/Natchez Pilgrimage Tours
Open: 9 a.m.–5 p.m., closed Christmas
Admission: Adults $4; youths (6-17) $2; three house package: adults $10; youths $6.50; five house package: adults $16; youths $8. Tours every 30 minutes.

Suggested Time to View House: 1 hour
Year House Built: 1820
Style of Architecture: Greek Revival
On-Site Parking: Yes

Description of House

This stately brick mansion was built on the former site of Fort Rosalie where the French suffered a massacre in the 18th century. The mansion was the dream home of Peter and Eliza Little, a wealthy Natchez couple. Little earned his considerable fortune from his lumber mill on the Mississippi, the first to use steam power. In 1858, the house was bought by Natchez millionaire Andrew Wilson who furnished it with family heirlooms, imported carpets, and exquisite Belter furniture. During the Civil War, Rosalie served as Union headquarters following the surrender of Natchez. In 1863, General Ulysses S. Grant occupied the mansion, followed by General Walter Gresham. The mansion is now the State Shrine of the Mississippi Daughters of the American Revolution, and is listed as a National Historic Landmark.

Traces of history can be seen in Rosalie's many fine furnishings and decorations. The white marble mantels over the fireplaces still show the smoke stains from the period that the soldiers were quartered here. Many of the original fine furnishings are on display in the period rooms including French mirrors and crystal chandeliers. The parlor has a complete set of Belter furniture which belonged to owner Andrew Wilson as well as his family banquet table. The house is surrounded by an unusual white picket fence which was constructed without the use of nails.

The House on Ellicot Hill

Corner of Canal and
Jefferson Streets
Natchez, MS 39121
(601) 442-2011

Contact: Natchez Garden Club/Natchez
Pilgrimage Tours

Open: Tues.-Sat. 9:30–4:30 p.m.,
Sun. 1:30–4 p.m.

Admission: Adults $4; youths (6-17) $2;
three house package: adults $10; youths
$5; four house package: adults $13;
youths $6.50. Guided tours, package
tours allow visitors to combine visits to
the ten other historic homes open to the
public on a regular basis.

Suggested Time to View House: 30 minutes

Year House Built: 1798

Style of Architecture: Modified Georgian

On-Site Parking: Yes

Description of House

The House on Ellicot Hill exemplifies the frontier elegance of the first years of the Mississippi territory. The house was built by James Moore, a wealthy Natchez merchant, as his residence. Just one year earlier in 1797, the site achieved fame when Major Andrew Ellicot defied the Spanish authorities and raised the American flag on this hill. The house has seen its share of danger during the days when outlaws frequented this area known as the Natchez Trace.

Throughout its colorful history, the house has served as home to many prominent Natchez citizens including one of the town's early physicians. In later years the house fell into disrepair, but since 1935 this stately home has been owned by the Natchez Garden Club and has been declared a National Historic Landmark.

This two-story frame house features lovely porches on the first and second floors. The original hand-made brick floors have been maintained on the first floor. In addition, this former tavern also exhibits primitive cooking utensils, a rare Waterford crystal chandelier, and a Natchez-made clock in the period rooms.

Lansdowne

1323 Martin Luther King Drive
Natchez, MS 39121
(601) 446-9401

Contact: Natchez Pilgrimage Tours

Open: Mon.-Fri. 10 a.m.–4 p.m.; Sat.-Sun. 10 a.m.–1 p.m.

Admission: Adults $4, youths (6-17) $2; three house package: adults $10; youths $6.50; five house package: adults $16; youths $8. Tours usually conducted by family members. Group tour dinners and luncheons. House also serves as bed and breakfast.

Suggested Time to View House: 30 minutes

Description of Grounds: Large park-like grounds surround house. A family cemetery (still in use) is on the property

Best Season to View House: Spring or fall

Year House Built: 1853

Number of Rooms: 6 open to public

Number of Yearly Visitors: 6000

Style of Architecture: Greek Revival

On-Site Parking: Yes **Wheelchair Access:** No

Description of House

Built on land given as a wedding gift for Charlotte Hunt and her husband, George Marshall, this gracious mansion was named after Marshall's good friend, the Marquis of Lansdowne. The couple's fathers, Lavin Marshall and David Hunt, were two of the wealthiest men in the South. Marshall was a cotton planter and a state legislator. He served in the Confederate Army and was wounded at the Battle of Shiloh. Several generations of Marshalls continued to reside at Lansdowne, and currently the daughter of George Marshall III lives here and opens the house to the public.

This one-story plantation home features a brick exterior stuccoed to resemble stone. Visitors enter through a columned front gallery and walk along a sixty-five-foot central hallway with fourteen-foot ceilings. The brick courtyard in the rear is flanked by two two-story dependencies with full galleries which were originally used for the kitchen, servants' rooms, a billiard room, and the school room. Lansdowne features the original *faux bois* woodwork and faux marble baseboards to match the marble mantels.

Most of the furnishings belonged to the original Marshall family, the builders of the house. French Zubor wallpaper and replicas of the original drapes decorate the parlor. The gasoliers (bronze chandeliers) located throughout the house were made by Cornelius Baxter of Philadelphia.

Notable Collections on Exhibit

In addition to the original furnishings, Lansdowne displays a collection of family silver, including the largest known piece of Natchez-made silver. Also exhibited are Thomas Sully portraits of Lavin Marshall, a miniature of Andrew Jackson by Ralph Erle, and a button from Robert E. Lee's uniform with a note from his daughter. Other notable collections include antique china, Bohemian glass, and a number of heirloom bronze pieces.

The Burn

712 North Union Street
Natchez, MS 39121
(601) 442-1344

Contact: Natchez Pilgrimage Tours
Open: Tues.-Sat. 9:30–4:30 p.m.,
  Sun. 1:30–4 p.m.
Admission: Adults $4; youths (6-17) $2;
  three house package: adults $10; youths
  $5; four house package: adults $13;
  youths $6.50. Guided tours, package
  tours allow visitors to combine visits to
  the 10 other historic homes open to the
  public on a regular basis.
Suggested Time to View House: 1 hour
Description of Grounds: The house has a
  unique garden with over 125 varieties of
  camellias
Best Season to View House: Spring
Year House Built: 1836

Style of Architecture: Greek Revival
On-Site Parking: Yes

Description of House

The Burn, beautifully detailed and proportioned, is one of Natchez's oldest and historically documented Greek Revival residences. Today, visitors will be able to see in the beauty of the house and its furnishings a home once linked with the social life of Natchez. During the Civil War, the Burn was the headquarters for the Federal Fort McPherson and later, a hospital for Union soldiers.

This three-story mansion is one of the earliest purely Greek Revival residences in Natchez. The front portico is supported by large Doric columns and the paneled doorway is surrounded in lights of blown glass. The house is especially noted for its beautiful semi-spiral staircase and its fine collection of 19th-century furnishings; the formal dining room is decorated with matching Regency servers while one of the bedrooms has furniture by Prudent Mallard carved in New Orleans. The Burn is listed on the National Register of Historic Places.

Additional Information

The Burn is also noteworthy for its exceptional gardens filled with many rare varieties of camellias. An original detached dependency known as a "garconierre" stands in the garden and has been adapted as a guest house.

Auburn

Contact: Natchez Pilgrimage Tours/Auburn Garden Club

Open: Tues.-Sat. 9:30–4:30 p.m., Sun 1:30–4 p.m.

Admission: Adults $4; youths (6-17) $2; three house package: adults $10; youths $5; four house package: adults $13; youths $6.50. Guided tours, package tours allow visitors to combine visits to the 10 other historic homes open to the public on a regular basis.

Suggested Time to View House: 1 hour

Description of Grounds: The mansion stands in a public park with grounds featuring nature trails, picnic areas, and moss-draped oak trees.

Year House Built: 1812

On-Site Parking: Yes

Style of Architecture: Greek Revival

Description of House

This imposing mansion set in the midst of Duncan Park was designed by architect Levi Weeks. In 1911, Auburn and its surrounding acreage were deeded to the city of Natchez as a public park. The building has also been designated a National Historic Landmark.

In 1820, Auburn was described as "the handsomest about Natchez" because of its elegant facade and beautiful interiors. Still impressive today, the red brick mansion is famous as the first house in the Mississippi territories to be built on architectural orders. The interiors hand-carved woodwork is one of the finest in the South. Auburn is particularly noteworthy for its beautiful, free-standing, elliptical stairway which rises unsupported to the second floor. The period rooms are decorated with fine early 19th-century furnishings.

Stanton Hall

401 High Street at Pearl
Natchez, MS 39121
(601)442-6282

Contact: Pilgrimage Garden Club/Natchez
Pilgrimage Tours
Open: 9 a.m.–5 p.m., closed Christmas
Admission: Adults $4, youths (6-17) $2;
three house package: adults $10; youths
$6.50; five house package: adults $16;
youths $8. Tours every 20 minutes
Suggested Time to View House: 1 hour
Facilities on Premises: Gift shop
Description of Grounds: A beautifully
landscaped courtyard
Year House Built: 1858
Style of Architecture: Greek Revival
On-Site Parking: Yes

Description of House

Stanton Hall is one of the most magnificent and princely edifices of antebellum America. This grand home was built for Frederick Stanton, a wealthy cotton commission broker using the design of a Natchez architect, Thomas Rose. The architect employed local skilled artisans, builders, and finishers to complete this extraordinary structure which occupies a full city block.

Stanton spared no expense in constructing his new home. The exterior has four immense Corinthian columns on the front gallery while the interior details, such as the silver knobs and hinges used throughout the mansion, are equally impressive. Stanton imported immense gilt mirrors from France, ordered unusual bronze chandeliers from Philadelphia, and brought in beautifully sculptured marble mantels from New York to decorate his regal home. Stanton Hall is registered as a National Historic Landmark.

Notable Collections on Exhibit

Stanton Hall exhibits a beautiful collection of Natchez antiques, including an elaborate Gothic-style hall stand and matching chairs, and exquisite *objets d'art*.

Additional Information

Visitors to Stanton Hall may combine a visit with many other the other historic homes located in the area such as The Burn and the House on Ellicot Hill. Contact Natchez Pilgrimage Tours for more information (800-647-6742).

Longwood

Lower Woodville Road
Natchez, MS 39121
(601) 442-5193

Contact: Pilgrimage Garden Club/Natchez Pilgrimage

Open: 9 a.m.–5 p.m., closed Christmas

Admission: Adults $4; youths (6-17) $2; three house package: adults $10; youths $5; four house package: adults $13; youths $6.50. Tours every 20 minutes.

Suggested Time to View House: 30 minutes

Description of Grounds: Landscaped gardens

Year House Built: c.1860

Style of Architecture: Octagonal

Number of Rooms: 9 open to public

On-Site Parking: Yes

Description of House

Considered the largest octagonal house still standing in America, Longwood is a superb example of the mid 19th-century "villa in the Oriental style". Also known as "Nutt's Folley", this unusual house was designed for the wealthy cotton planter and physician, Haller Nutt. The house's construction was begun in 1860 but, unfortunately the onset of the Civil War caused the Yankee artisans to leave the house without finishing the massive structure. The family moved into the basement and created a "temporary habitat"; these rooms are now the only ones open to the public.

The most ornate octagonal house in the country, Longwood stands five stories high and is topped with a Byzantine onion-shaped dome. The house contains an exhibit of the architect's drawings of the mansion as it was to have been—a six-story structure of brick, plaster and marble with eight rooms on each floor centered around a rotunda. Today, only the basement rooms are furnished as they were during the period of the family's occupancy with heirlooms and period furnishings.

Magnolia Hall

Corner Pearl and Washington Streets
Natchez, MS 39121
(601) 446-6742

Contact: Pilgrimage Garden Club/Natchez
Pilgrimage
Open: 9 a.m.–5 p.m., closed Thanksgiving
and Christmas
Admission: Adults $4; youths (6-17) $2;
three house package tour, adults $10;
youths $5; four house package: adults
$13; youths $6.50. Guided tours.
Suggested Time to View House: 30 minutes
Facilities on Premises: Gift shop
Year House Built: 1858
On-Site Parking: Yes

Style of Architecture: Greek Revival

Description of House

Magnolia Hall was one of the last great mansions erected in Natchez prior to the Civil War. Constructed in 1858 by Thomas Henderson, a prominent planter and merchant, the house recalls the splendor of the antebellum South.

The Greek Revival exterior features a brownstone facade with large white columns at the entrance to the mansion. The renovation of Magnolia Hall began in 1976 and is still continuing today. Inside, the period rooms display a fine collection of 18th and 19th-century furnishings and decorations. The mansion is listed on the National Register of Historic Places.

Notable Collections on Exhibit

In addition to the period furniture, Magnolia Hall contains the Natchez Costume Museum with many Pilgrimage costumes including the gowns of former queens.

Monmouth

John A. Quitman Parkway
and Melrose Avenue
Natchez, MS 39121
(601) 452-3852

Contact: Pilgrimage Garden Club/Natchez
Pilgrimage Tours
Open: 9:30 a.m.–4:30 p.m., closed Christmas
Admission: Adults $4; youths (6-17) $2;
three house package: adults $10; youths
$6.50; five house package: adults $16;
youths $8. Tours every 45 minutes.
Suggested Time to View House: 1 hour
Facilities on Premises: Gift shop, bed and
breakfast
Year House Built: 1818
Style of Architecture: Greek Revival
On-Site Parking: Yes

Description of House

This stately mansion was home to General John Anthony Quitman, a hero of the Mexican American War. In addition to his war achievements, Quitman also served as a U.S. Congressman and governor of Mississippi. Quitman was a member of an outspoken group who advocated secession from the Union, but he died in 1858 before the Civil War began. Family members continued to live in the home which suffered considerable damage during the war. In 1914, the mansion was sold, and by the 1970s much of the building was falling apart. Considerable research and effort has gone into the accurate historical restoration since then.

Monmouth has an impressive facade with its massive square columns and its symmetrically placed windows. Built in 1818, the mansion has now been meticulously restored to its former beauty and furnished to represent the period of its most illustrious owner, General Quitman. Monmouth is listed on the National Register of Historic Places.

Notable Collections on Exhibit

Many of Quitman's personal effects are currently exhibited, including a gold sword presented to him for his valor in the Mexican War. The general's desk and his original New Orleans Empire bed are also on display.

Additional Information

As part of the Natchez Pilgrimage Tours, visitors may combine a visit to Monmouth with other Natchez homes such as Magnolia Hall and Dunleith, for a reduced admission price.

Rowan Oak

Old Taylor Road, P.O. Box 965
Oxford, MS 38655
(601) 234-4651

Contact: Oxford Tourism Council
Open: Tues.-Sat. 10 a.m.–12 p.m.;
Sun. 2–4 p.m., closed holidays
Admission: Free. Guided tours.
Facilities on Premises: 1 hour
Description of Grounds: A 32-acre
estate known as Bailey's Woods
Best Season to View House: Summer-fall
Year House Built: 1840s
Style of Architecture: Greek Revival
Number of Rooms: 10
On-Site Parking: Yes

Description of House

Rowan Oak, built by a pioneer settler in the 1840s and situated in a grove of oak and cedar trees, is best known as the home of author William Faulkner. He bought the house in 1930 and named it after the Rowan tree which, according to legend, was supposed to ward off evil spirits and give the occupants a place of refuge, privacy, and peace. After 1930, Faulkner did most of his writing at Rowan Oak. In 1950, shortly after he was awarded the Nobel Prize, he added a small office which became his sanctuary. It was in this office that he prepared the outline for his Pulitzer prize-winning novel *The Fable*, and inscribed it on the wall in his close, vertical handwriting which is still visible today. Faulkner lived at Rowan Oak until his death in 1962.

A visit to Rowan Oak provides a fascinating view of one of America's most important literary figures. The two-story frame dwelling survived the burning of Oxford during the Civil War and contains many rooms which reflect Faulkner's lifestyle. The first-floor library contains many of his artifacts including a favorite chair, manuscript papers, and his pipe and glasses. The parlor contains his wife's favorite Chickering piano; while Faulkner's office off the back hall exhibits many items related to his work. In addition to the main house, the grounds also contain a cook's house and kitchen, a stable constructed of hand-hewn logs, and the formal gardens which Faulkner himself designed. All of the furnishings date from 1930 to 1962, the period the that Faulkners lived here.

Notable Collections on Exhibit

Rowan Oak exhibits a comprehensive display of Faulkner memorabilia and will delight anyone familiar with his writing. Some of the notable items include his typewriter, his desk, portraits of the family, and a photograph exhibit on the author's life.

Cedar Grove Mansion

2300 Washington Street
Vicksburg, MS 39180
(800) 448-2800

Contact: Cedar Grove Mansion

Open: Daily 9 a.m.–5 p.m

Admission: Per person $5; students $4. Guided tours and bed and breakfast.

Suggested Time to View House: 30 minutes

Facilities on Premises: Gift shop

Description of Grounds: Formal gardens, gazebos, fountains, courtyard, and recreational facilities

Best Season to View House: Spring

Number of Yearly Visitors: 500,000

Year House Built: 1840

Style of Architecture: Greek Revival

Number of Rooms: 35

On-Site Parking: Yes **Wheelchair Access:** Yes

Description of House

Cedar Grove was built by John A. Klein as a wedding present for his bride Elizabeth, a cousin of General William T. Sherman. It took him eighteen years to complete this impressive mansion. During the Civil War, the house barely escaped destruction during the siege of Vicksburg when it was used as a hospital. To this day, a Union cannonball remains lodged in the parlor wall.

Cedar Grove is one of the South's largest and loveliest historic mansions which now functions as a bed and breakfast inn. The basement was used as the original slave quarters, and the main floor is available for tours. The mansion is exquisitely furnished with many original antiques, gaslit chandeliers, gold leaf mirrors, and Italian marble mantels. The second and third floors contain the guest rooms.

Notable Collections on Exhibit

Cedar Grove displays many fine period furnishings, many of which belonged to the Klein family. There are also many fascinating artifacts on display including a 3,000-pound cast-iron safe and the original king-sized canopy bed which General Grant slept in after the Vicksburg siege.

Duff Green Mansion

1114 First East Street
Vicksburg, MS 39180
(601)636-6968

Contact: Duff Green Mansion

Open: 9 a.m.–5 p.m., closed Christmas and
New Year's Day

Admission: Adults $5, children (6-12) $3.
Guided tours.

Suggested Time to View House: 30 minutes

Facilities on Premises: Mansion houses a
bed and breakfast

Description of Grounds: Located in
Vicksburg's historic district

Best Season to View House: Year round

Year House Built: c. 1856

Number of Rooms: 5 open to public

Style of Architecture: Palladian

On-Site Parking: Yes

Description of House

The mansion was built by Duff Green, one of the most prosperous merchant's in Vicksburg, for his wife, Mary Lake Green. Many parties were held here during the antebellum days but it was hastily converted to a hospital for both Confederate and Union soldiers during the siege of Vicksburg and the remainder of the Civil War. While the city was under siege, the couple lived with Mary's parents in a cave near the mansion. During this time, Mary gave birth to a son and appropriately named him Siege Green. Several other families lived in the home until the Salvation Army bought it in 1931 for just $3000. After using the mansion as their headquarters, the Sharp family bought the building and restored it to its original beauty.

This impressive Palladian structure maintains many of its original features. The dining room has sliding doors made of solid cypress. Unlike other antebellum homes in which the kitchen was located in a separate room, in Duff Mansion the kitchen was built directly under the dining room, and food was brought up by a dumb waiter in the corner. There are fifteen coal-burning fireplaces located throughout the house. In addition, one of the upstairs bedrooms features a glass ceiling through which visitors may see a beam with a hole made by a Union cannonball. The mansion is listed on the National Register of Historic Places.

Notable Collections on Exhibit

Duff Mansion contains many original furnishings and fixtures from the 19th century. The elegant dining room features a 200 year-old English Jacobean table and a Waterford chandelier. The ballroom displays French crystal chandeliers while the main hallway showcases an impressive crystal and bronze chandelier and a large Italian painting (c. 1837).

McRaven

1445 Harrison Street
Vicksburg, MS 39180
(601) 636-1663

Contact: McRaven Tour Home

Open: Fall and spring, Mon.-Sat.
9 a.m.–5 p.m., Sun. 10 a.m.–5 p.m.;
June 1-Labor Day, Mon.-Sat.
9 a.m.–6 p.m., Sun. 10 a.m.–6 p.m.

Admission: Adults $4.50; senior citizens $4;
children (12-18) $2; children (6-11)
$1.50. Guided tours.

Description of Grounds: The original
pre-war strolling gardens date from 1849
and were the scene of a famous murder,
and a confederate campsite

Year House Built: 1797

Style of Architecture: Frontier (1797);
Empire (1836); Greek Revival (1849)

On-Site Parking: Yes

Description of House

Andrew Glass, a Natchez Trace highwayman built the first section of the house in 1797. Following his residency, the buildings and grounds were used as a way station during the Indian removal program of the early 1830s which historians now call "The Trail of Tears." Shortly thereafter, Sheriff Stephen Howard of Vicksburg moved in and added the second section. The last resident was John H. Bobb in 1849.

McRaven's restoration and furnishings reflect the three distinct and separate periods of ownership. The first section was built in 1797, the furnishings are typical of the frontier dwelling of that era of Spanish governmental dominion. The second or "middle" section of the house was built in 1836 in the Federal style, and the furnishings are of the American Empire period. The final section was built in 1849 in the Greek Revival style with furnishings of the Rococo Revival style. In addition to the beautiful period pieces, the interior features a flying wing staircase, jib doors, floor-to-ceiling windows, carved millwork, elaborate plaster friezes and ceiling medallions throughout the entire 1849 section of the house.

Notable Collections on Exhibit

One of the most notable items on display is the collection of rose medallion export porcelain, which is larger than the Roosevelt collection at the White House; it comprises over 1400 pieces and dates from 1730 to 1860. In addition, there are first editions of works by the American artist, John James Audubon. There is a large collection of Civil War artifacts on display, all original to McRaven's grounds. Signed pieces of Sevres Porcelain that once belonged to Louis-Phillipe, King of France, are also on exhibit.

Anchuca

**1010 First East
Vicksburg, MS 39180
(800) 262-4822**

Open: 9 a.m.–5 p.m.

Activities: Guided tours

Suggested Time to View House: 30 minutes

Facilities on Premises: Mansion serves as bed and breakfast and has dining facilities.

Description of Grounds: Located in historic district of Vicksburg, the mansion has landscaped formal gardens and a courtyard.

Best Season to View House: Year round

Year House Built: 1830, 1845 addition

Style of Architecture: Greek Revival

Number of Rooms: 11

On-Site Parking: Yes

Description of House

This lovely antebellum home was the first mansion in Vicksburg and the first house in the city to use Greek Revival architecture. A city alderman, J.W. Mauldin, was the first person to live here in 1830. Five years later he sold the house to a woman, Hanna Giles, an unusual occurrence for the time. Mississippi was ahead of other states in the South in its position on women's rights; it was the first to give women property rights and also claims to have the first female college graduate. Anchuca is also noted for having been the site of a historic speech by Jefferson Davis to the troops during the Civil War.

This gracious mansion continues to exhibit many of the fine features created by its former owners. The structure is comprised of over 55,000 bricks manufactured on the grounds. The slave quarters, which were originally separated from the main house, are now joined and serve as guest accommodations. The original painted glass decorates the second floor as well as the gas-lit chandeliers. All of the rooms are furnished according to the different periods of occupancy and include a music room decorated with furniture from 1845 and a gentleman's parlor displaying furnishings from the 1860s. The original living quarters are furnished to represent the period from 1830.

Notable Collections on Exhibit

The many fine furnishings on display include a Sheraton dining table and sideboard, family-owned Chippendale chairs, and a china cabinet signed by Duncan Phyfe.

Martha Vick House

1300 Grove Street
Vicksburg, MS 39180
(601) 638-7036

Open: Mon.-Sat. 9 a.m.–5 p.m.,
Sun. 2–5 p.m.
Admission: Adults $5; children (6-11) $2.50.
Guided tours.
Suggested Time to View House: 30 minutes
Description of Grounds: An enclosed
gallery filled with greenery and flowers
Year House Built: 1830
Style of Architecture: Greek Revival

Description of House

This attractive "mini-mansion" was built in 1830 for Martha Vick (1800-1851), an unmarried daughter of Reverend Newit Vick, the founder of Vicksburg. This last remaining Vick house has been described as "light and airy, of generous proportions." For visitors today the house provides an illuminating sense of the wealth and elegance of the deep South in the years before the Civil War. The house is furnished with distinctive pieces of 18th and 19th-century furniture and decorated with late French impressionist paintings. The dining room table is set with Haviland china and sterling silver, as if Martha Vick herself were about to entertain guests.

Additional Information

Visitors to Vicksburg should not miss the opportunity to see many of the other notable historic homes open to the public including Duff Mansion (1114 First East Street) and Grey Oaks (4142 Rifle Range Road), a fine example of Federal architecture surrounded by acres of landscaped grounds.

Rosemont Plantation

Highway 24 East
Woodville, MS 39669
(601) 888-6809

Contact: Rosemont Plantation

Open: March-Dec., Mon.-Fri. 10 a.m.–5 p.m.

Admission: Adults $6; students $3. Guided tours, audiovisual presentations.

Suggested Time to View House: 1 hour

Facilities on Premises: Rest rooms

Description of Grounds: Family cemetery

Best Season to View House: Spring and fall

Number of Yearly Visitors: 5,000

Year House Built: 1810

Style of Architecture: Planter-style raised cottage

Number of Rooms: 7

On-Site Parking: Yes **Wheelchair Access:** No

Description of House

The house was the boyhood home of Jefferson Davis. This attractive cottage was built by his parents and was owned by the family until 1895. Jefferson Davis is best known for his four years as President of the Confederacy. Less well known are the several other careers he pursued during his eighty-one years, any one of which could qualify as a lifetime achievement for most men. He was a soldier, planter, a U.S. Senator, secretary of war, and author of a multi-volume history of the Confederacy. Davis was effective on the battlefield, in the drawing rooms of southern plantations and on the speakers platform. Many states have reminders of the fortunes and tragedies of his life, which ended with the greatest funeral the South has ever known.

The one-and-a-half story Rosemont features front and rear verandas and Palladian windows. Inside, large wood-grained doors open at either end onto galleries running the length of the home. Many of the furnishings are original Davis pieces.

Notable Collections on Exhibit

Notable furnishings include the Davis four-poster bed, several family portraits, and a magnificent whale oil chandelier dominating the center hall.

North Carolina

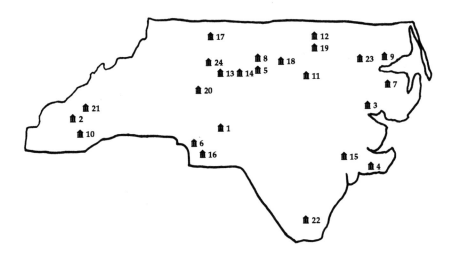

1. **Albemarle**
   Snuggs House
   Marks House

2. **Asheville**
   Thomas Wolfe Memorial
   Smith-McDowell House
   Biltmore House

3. **Bath**
   Historic Bath
   Williams 'Glebe' House

4. **Beaufort**
   Historical Beaufort

5. **Chapel Hill**
   Horace Williams House

6. **Charlotte**
   Hezekiah Alexander Homesite

7. **Creswell**
   Somerset Place

8. **Durham**
   Bennett Place
   Duke Homestead
   Richard Bennehan House

9. **Edenton**
   Barker House
   Cupola
   James Iredell House
   State Historic Site

10. **Flat Rock**
    Carl Sandburg Home

11. **Fremont**
    Charles B. Aycock Birthplace

12. **Halifax**
    Owens House
    The Sally-Billy House

13. **High Point**
    Haley House

14. **Jamestown**
    The Mendenhall Plantation

15. **New Bern**
    Dixon-Stevenson House
    John Wright Stanly House
    Tryon Palace

16. **Pineville**
    James K. Polk Memorial

17. **Pinnacle**
    Horne Creek Living
    Historical Farm

18. **Raleigh**
    Mordecai Historic Park
    "Wakefield"–Joel Lane House
    Executive Mansion
    Haywood Hall

19. **Rodey Mount**
    Stonewall Manor

20. **Salisbury**
    The Michael Braun House
    The Utzman-Chambers House

21. **Weaverville**
    Zebulon B. Vance Birthplace

22. **Wilmington**
    Burgwin Wright House
    and Gardens

23. **Windsor**
    Hope Plantation

24. **Winston-Salem**
    Old Salem
    Reynolda House–
    Museum of American Art

Snuggs House

112 N. Third
Albemarle, NC 28001
(704) 983-7316

Contact: Albemarle Stanly County
Historical Preservation Commission
Open: Mon.-Thur. 9 a.m.–5 p.m.; closed all
major holidays
Admission: Free. Guided tours.
Suggested Time to View House: 1 hour
Facilities on Premises: Gift shop
Description of Grounds: Small lawns with
period flowers
Best Season to View House: Spring
Number of Yearly Visitors: 4,200
Year House Built: c. 1870
Number of Rooms: 3

On-Site Parking: Yes **Wheelchair Access:** Yes

Description of House

This charming, white frame house has witnessed much local history as the home of Sheriff Isaiah "Buck" Wilson Snuggs (1846-1904).

At 17, Buck Snuggs served in the 14th North Carolina State Troops in the Civil War, and lost a leg at Spotsylvania Court House. In the years following the war, he turned to a career of public service, first as register of deeds, and later as county treasurer. But it is as Stanly county's ninth sheriff that Snuggs is best remembered. A sheriff's job in rural North Carolina in the 19th century was not all paperwork and tax collection. Citizens still recall the quiet courage and good sense he embodied in times of trial and distress.

The Snuggs House is the third oldest house in Albemarle. The precise date of construction is unsure, but the building appears to have its origins in the 1850s as a two-room log cabin, a type common to the region. After the war, Mr. Snuggs purchased the property in 1873, added the south front room downstairs, the staircase and second story. He sealed the inside of the log rooms and weather-boarded the exterior. In time, he built several rooms to the rear of the house as his family expanded. The second floor recreates a bedroom, circa 1870, and a Victorian parlor. The rooms exhibit furnishings, appointments, and costumes true to the period and region, including several original Snugg pieces. The house is preserved not so much in memory of a man, but more as a model of life in this section of North Carolina.

Notable Collections on Exhibit

In addition to the period furnishings, the main gallery on the first floor displays relics from the community's past and is the location of a series of ongoing exhibits.

Marks House

112 N. Third
Albemarle, NC 28001
(704) 983-7316

Contact: Albemarle Stanly County
Historical Preservation Commission

Open: Mon.-Thur. 9 a.m.–5 p.m.; closed all
major holidays

Admission: Free. Guided tours.

Suggested Time to View House: 1 hour

Facilities on Premises: Gift shop

Description of Grounds: Small lawns with
period flowers

Best Season to View House: Spring

Number of Yearly Visitors: 4,200

Year House Built: c. 1850

Number of Rooms: 4

On-Site Parking: Yes **Wheelchair Access:** Yes

Description of House

As the oldest house in Albermarle, the Marks House is synonymous with the settlement of the area. The first owner was Daniel Freeman, a prominent local merchant. From Freeman, the house passed through a succession of owners. The most notable residents include James Marshall McCorkle, a leading lawyer in the state, who utilized the building from 1850 to 1861 as a law office and private residence. Another famous inhabitant was Samuel James Pemberton, co-author of *The North Carolina Criminal Code and Digest*, published in 1892 which he compiled while living in this modest dwelling. This reference work is still used by lawyers today. In 1884, the property was purchased by Whitson a Marks, an Albermarle farmer and businessman. Marks maintained the building as his home until 1906, when he built a larger brick structure for his residence. At that time he moved the Marks House to accommodate his new home. In August 1975, the city designated the house an historic property and later that year the building was moved to its present location behind the Snuggs House.

The house has been fully restored to its late 1840s appearance as a combination residence and law office. Visitors will find authentic period furnishings in the child's and adult bedrooms, as well as the attorney's office and the parlor. Several pieces are original to the house and the Marks family.

Additional Information

A combined visit to the Marks House and the Snuggs House provides visitors with a rare view of 19th-century life in a former county seat.

Thomas Wolfe Memorial

48 Spruce Street, P.O. Box 7143
Asheville, NC 28807
(704) 253-8304

Contact: Department of Cultural Resources
Open: April 1-Oct. 31, Mon.-Sat.
  9 a.m.–5 p.m., Sun. 1–5 p.m.; Nov.
  1-March 31: Tues.-Sat. 10 a.m.–4 p.m.,
  Sun. 1–5 p.m.
Admission: Adults $1; children $.50.
  Guided tours.
Year House Built: c. 1890s
Style of Architecture: Victorian

Description of House

Of all this country's major novelists, Thomas Wolf was the most overtly autobiographical, his own family and boyhood providing the material for many memorable passages and characters in the first two and most successful of his novels, *Look Homeward, Angel* and *Of Time and the River*. The scene of his boyhood was Asheville and, most specifically, "The Old Kentucky Home," a rambling Victorian boarding house run by his mother, Julia. Called "Dixieland" in his book, it provided the author with an abundance of diverse characters and was the scene of some of Wolfe's most powerfully written episodes. The home, preserved as a memorial to Wolfe, stands as a striking monument to him and his work. Those who are familiar with his writing will feel the intimate relationship of the old home to his work; other visitors will receive a wonderful introduction to this literary master.

This Victorian boarding house, has a gabled roof with many porches. The home remains virtually unchanged since Thomas Wolfe's childhood with all of the furnishings and personal effects. When the Wolfe Memorial was first opened to the public, Tom's surviving brother and sister arranged the interior of the house to look as it had during the period described in his first novel, *Look Homeward, Angel*. The house and its period furnishings are typical of early 20th-century American homes of middle class families.

Notable Collections on Exhibit

One room in the house contains the furnishings from the author's last New York apartment, including his writing table and typewriter.

Biltmore House

One North Pack Square
Asheville, NC 28801
(704) 255-1700

Contact: Biltmore Estate

Open: Daily 9 a.m.–5 p.m.; closed
Thanksgiving, Christmas, New Year's Day

Admission: Adults $21.95; students (10-15)
$16.50; under 9 (accompanied by a
parent) free. Audio tour (for rent),
behind-the-scenes tours (additional $10).

Suggested Time to View House: 2–2½ hours

Facilities on Premises: Gift shops,
restaurants

Description of Grounds: The formal garden
grounds, designed by Frederick
Olmstead, cover 75 acres. The entire
estate is approximately 8,000 acres and
contains a working vineyard.

Best Season to View House: Mid
March-mid Oct.

Number of Yearly Visitors: 715,000

Year House Built: 1895

Style of Architecture: French Renaissance

Number of Rooms: 250

On-Site Parking: Yes **Wheelchair Access:** Yes

Description of House

Grandeur is the best term to describe visitors' first impression of seeing
Biltmore, the largest private residence in America and the home George
Vanderbilt. George was the grandson of Commodore Cornelius Vanderbilt,
the railroad magnate. A scholar and intellect, the young Vanderbilt spoke
eight foreign languages and amassed a book collection totaling over 23,000
volumes. As a member of one of America's dynasties, George and his wife,
Edith Stuyvesant Dresser, used this magnificent mansion, modeled after the
French chateaus he loved so much, to entertain the many guests who would
come to enjoy the beauty of the North Carolina mountains.

Vanderbilt asked architect Richard Morris to design this impressive
structure in the style of the chateaus found in the Loire Valley in France.
Vanderbilt and Hunt assembled materials from around the world, including
tons of Italian marble and train loads of Indiana limestone. It took an army

of stonecutters and artisans five years to construct this massive structure which covers approximately four acres of floor space. When the house was completed, it required a staff of eighty to manage the over 200 rooms. The house was fully electric, had central heat, two elevators, two dumbwaiters, an indoor bowling alley and an indoor swimming pool. Upon entering the house, visitors experience another world filled with grace and beauty ranging from a skylit court of palms and tropical greenery to the grand library built to house an Italian master painting seventy feet in length. The rooms are filled with a remarkable collection of turn-of-the-century furnishings and art collected by the Vanderbilt family over the years. Biltmore House is still privately owned by Vanderbilt's grandson, William A.V. Cecil, and remains self-sufficient, receiving no governmental funding of any kind.

Notable Collections on Exhibit

Visitors will not be disappointed by the tremendous array of antique furnishings including a chess table owned by Napoleon and a magnificent collection of Oriental carpets. The fine paintings hanging on the wall include two Renoirs, seven John Singer Sargents, two Whistlers, and several Durers. Also displayed is are collections of 16th-century Flemish tapestries, 19th-century French bronzes, and Ming Dynasty china.

Additional Information

The hand Frederick Olmstead, designer of New York's Central Park, is evident in every acre of the formal gardens and grounds surrounding Biltmore. The estate's English walled garden is said to be the finest of its kind in America with its over 50,000 tulips. In addition, the estate's winery produces award-winning wines available for purchase in the gift shop.

Smith-McDowell House

283 Victoria Road
Asheville, NC 28801
(704) 253-9231

Contact: Smith-McDowell House Museum
Open: May 1-Oct. 31, Tues.-Sat.
10 a.m.–4 p.m., Sun., 1–4 p.m.;
Nov. 1-April 30, Tues.-Fri. 10 a.m.–2 p.m.
Admission: Adults $3; children $1.50;
special events extra. Guided tours,
seasonal exhibits, Heritage Alive Crafts
Fair (school children).
Suggested Time to View House:
30–50 minutes
Facilities on Premises: Gift shop
Description of Grounds: Beautifully
landscaped grounds designed by
Frederick Law Olmstead
Best Season to View House:
Spring-summer
Number of Yearly Visitors: 5,000
Year House Built: c. 1840
Number of Rooms: 12

Style of Architecture: Federal
On-Site Parking: Yes **Wheelchair Access:** No

Description of House

James McConnell Smith, the builder of this fine brick house, was one of the most influential men in Asheville. He owned a store, the Buck Hotel, and a tanyard. In addition, when the Buncombe Turnpike connecting Greenville, South Carolina with Greenville, Tennessee was completed in 1827, Smith built and operated the first toll bridge over the French Broad River. The house was built for James's son, John Patton Smith (1823-1857), who never married. It was later purchased by James' daughter, Sarah Lucinda Smith (1826-1905) and her husband William Wallace McDowell (1823-1893). The McDowells reared nine children and lived in this attractive home for twenty-five years. During the Civil War, McDowell organized the "Buncombe Rifleman", the first company to leave Asheville for Confederate service. Economic reversals forced McDowell to sell the house in 1881 to Alexander Garrett. Garrett organized and served as first mayor of the town of Victoria, a colony of homes located near Asheville on Victoria Road. The Smith-McDowell House is notable as Asheville's oldest brick structure. Many of the original features of the house have been maintained, including the original Victorian wallpaper. The rooms are furnished with an excellent selection of Victorian furniture and decorations, collected and appropriate for the period. This Asheville landmark is listed on the National Register of Historic Places.

Notable Collections on Exhibit

The Smith-McDowell House features a series of changing exhibits related to the history of western North Carolina in addition to the elegantly furnished period rooms.

Historic Bath

Box 124
Bath, NC 27808
(919) 923-3971

Contact: Department of Cultural Resources
Open: Mon.-Sat. 9 a.m.–5 p.m.,
Sun. 1–5 p.m.
Admission: Adults $1; children $.50.
Guided tours; introductory film.
Facilities on Premises: Visitor center,
snack bar
Description of Grounds: Historic district
Year House Built: Van der Veer
House-c. 1790, Palmer House-1740,
Bonner House-1830

Description of House

A walking tour of historic Bath puts visitors in close touch with the history and charm of North Carolina's oldest town, chartered in 1705. Bath was the colony's official port of entry and the site of the first meeting of the Colonial assembly. Today, visitors are able to see several houses within the historic district which have survived from the 18th and 19th centuries. All of the houses have been restored and exhibit selected period furnishings and artifacts of historical significance.

Near the visitor's center stands the Van Der Veer House, a fine example of a frame, gambrel roof dwelling. This house was relocated from the waterfront on the north edge of town and is still undergoing restoration. The next home on the tour, the Palmer Marsh House is one of the oldest remaining homes in North Carolina. This distinctive colonial structure features a large double chimney and has been designated a National Historic Landmark. In contrast, the Bonner House provides an excellent example of early 19th-century Carolina architecture and was home to one of the most distinguished families in Beaufort county. St. Thomas's Episcopal church and the adjoining Glebe House (c. 1835), home to several notable Bath citizens are two other buildings of note on the tour. In addition to the historic structures, visitors are also encouraged to wander to Harding's landing, a public boat dock which provides an excellent view of the town shoreline.

Additional Information

One of Bath's other claims to fame is as the home of the notorious pirate Blackbeard. Each year the Blackbeard Amphitheater presents an outdoor drama entitled "Blackbeard, Knight of the Black Flag" which portrays life in the town during the early 18th century when Bath was a bustling port. Contact the visitor's center at (919) 923-3971 for more information.

Williams "Glebe" House

Bath, NC 27808

Contact: Episcopal Diocese of East Carolina
Open: Mon.-Sat. 9 a.m.–5 p.m.,
  Sun. 1–5 p.m.
Activities: Historic walking tour;
  orientation film
Facilities on Premises: Visitor center
Description of Grounds: Historic village
Best Season to View House: Year round
Year House Built: 1827 to 1832

Description of House

The Williams House, or Glebe House, provides a stop along Historic Bath's walking tour for visitors. This charming frame house was built by Samuel Lucas; his family maintained it until 1847. For the next thirty years the house was owned by several members of the Bonner family. The most significant owner of the house was a relative of the Bonners, Dr. John F. Tompins, a noted antebellum reformer, a founder of the North Carolina State Fair, and publisher of *The Farmers Journal* during the 1850s. The Williams family of Bath purchased the house in 1877, and it derives its name from the sixty years of occupancy by the Williams family. In 1945, the building was acquired by the Episcopal Dioceses of East Carolina to use as the rectory for the historic St. Thomas. At this time the dwelling was also referred to as Glebe House, a term handed down from colonial times when a "glebe" meant church land given to the minister for his financial support.

Additional Information

Another important site for visitors to Bath is the nearby St. Thomas Church, the oldest existing church in North Carolina and one of the earliest to be built in the state. The church continues to serve as a house of worship and displays an original 1703 Bible, a silver chalice and a pair of silver candelabra from the Colonial period, and a church bell known as Queen Anne's Bell, which was recast in 1872 from the 1732 original.

Historic Beaufort

100 Block Turner Street
P.O. Box 1709
Beaufort, NC 28516
(919) 728-5225

Contact: Beaufort Historical Association
Open: Mon.-Sat. 9:30 a.m.–4:30 p.m.
Activities: Special tours for groups; English double-decker bus; guided tours of Old Burying Grounds.
Facilities on Premises: Various shops and restaurants
Description of Grounds: Historical village
Year House Built: Various 18th and 19th-century houses

Description of House

Beaufort, the third oldest town in North Carolina was surveyed in 1713, nearly twenty years before the George Washington was born. Today, Beaufort remains a lovely, unspoiled historic part of North Carolina. The walking tour of this seaside town includes several fine historic houses open to the public on a regular basis. The tour includes the Joseph Bell House (c. 1767), the former home of well-to-do plantation owner. The exterior is painted conch red with white shutters, and has double front doors, a typical feature of early Beaufort architecture. The interior is decorated with appropriate 18th-century furnishings which enhance the charm of this lovely house. Nearby stands the Josiah Bell House (c. 1825), furnished in a comfortable, but lovely, Victorian manner. The beautiful side garden is maintained by the local garden club. In contrast, the Rustell House (c. 1732) is a frame, tin roof dwelling for which only the exterior has been restored. The final house, Samuel Leffer's Cottage (c. 1778) represents a school master's dwelling. This recently restored building features a typical early Beaufort roofline.

Additional Information

A full tour of Historic Beaufort will include visits to several other notable structures such as an 18th-century apothecary shop, the old courthouse and the local jail. In addition, the famous Old Burying Grounds are a few steps away with gravesites of many notable Beaufort citizens.

Horace Williams House

610 East Rosemary Street
Chapel Hill, NC 27514
(919) 942-7818

Contact: Chapel Hill Preservation Society
Open: Mon.-Fri. 10 a.m.–5 p.m.;
Sun. 1–5 p.m.
Admission: Free. Video presentations.
Suggested Time to View House:
30–60 minutes
Description of Grounds: Large open grassy
areas and old trees, very pleasant and
typical of Old Chapel Hill

Best Season to View House: All seasons
Number of Yearly Visitors: 1,200-1,500
Year House Built: In three stages—1840s,
1850s, 1890s
Style of Architecture: Mostly Greek Revival
Number of Rooms: 6 principle, others are
storage, etc.
On-Site Parking: Yes **Wheelchair Access:** No

Description of House

This charming farmhouse has been home to several professors from the University of North Carolina over the years since it was first built in 1840. The house is named for a tremendously popular professor Horace Williams who donated the house to the university. Williams was immortalized in print by one of his former students, Thomas Wolfe, in his novel *You Can't Go Home Again*.

The Horace Williams House evolved over several architectural periods. The farmhouse retains its original pine floor boards, mantel, and high window woodwork. The parlor and entrance hall were built between 1880 and 1900, the latter built from what may have been a covered dog trot. The parqueted ceilings in both rooms are particularly noteworthy. The octagon room, the major gallery space since restoration of the house, was built between 1852 and 1855 during the residency of professor Benjamin Sherwood Hedrick. Hedrick was "denounced from nearly every pulpit in the state" and dismissed by the university for his outspoken opposition to slavery. The period furnishings on display have been collected and are appropriate to the period. The house is currently maintained as a cultural center by the Preservation Society.

Additional Information

The society sponsors free chamber music concerts in the house and a changing art exhibit. Artists and craftsmen are encouraged to apply to the society to schedule a showing of their work.

Hezekiah Alexander Homesite

3500 Shamrock Drive
Charlotte, NC 28215
(704) 568-1774

Contact: The Charlotte Museum of History
Open: Tues.-Fri. 10 a.m.–5 p.m.,
   Sat.-Sun. 2–5 p.m.
Admission: Adults $2; children $1.
   Guided tours; colonial cooking
   demonstrations.
Facilities on Premises: Museum shop
Best Season to View House: Year round
Year House Built: 1774

Description of House

Hezekiah Alexander was a signer of the May 20, 1775 Mecklenburg Declaration of Independence, and a delegate to the Fifth Provincial Congress which established a permanent government for the State of North Carolina. He helped draft the North Carolina State Constitution and Bill of Rights. Born in 1728, Alexander was a blacksmith by trade, and after moving to Mecklenburg County in 1767, he became a justice of the peace and listed himself as a planter. He built this "Rock House", as it is fondly known, for his wife and ten children in 1774 on the site where it presently stands.

The Hezekiah Alexander Homesite is the oldest dwelling still standing in Mecklenburg County. The house was built of stone quarried from the nearby hillsides. The homesite has been carefully refurnished with authentic Piedmont, North Carolina antiques.

Additional Information

Water still flows through the reconstructed two-story spring house which borders the Alexander House. This building can still function as it did in the 18th century, providing a cool, damp place for keeping cheese, butter, and milk. A working log kitchen with stone fireplace has been built adjacent to the house providing an excellent site for frequent colonial kitchen demonstrations.

Somerset Place

P.O. Box 215
Creswell, NC 27928

Contact: Department of Cultural Resources
Open: Mon.-Sat. 9 a.m.–5 p.m.,
   Sun. 1–5 p.m.
Activities: Guided tours
Description of Grounds: Plantation with
   spacious lawns lined with majestic oak
   and cypress trees as well as original
   brick walks and formal gardens
Year House Built: 1830

Description of House

The mansion was built by Josiah Collins III, on the plantation developed by his grandfather and later run by his father. Josiah was a successful merchant, manufacturer, and planter. A staunch churchman, Collins provided a chapel and chaplain for the benefit of his slaves's spiritual well-being; he and has family participated in worship there. Unfortunately, the Civil War drove Collins from his beautiful home, and ruined his magnificent estate. He died broken and impoverished in Hillsboro, North Carolina. Despite the efforts of his wife and sons to revive the place, they were finally forced to sell the plantation.

The mansion was known as the "Big House", Somerset's most elegant establishment. At the time, costly furniture, interesting books, and treasures of art were the setting in which generous hospitality, culture, and refinement prevailed in a religiously oriented atmosphere. Today, the beautifully preserved mansion and cluster of outbuildings at Somerset are the result of restoration work which began in 1951 and still continues. Extensive documentary and archaeological research was completed before considerable authentic restoration of the buildings and grounds was accomplished. Archaeological studies have exposed the remains of slave buildings, including the hospital and chapel, and the overseer's house.

Bennett Place

**4409 Bennett Memorial Road
Durham, NC 27705
(919) 383-4345**

Contact: Department of Cultural Resources
Open: April 1-Oct.31: Tues.-Sat.
9 a.m.–5 p.m., Sun. 1–5 p.m.;
Nov. 1-March 31: Tues.-Sat.
10 a.m.–4 p.m., Sun. 1–4 p.m.
Activities: Tours and audiovisual
presentation
Facilities on Premises: Visitor center
Year House Built: c. 1850

Description of House

In April 1865, this simple farmhouse housed a series of famous discussions between Joseph Johnston and William Sherman regarding an end to the Civil War. After three meetings, the Bennett's dwelling became the site of the largest troop surrender of the War.

Ordinary people, the Bennetts had no idea that their house would secure such an important place in history. James Bennett, his wife, Nancy, and their three children had settled on the 325-acre farm in Orange County in 1846. Striving to be self-sufficient, the family cultivated corn, wheat, oats, and potatoes, and raised hogs. Although a yeoman farmer, Bennett practiced a number of trades to add to his income; he was a tailor, cobbler, and sold horse feed, tobacco plugs, and distilled liquor. Bennett's grandchildren lived on the property until 1890, when they left the farm to work in the mills in Durham.

In 1921 a fire destroyed the Bennett family farmhouse and kitchen; only the stone chimney survived. The present buildings were carefully reconstructed in the 1960s using Civil War sketches and early photographs as a guide. The simple farm dwelling and log kitchen convey what life was like during a tragic period of our nation's history.

Notable Collections on Exhibit

A modern visitor center with exhibits and audiovisual programs help tell the Bennett Place story. Other displays illustrate North Carolina's contributions to the Civil War.

Duke Homestead

2828 Duke Homestead Road
Durham, NC 27705
(919) 477-5498

Contact: Department of Cultural Resources
Open: April-Oct., Mon.-Sat. 9 a.m.–5 p.m.,
Sun. 1–5 p.m.; Nov.-March, Tues.-Sat.
10 a.m.–4 p.m., Sun. 1–4 p.m.
Activities: Tours with costumed guides,
audiovisual program, special events
Facilities on Premises: Visitor center
Year House Built: 1852
Style of Architecture: Farmhouse

Description of House

When Washington Duke returned from the Civil War, he and his children began a factory in a tiny log building on the homestead. Their product was smoking tobacco; cured Bright Leaf was flailed, sifted, and packed into cloth bags to be sold. Within a few years, Duke's business had grown enough so that he needed a second and then third tobacco processing factory at the homestead. In 1869, with his father's help, Brodie Duke began a small smoking tobacco factory within the town of Durham, taking advantage of the railroad shipping service and the farmer's tobacco market there.

Duke and his sons formed a successful business team and began, in the 1880s, the first mechanical mass production of cigarettes. With this advantage, the Duke family eventually controlled the largest tobacco company in the world. Certain colleges, such as Trinity, later to become Duke University, benefitted from Duke family contributions.

This historic site includes the main house consisting of a simple four room dwelling with a kitchen addition; the reconstructed first tobacco processing factory; the original third factory; two outbuildings; a tobacco pack house; and a curing barn. In 1966, the homestead was added to the National Historic Landmark Register.

Notable Collections on Exhibit

The buildings contain exhibits and programs depicting the history of the Dukes and tobacco culture, tobacco farming and early manufacturing processes. The displays include advertisements, signs, machinery, and even an authentic cigar store Indian. The area is also periodically staffed with costumed interpreters portraying the life of a middle class Piedmont farm family during the 1870 period.

Richard Bennehan House

Box 71217
Durham, NC 27722-1217
(919) 620-0120

Contact: Stagville Center
Open: Mon.-Fri. 9 a.m.–5 p.m.
Activities: Guided tour; self-guided tour to antebellum slave quarter area and 1869 barn; slide presentation.
Suggested Time to View House: 45 minutes
Best Season to View House: Year-round
Year House Built: 1787 to 1799
Style of Architecture: Vernacular Georgian
Number of Rooms: 8

Description of House

Richard Bennehan, the builder of this attractive home, was a merchant who moved to North Carolina from Virginia in 1769. He began to acquire land in the Piedmont region in 1776 and by the end of the century was one of the largest plantation owners in Orange County. The house and plantation later belonged to Bennehan's descendants, the Cameron family, whose plantation holdings in Piedmont, North Carolina were among the largest in the South, encompassing approximately 30,000 acres.

The Bennehan House was built in two sections; the 1787 wing of the house is a one-and-a-half story hall-parlor house with two shed rooms. The 1799 addition is two stories tall, with three bay windows across the front and rear facades. The house represents the type of dwelling constructed by prosperous planters in North Carolina during the late 18th century. The dwelling features molded window sills and weatherboarding, nine-over-nine sash windows, six panel doors, paneled wainscot and mantels, and a double-shoulder chimney. As was typical, the assemblage of these details was unique for each structure, no two were exactly alike and were thus unique in that sense. Several of the rooms feature furniture appropriate to the period and include family pieces.

Additional Information

Stagville uses the historic site buildings as a means of providing periodic classes in historic preservation. In addition, the center offers programs in African-American history, making use of the two-story, four-room slave houses which still stand at the site and date to the 1850s. These buildings are a rare survival from the pre-Civil War period.

Barker House

P.O. Box 474
Edenton, NC 27932
(919) 482-2637

Contact: Historic Edenton

Open: April 1-Oct. 31; Mon.-Sat.
9 a.m.–5 p.m., Sun. 1–5 p.m. and
Nov. 1-March 31; Tues.-Sat.
10 a.m.–4 p.m.

Admission: Adults $5; students (grades
K-12) $2.50; families $12. Guided tours
and audiovisual programs.

Suggested Time to View House: Historic
Edenton tour 120 minutes

Facilities on Premises: Gift shop

Description of Grounds: The waterfront
setting, well-tended gardens and trees
make this a stroller's paradise.

Best Season to View House: Year-round

Number of Yearly Visitors: 26,000

Year House Built: 1782

Style of Architecture: Georgian with Greek
Revival addition

Number of Rooms: 10

On-Site Parking: Yes **Wheelchair Access:** No

Description of House

The house was the home of Thomas Barker, the London agent for the colonies. Tradition holds that his wife, Penelope, presided over the famous Edenton Tea Party on October 25, 1774. This has been called the first political activity of women in the American colonies. The Barker House is a two-story frame structure with a finished attic below a gable roof. Covered with beaded weatherboards and raised on a brick foundation, the house has at both ends a pair of single-shoulder exterior chimneys laid in one-to-three common bond. The front and rear facades are marked by three bays on either side of a slightly off-center entrance. This arrangement somewhat disguises the fact that the two sides of the house are unequal in size. The front facade, overlooking the water, is dominated by a full-length, two-tiered porch carried on superimposed fluted pillars under a shed roof.

Until recently, the house has been used as the visitor center for Historic Edenton and is unfurnished. The building has a fabulous waterfront location with a magnificent view of Edenton Bay on three sides.

Additional Information

The Barker House was moved from its original location to its present location on the waterfront in 1952.

Cupola House

P.O. Box 474
Edenton, NC 27932
(919) 482-2637

Contact: Historic Edenton

Open: April 1-Oct. 31; Mon.-Sat.
9 a.m.–5 p.m., Sun. 1–5 p.m. and Nov.
1-March 31; Tues.-Sat. 10 a.m.–4 p.m.

Admission: Adults $5; students (grades
K-12) $2.50; families $12. Guided tours,
audiovisual programs, holiday
celebrations.

Suggested Time to View House: Historic
Edenton tour 2 hours

Facilities on Premises: Gift shop

Description of Grounds: The vegetable
garden at the back and the formal
garden in the front have been restored
with the Sauthier map of 1769.

Style of Architecture: Exterior Jacobean
with interior Georgian woodwork

Best Season to View House: Year-round

Number of Yearly Visitors: 26,000

Number of Rooms: 9

Year House Built: 1758

On-Site Parking: Yes **Wheelchair Access:** No

Description of House

The Cupola House has been called "the best example of an existing wooden house in the Jacobean tradition in the South." This architectural gem was acquired by Samuel Dickinson in 1777 and his descendants owned it until 1918.

Probably the oldest and most famous house in Edenton, the Cupola House is a fascinating architectural composition. The two-story frame house is an assemblage of Jacobean, Queen Anne, and Georgian architectural featurers, and seems more New England in scale and character than Southern. The rare Jacobean features include the large chimneys and decorative finials. Of particular interest is the New England type over-hang of the second floor on the facade, and the octagonal cupola from which the house derives its name. Francis Corbin, land agent for Lords Proprietor Lord Granville, may have added the interior woodwork. Part of the woodwork was sold to the Brooklyn Museum of Fine Arts, but has been carefully reproduced. Other notable details include the original window pane etchings dating from the 1830s. The furnishings generally represent the 1725 to 1775 period and feature some locally-made Chowan River Basin pieces.

Notable Collections on Exhibit

Collections on exhibit include 1756 paintings of Thomas and Penelope Barker and Thomas Hodgson by artist John Wollaston. Also on display are early American and British furnishings including a joined chest with carved geometric design, (c. 1650 to 1680); a dropleaf dining table, and a corner chair. A Newhall English china tea set (Staffordshire c. 1800) can also be seen.

James Iredell House State Historic Site

**P.O. Box 474
Edenton, NC 27932
(919) 482-2637**

Contact: Historic Edenton

Open: April 1-Oct. 31; Mon.-Sat.
9 a.m.–5 p.m., Sun. 1–5 p.m. and
Nov. 1-March 31; Tues.-Sat.
10 a.m.–4 p.m.

Admission: Adults $5; students (grades
K-12) $2.50; families $12. Guided tours
and audiovisual programs

Suggested Time to View House: Historic
Edenton tour 2 hours

Facilities on Premises: Gift shop

Description of Grounds: The house is
located on one-acre of land with formal
gardens and four outbuildings including
a kitchen.

Best Season to View House: Spring

Number of Yearly Visitors: 26,000

Year House Built: 1773

Style of Architecture: Georgian with
Federal addition

Number of Rooms: 6

On-Site Parking: Yes

Wheelchair Access: No

Description of House

The Iredell House was the home of both James Iredell and his son, James Iredell, Jr., governor of North Carolina (1827-28). Iredell came to America in 1768, at the age of seventeen and studied law under his future brother-in-law, Samuel Johnston. He became Attorney General of North Carolina and was later appointed by George Washington as an Associate Justice of the first United States Supreme Court. Judge James Iredell and James Wilson of Pennsylvania co-authored the eleventh amendment to the Constitution. The amendment was passed into law shortly before Iredell's death in 1799. The house is of particular historical interest for having served as a meeting place for many prominent political figures of the late 18th and early 19th centuries such as Joseph Hewes, James Wilson (both signers of the Declaration of Independence), and Samuel Johnston, who served North Carolina as senator and governor.

Architecturally, the house is an unusual but extremely well-executed combination of Georgian and Federal motifs. The earliest section of the house was built around 1776 as a rectangular two-story structure. In 1816, a two-story frame addition was built perpendicular to the west facade, thus forming the house's present structure. This attractive house features a full-length two-tier porch covering the five-bay 1816 addition. A six-panel door on each floor opens on to he porch. The interior features refined Federal details including several unadorned mantels and simple stairway with a rounded handrail rising to the second floor. The furnishings are of the same period; some are original pieces, others are collected or reproductions.

Notable Collections on Exhibit

Oil canvas paintings on display include portraits of James Iredell, Hannah Iredell, and James Iredell, Jr. The collected period furnishings feature British and American furniture from the late 18th to early 19th centuries including examples of Queen Anne, Sheraton, Chippendale, Hepplewhite, and Duncan-Phyfe styles.

Carl Sandburg Home (Connemara)

1928 Little River Road
Flat Rock, NC 28731
(704) 693-4178

Contact: National Park Service

Open: 9 a.m.–5 p.m., closed Christmas day

Admission: Adults $2, students and seniors free. Guided tours, audiovisual programs, dramatic presentations and demonstrations during the summer months.

Suggested Time to View House: 2 hours for entire site

Facilities on Premises: Gift shop

Description of Grounds: Beautiful rolling pastures and mountain woods with nature trail and paths for walking

Best Season to View House: Summer

Number of Yearly Visitors: 25,000

Year House Built: 1838

Number of Rooms: 8

Style of Architecture: Farmhouse

On-Site Parking: Yes **Wheelchair Access:** Yes

Description of House

Although originally built for Christopher Memminger, the secretary of the treasury for the Confederacy, this charming farmhouse is best known as the home of writer Carl Sandburg. This poet, Pulitzer-prize winning author, lecturer, and onetime political activist and thinker came to the mountains of North Carolina in 1945 and spent the last twenty-two years of his long, productive life on this Flat Rock farm. The house and farm had everything the Sandburg family wanted, including ample pasture for their goats and seclusion for his writing. The Sandburgs moved from Michigan with their three daughters and two grandchildren, their library of more than 10,000 volumes, all their personal belongings, and their herd of Chikaming goats. Sandburg had already written his prize-winning biography of Abraham Lincoln before moving here, but the years spent at Connemara were also productive. Among other things, in 1948 he published his only novel *Remembrance Rock,* which traced the American epic from Plymouth Rock to World War II, in 1953 he published his autobiography, and in 1951 his *Complete Poems* won the Pulitzer prize for poetry.

His wife and the other members of the family took care of the farm business so that Sandburg could devote himself to writing. Many guests frequented the household, including Mrs. Sandburg's famous brother, Edward Steichen. Carl Sandburg died here in 1967 and the following year the house was opened to the public by the National Park Service.

Additional Information

In addition to the main house, visitors are encouraged to wander outside and see the beautiful countryside and the various outbuildings including a springhouse, a barnyard, a gazebo, and a greenhouse. The Swedish House contains Sandburg's magazines, books, and research materials.

Charles B. Aycock Birthplace

P.O. Box 207
Fremont, NC 27830
(919) 242-5581

Contact: Department of Archives and
History
Open: April 1-Oct. 31: Mon.-Sat.
9 a.m.–5 p.m., Sun. 1–5 p.m.; Nov.
1-March 31: Tues.-Sat. 10 a.m.– 4 p.m.,
Sun. 1–4 p.m.
Activities: Tours
Facilities on Premises: Visitor center
Year House Built: mid-1800s
Style of Architecture: Farmhouse

Description of House

This modest farm was the birthplace of Charles B. Aycock, the former governor inspired the growth of public education in North Carolina. After spending his formative years on the farm, Aycock went on to become a lawyer, and was elected governor of North Carolina in 1900. Politics became the vehicle through which he brought his campaign for public school education in North Carolina to the people. He launched a public crusade which resulted in a dramatic improvement in the state's educational facilities. According to Aycock we should educate for three things: to know something; to be able to do something; to be able to be something. By the end of Aycock's four-year term as governor, the state school system had improved demonstrably; many new schools had been built, enrollment figures were higher, and teaching and supervisory personnel had been improved.

The restored birthplace of Charles B. Aycock is typical of an eastern North Carolina farmhouse of the mid-1800s. Established at the site in addition to the dwelling itself and a reconstructed kitchen, are a large granary, or corn barn, a large and small smokehouse, and the stable, all of which were part of the original Aycock farm. A small one-room schoolhouse of 1870 vintage stands nearby on the farm grounds.

Notable Collections on Exhibit

The visitor center contains exhibits portraying the life of Governor Aycock.

Owens House

P.O. Box 406
Halifax, NC 27839

Contact: Historic Halifax

Open: April-Oct., Mon.-Sat.
9 a.m.–5 p.m.,Sun. 1–5 p.m.,
Nov.-March, Tues.-Sat. 9 a.m.– 4 p.m.,
Sun. 1– 4 p.m., closed state holidays

Admission: Free. Self-guided tours,
audiovisual presentation

Facilities on Premises: Visitor center

Description of Grounds: Gardens as part
of the historic village

Year House Built: c. 1760

Style of Architecture: 18th-century English
style town house

Description of House

The Owens House was named for George Owens, Sr., a successful Halifax merchant who owned the property in the mid 1800s.

The building is patterned after a typical 18th-century English style town house. The interior has Georgian-style mantels; the exterior features a gambrel roof. According to one theory, the gambrel roof house was popular because it offered its owner a tax advantage, giving two stories of room but having a property tax based on a single-story dwelling. The kitchen, a separate building, was located behind the main dwelling.

The house is furnished, with period furniture including gifts of the Halifax Restoration Association, as the home of a typical merchant of the late to early colonial to early statehood period.

Notable Collections on Exhibit

The exhibited furnishings feature many North Carolina pieces including a chest dating from the early 1700s, a bed, dressing table, corner chair, chest of drawers, and a blanket chest.

The Sally-Billy House

P.O. Box 406
Halifax, NC 27839

Contact: Historic Halifax

Open: April-Oct., Mon.-Sat.
9 a.m.–5 p.m.,Sun. 1–5 p.m.,
Nov.-March, Tues.-Sat. 9 a.m.– 4 p.m.,
Sun. 1– 4 p.m., closed state holidays

Admission: Free. Self-guided tours, audiovisual presentation

Facilities on Premises: Visitor center

Description of Grounds: Gardens as part of the historic village

Year House Built: c. 1808

Description of House

The Sally-Billy House was constructed for a Roanoke Valley planter named Lewis Bond. The surrounding property passed through several ownerships until 1834. In that year, the house and 375 acres of land were sold to William Ruffin Smith, Sr., who moved there with his wife. Smith, nicknamed "Billy," was a Roanoke Valley planter who served for many years as a county court justice and whose hobby was the breeding and racing of thoroughbred horses. Around 1800, Smith married Sarah Walton Norfleet, whom he call "Sally," and the couple raised six children in the house.

The Sally-Billy House has been located on a plot that has an environment similar to its original site. The structure is a tripartite building, with a central two-story section and flanking, single-story wings. This striking style was popular in the Roanoke Valley from about 1790 to 1820—the Federal period of American architecture. The Sally-Billy House reveals not only its Federal style, but also the fine craftsmanship of the Roanoke Valley's early builders. Currently, the house is being furnished through a special bicentennial project.

Additional Information

Visitors to Halifax are encouraged to take advantage of the full walking tour and visit Market Square, the old cemetery, the 1820 Burgess Law Office and the archeological museum built over the ruins of the 1762 Montfort home.

Haley House

1805 E. Lexington Avenue
High Point, NC 27262
(919) 885-6859

Contact: The High Point Museum
Open: Tues.-Sat. 10 a.m.–4:30 p.m., Sun. 1–4:30 p.m.
Facilities on Premises: Museum store
Year House Built: 1786

Admission: Free. Guided tours, group tours by reservation
Description of Grounds: Historical park

Description of House

In 1786, John and Phebe Haley built their new brick, Quaker-style home by the road running from Petersburg, Virginia to Salisbury, North Carolina. John Haley was a blacksmith by trade and was active in the political and civic life of the area, serving as sheriff, tax collector, and road commissioner.

Built of brick with careful attention to finishing details, the Haley House was far larger and more substantial than the log houses in which most of their neighbors resided. In design, it was similar to houses that had been built fifty years earlier by colonists living in the Virginia and North Carolina tidewater areas. The house is furnished (based upon Haley's will) with late 18th and early 19th-century furniture, ceramics and household goods— many of which were hand-made in the North Carolina Piedmont.

Additional Information

The house is part of the High Point Museum and Historical Park. The property contains a working blacksmith shop, equipped with tools and materials similar to those John Haley used in his trade. Another nearby log house features a floor loom and other textile production artifacts of the early 19th century. The exhibits at the High Point Museum showcase a broad range of topics and interests such as early telephone communication equipment, textiles, machinery, products of local industry, and toys. In addition, the museum offers a variety of materials illustrating life in the Piedmont area during the past three centuries.

The Mendenhall Plantation

U.S. 29A and 70-A
P.O. Box 512
Jamestown, NC 27282

Contact: Historic Jamestown Society, Inc.
Open: Sun. 2–5 p.m.
Activities: Guided tours
Suggested Time to View House: 45 minutes
Facilities on Premises: Gift shop
Description of Grounds: Located in historic Jamestown, the plantation has landscaped grounds and a nature trail through an old field and orchard.
Best Season to View House: Spring-fall
Year House Built: 1811
Style of Architecture: Farmhouse
Number of Rooms: 10
On-Site Parking: Yes

Description of House

Mendenhall Plantation provides a fascinating view of "the other South", the South of the small farmer and tradesman, of plain speech and plain dress. The Mendenhalls were Quakers who moved to the area in 1762, and established the village now known as Jamestown. James Mendenhall built a mill which his son, George, later took over. In 1800, George laid out the town with streets and named it Jamestown after his father. His sons, Richard and Nathan, were leaders in the Manumission Society. Richard held a free night school which welcomed all races. Another son, George, trained law students and on at least one occasion successfully defended in court a neighbor who had helped a runaway slave. As Quakers, the Mendenhalls were pacifists and refused combat roles in the Civil War.

This lovely brick plantation was built by Richard Mendenhall and forms part of a complex which also includes the Mendenhall Store (where he worked) and a Quaker meetinghouse. Six of the rooms are furnished as period rooms with early 19th-century furniture. The kitchen, once a separate building, has been joined to the main portion of the house and is completely furnished with appropriate utensils and artifacts. One of the rooms on the first floor features exhibits related to local history. The plantation complex is listed on the National Register of Historic Places.

Mendenhall Plantation has been restored to depict Quaker life in the 19th century. In addition to the main house, the grounds also feature a large Pennsylvania-style log barn.

Dixon-Stevenson House

Pollock Street, P.O. Box 1007
New Bern, NC 28563
(919) 638-1560

Contact: Tryon Palace Historic Sites and Gardens

Open: Tues.-Sat. 9:30 a.m.–4 p.m., Sun. 2:30–4 p.m.; closed Thanksgiving, Dec. 24, 25, 26, and Jan. 1st

Admission: Adults $4, youths (6-18) $3, special rates for combined entrance to other houses at Tryon Palace Historic Sites. Guided tours with costumed interpreters, audiovisual presentation, craft demonstrations.

Suggested Time to View House: 2 hours

Facilities on Premises: Gift shop, visitors center

Description of Grounds: The house has a garden in the rear with an arrangement of seasonal flowers, all in white

Best Season to View House: Year round

Year House Built: 1820s

Style of Architecture: Neoclassical

On-Site Parking: Yes

Description of House

Erected in the late 1820s on a lot that was originally part of Tryon Palace's garden, the Dixon-Stevenson House epitomizes New Bern's lifestyle in the first half of the 19th century when the town remained a prosperous port and one of the state's largest cities. This gracious house was home to the mayor of New Bern who was also a successful merchant. In addition to serving as a residence, the house also served as a regimental hospital when Union troops occupied New Bern during the Civil War.

The house is a fine example of Neoclassical architecture which was typically used by many homes along the Carolina coast. The interior features splendid hand-carved woodwork. The furnishings, reflecting the Federal period, reveal the changing tastes of early America.

Additional Information

Located near the Tryon Palace, the house is a good starting point for visitors exploring the many other historic sites of picturesque New Bern. Visitors are encouraged to see the New Bern Academy Museum where exhibits show the city's history from the earliest European settlements of 1710 through the Civil War. In the museum, special focus is given to the topics of early education, New Bern's architecture and builders, and New Bern as a Union city in the midst of the Confederacy.

John Wright Stanly House

George Street, P.O. Box 1007
New Bern, NC 28563
(919) 638-1560

Contact: Tryon Palace Historic Sites and Gardens

Open: Tues.-Sat. 9:30 a.m.–4 p.m., Sun. 2:30–4 p.m.; closed Thanksgiving, Dec. 24, 25, 26, and Jan. 1st

Admission: Adults $4, youths (6-18) $3. Guided tours with costumed interpreters, audiovisual presentation, craft demonstrations

Suggested Time to View House: 2 hours

Facilities on Premises: Gift shop, visitor's center

Description of Grounds: 13 acres of beautifully landscaped gardens for the entire Tryon Palace complex

Best Season to View House: Year round

Year House Built: 1780s

Style of Architecture: Georgian
On-Site Parking: Yes

Description of House

This carefully restored home was built by the successful ship owner John Wright Stanly in the early 1780s. Stanly made his fortune during the Revolutionary War; his merchant ships plied the waters as privateers, capturing British ships to aid the American cause. George Washington is reported to have stayed in the house for two nights during his southern tour in 1791. Although he spent most of his time in the more luxurious surroundings of the nearby Tryon Palace, he described his stay at Stanly's house as "exceedingly good lodgings".

The elegance of Stanly's house reflects the wealth of its owner. The design has been attributed to the architect John Hawkes. The striking white facade is topped by a roof with detailed balustrades. The interior is notable for the exceptionally fine woodwork and is considered to be some of the finest in the state. The period rooms display an impressive collection of American and imported (mainly English) furniture and decorations from the late 18th century.

Additional Information

The John Wright Stanly House forms part of the Tryon Palace complex. In addition to the palace, the beautifully landscaped grounds also feature the Dixon-Stevenson House and the New Academy Museum. Visitors to the site will find a rich examination of historic New Bern's heritage through the demonstrations of colonial crafts and domestic activities, the summer drama tours, workshops, and a variety of other special events.

Tryon Palace

George Street, P.O. Box 1007
New Bern, NC 28563
(919) 638-1560

Contact: Tryon Palace Historic Sites and Gardens

Open: Tues.-Sat. 9:30 a.m.–4 p.m., Sun. 2:30–4 p.m.; closed Thanksgiving, Dec. 24, 25, 26, and Jan. 1st

Admission: Adults $8, youths (6-18) $4 (for both palace and gardens) Guided tours with costumed interpreters, audiovisual presentation, craft demonstrations

Suggested Time to View House: 2 hours

Facilities on Premises: Gift shop, visitor's center

Description of Grounds: 13 acres of beautifully landscaped gardens for the entire Tryon Palace complex

Best Season to View House: Year round

Year House Built: 1767

Style of Architecture: Georgian
On-Site Parking: Yes

Description of House

In colonial times, Tryon Palace was spoken of as the most beautiful public building in North America. The mansion was built for the Royal Governor William Tryon and served as both his residence and as the capitol for the Royal colony. The palace provided elegant surroundings for talk of England for Governor Tryon's official business meetings and for the many social engagements hosted by he and his wife, Margaret Wake Tryon. After the Revolution, Tryon Palace became North Carolina's first state capitol.

Burned in 1798, the palace was reconstructed in the 1950s from the John Hawke's (the original architect) plans. Today, it stands as a living example of the fashionable taste Governor Tryon brought with him from England. The rooms on display show the many functions the house served: a council room where official business transpired; the kitchen where elegant meals were prepared; and the drawing room where guests were entertained.

The palace is furnished with objects dating from the late 18th century. These rare English and American antiques were selected to approximate an inventory of Governor Tryon's possessions made two years after he left New Bern to become governor of the colony of New York.

Additional Information

The palace is surrounded by formal period gardens which visitors may walk through and relax in after their tour. In addition, the complex contains the John Wright Stanly House and the Dixon-Stevenson House.

James K. Polk Memorial

Box 475
Pineville, NC 28134
(704) 889-7145

Contact: Department of Archives and
History
Open: April 1-Oct. 31: Mon.-Sat.
9 a.m.–5 p.m., Sun. 1–5 p.m.;
Nov. 1-March 31: Tues.-Sat.
10 a.m.–4 p.m., Sun. 1–4 p.m.
Activities: Tours
Description of Grounds: A 21 acre tract
encompasses the original Polk
homestead.
Year House Built: Buildings date to the
early 1800s
Style of Architecture: Log buildings

Description of House

Born in 1795 on the 250-acre farm worked by his parents, Jane and Samuel, James Knox Polk, eleventh President of the United States, spent most of his childhood here. A successful lawyer, Polk entered politics as a representative in the Tennessee House. Then for fourteen years he served as a representative in the U.S. Congress, including four years as the Speaker of the House. His eloquent speeches, unfailing support of Andrew Jackson, and firm belief in the Jeffersonian principles—equal rights for all, special privileges for none, and a friend of the common people—won him the nickname "Napoleon of the Stump." Polk became the first "dark horse" in American politics when he was the party's choice over Martin Van Buren as the Democratic nominee for President against Henry Clay of the Whig party. With the campaign slogan of "Fifty-Four Forty or Fight," in reference to his position on the northern boundary of the Oregon territory, Polk rode into the White House.

The original buildings of the Polk homestead were torn down around 1920. The reconstructed buildings stand within a few hundred yards of the original homestead location. All of the log structures were brought from other Meklenburg County sites and date back to the early 1800s. The squared logs of each structure are notched with half-dovetail joints, the interstices plugged with cement colored to resemble clay. Each building has a gable roof covered with cedar or cypress shingles, slightly overhanging eaves, and weatherboarded gables. The shingles are overlapped with small openings for ventilation; they swell and close with rain. Both the dwelling and the kitchen have single exterior end chimneys. The furnishings are not original to the Polk homestead, but are period pieces which date from the early 1800s.

Horne Creek Living Historical Farm

Rte. 2, Box 118-A
Pinnacle, NC 27043
(919) 325-2298

Contact: Department of Cultural Resources
Open: April 1-Oct.31: Tues.-Sat.
9 a.m.–5 p.m., Sun. 1–5 p.m.; Nov.
1-March 31: Tues.-Sat. 10 a.m.–4 p.m.,
Sun. 1–4 p.m.

Activities: Educational programs
Description of Grounds: Reconstruction of a
family farm dating back 100 years.
Year House Built: c. 1900

Description of House

The Horne Creek Living Historical Farm represents the physical environment and seasonal work cycle of a North Carolina family farm from a century ago. The project is located on the site of a farm formerly owned by the Hauser family. Here visitors will encounter archaeologists investigating the site of an early farm building, or may watch as staff experiment with traditional log construction techniques. One can try their hand at cutting grass with a scythe, or listen to an 80-year old woman explain how to make lye soap. Through educational programs ranging from white oak basket-making workshops to an annual cornshucking frolic, Horne Creek Living Historical Farm provides a unique opportunity to see a work in progress and learn more about North Carolina's rural past.

Additional Information

Horne Creek Living History Farm is located just a few miles away from Winston-Salem on Route 52. Visitors with an interest in living history demonstrations are also encouraged to visit Historic Bathabara Park (on University Parkway in Winston-Salem), the site of the first Moravian settlement in the state. Here costumed interpreters will guide visitors through 18th and 19th-century restored buildings representing Moravian culture and traditions.

Mordecai Historic Park

1 Mimosa Street
Raleigh, NC 27604
(919) 834-4844

Contact: Capital Area Preservation

Open: March-mid Dec., Tues.-Fri.
10 a.m.–3 p.m., Sat.-Sun. 1:30–3:30 p.m.

Admission: Free every third Sun. of the month.

Facilities on Premises: Gift shop

Description of Grounds: The garden was designed based on descriptions in *Gleanings From Long Ago,* by Ellen Mordecai.

Year House Built: 1785

Style of Architecture: Plantation house

Description of House

The first residents of Mordecai House, Henry and Polly Lane, were descendants of two Wake County pioneer families. The home acquired its name from its second owner, Moses Mordecai, who married the Lane's daughter, Margaret. The house remained in the Mordecai family until 1968.

The house is a wonderful combination of 18th and 19th-century architectural styles. In 1785, the plantation home consisted only of the north (rear) portion of the present house, then one and a half stories. In 1826, state architect William Nichols (who remodeled the State House) added the five south (front) rooms and converted the north portion to two stories. The Mordecai House remained a country manor until 1907 when Raleigh's second extension of the city limits encompassed part of the plantation. Subsequently, portions of the estate were gradually sold.

Many of the furnishings are original to the house and include furniture, portraits and books owned by the Mordecai family and donated by the family's descendants. These have been supplemented by gifts, bequests, and purchases of needed items.

Additional Information

Also set in the park in the village setting is the tiny, gambrel-roofed house (ca. 1795) in which Andrew Johnson, the seventeenth President was born in 1808. The modest frame building was both kitchen and dwelling in the yard of Peter Casso's Inn near the corner of Raleigh's Fayetteville and Morgan streets, where Johnson's parents were employed. The house, which was transported to the park in 1975, has been restored to its probable appearance at the time of Johnson's birth, and displays collected furnishings of the same period.

"Wakefield"–The Joel Lane House

729 West Hargatt
P.O. Box 10884
Raleigh, NC 27605
(919) 733-3456

Contact: National Society of
Colonial Dames

Open: March-Nov., Tues., Thurs.-Fri.
10 a.m.–2 p.m.; two day Christmas
tour, mid Dec.; open for special tours
upon request

Activities: Guided tours by costumed
hostesses; planned tours for students;
available for luncheons, teas, receptions

Year House Built: c. 1760

Description of House

The house is considered the oldest in the capital, and was home to one of its most noteworthy citizens. Colonel Joel Lane was born in Halifax, North Carolina, one of six sons of Joseph Lane and Patience McKinnie, both members of prominent southern colonial families. In 1762, he married Martha Hinton, and, after her death, married Mary Hinton in 1772. Both were daughters of Colonel John Hinton, a distinguished statesman and Revolutionary soldier of Wake County, and his wife, Grizelle Kimbrough. Joel Lane was known as "Father of Wake County" because as a representative from Johnston County to the Colonial Assembly at New Bern in 1770, he introduced the bill for its creation. He was also known as the "Father of Raleigh" because the city was planned on land he deeded to the state.

The Joel Lane House, also known as "Wakefield", has been restored to the 1790 to 1795 period when it was remodeled by Joel Lane. Architectural evidence remains visible of the house as originally built with a gable, rather than gambrel roof, and a porch extending across the front. Much of the interior woodwork and flooring are original. The exterior of the house features such restored details as beaded siding, chimneys constructed of handmade brick, and a roof of hand hewn and shaped shingles. The furnishings are authentic 18th-century pieces and almost all are American. Several pieces of furniture were made in Wake County, and believed to have been owned and used by the Lane family.

Notable Collections on Exhibit

In addition to the fine period furnishings, the house displays artifacts, such as buttons and shoe buckles, unearthed at the time of the restoration.

Executive Mansion

301 North Blount Street
Raleigh, NC 27601
(919) 733-1991

Contact: North Carolina's Executive
Mansion

Open: Please call to schedule tour

Activities: Guided tours

Description of Grounds: Outside the
mansion lie flower beds filled with
azaleas, camellias, hollies, and a variety
of annual plantings as well as a
Victorian garden dedicated to a former
first lady.

Year House Built: 1890s

Style of Architecture: Victorian

Description of House

Twenty-five Tar Heel governors and their families have lived in this lovely Victorian home for more than a century. This mansion is one of the oldest in America specifically built and continuously used as the home of governors.

Designed by noted architects Samuel Sloan and A.G. Bauer, the mansion's exterior features the characteristic elements of Victorian architecture: steeply pitched roofs, a cupola, richly colored textural surfaces, porches and pavilions, and projecting patterned chimneys. The mansion's first-floor plan has not changed substantially since the 1890s, and the ease with which this layout adjusts to public or private uses remains a frequently praised attribute. The large central hall runs from west to east and divides the major public rooms. This entrance hall is distinguished by elegant Corinthian columns framing the grand staircase which is carved on native heart pine and features carved oak leaves as decoration. A secondary hall on the north side of the house runs north to south and separates the ladies' parlor and dining room. On the south side of the central hall are the gentlemen's parlor, the ballroom and the library. These spacious rooms and halls provide the circulation needed for large social events.

The second floor is for the private use of the first family. It provides a handsome formal living room and dining room, six bedroom suites, a den and a small kitchen.

Notable Collections on Exhibit

The Executive Mansion is filled with many fine furnishings and decorations including a Victorian dining set made of mahogany, Chippendale chairs, French mirrors, and a variety of chandeliers ranging from Austrian crystal to ones of Sheffield manufacture.

Additional Information

A handsome wall of brick and wrought iron encloses the grounds, which consist of numerous gardens filled with a large variety of trees and flowers.

Haywood Hall

211 New Bern Place
Raleigh, NC 27601
(919) 832-4158

Contact: The Friends of Haywood Hall, Inc.
Open: March-mid Dec., Thurs.
10:30 a.m.–1:30 p.m.
Activities: Tours; educational programs;
symposiums
Description of Grounds: The garden
closely resembles the design and
planting organized by former resident
Eliza Haywood
Year House Built: Late 1790s
Style of Architecture: Classical

Description of House

As a member of the Council of State of North Carolina, John Haywood was required to purchase land in Raleigh, the new permanent capital of the State of North Carolina. He served as the first elected treasurer of the state for forty years and as the first Mayor of Raleigh. He lived here with his wife Eliza. The Haywood family and their descendants occupied Haywood for 175 years.

Haywood Hall holds the distinction of being the only house, built before 1800, (within the original city limits of Raleigh) that remains on its original foundations. Built during the Federal period and in the Classical style, the house has undergone little exterior alteration since that time. The mantel and surround in the main parlor of Haywood Hall is the most striking example of restoration in the house to date. It has been completely restored to the original faux marble finish. Small chips of paint were removed and examined by the North Carolina Division of Archives and History, which revealed the dramatic colors and textures seen today. The period furnishings have been collected and are appropriate for the late 18th-century interpretation of the house.

Stonewall Manor

100 Salem Street
Rodey Mount, NC 27804
(919) 443-6708

Contact: Nash County Historical Association, Inc.

Open: Every 2nd Sun., 2–4:30 p.m.; other times by appointment

Admission: Adults $2.50; groups and seniors $2; students (to 18 years old) $1. Guided tours.

Suggested Time to View House: 45 minutes

Description of Grounds: Large expanse of lawn with large trees

Best Season to View House: Spring and Summer

Year House Built: c. 1830

Style of Architecture: Late Federal

Number of Rooms: 12

On-Site Parking: Yes **Wheelchair Access:** Yes

Description of House

The original owner and builder of this impressive home was Bennett Bunn, a prosperous cotton planter. After his death in 1849, another cotton planter, Richard Harrison, took up residence in the home. Harrison's nephew, Kehelm Lewis, lived here until 1868 and his widow continued to make the house her home until her death in 1916.

The three-story manor features a brick exterior lain in a Flemish bond pattern. The first floor at the ground level is actually the basement and has brick walls and a cement floor. The other two floors are formal in appearance with marbleized baseboards running throughout most of the main floor and third floor. A twin or "wishbone" staircase joins the second and third stories of this large country house. Highlights of the interior decor include period reproduction wallpaper in many of the rooms and outstanding trim in the main rooms and front hall. Stonewall Manor features a collection of period furnishings appropriate for the mid 19th century. None of the items on display belonged to any of the original owners.

The Michael Braun House

Salisbury, NC 28144
(704) 633-5946

Contact: The Old Stone House
Open: April-Nov., Sat.-Sun. 2–5 p.m.
Admission: Adults $1; children $.50.
  Tours by appointment.
Description of Grounds: Family cemetery
  across road which contains a marker to
  the memory of Michael Braun
Year House Built: 1758 to 1766
Style of Architecture: Colonial

Description of House

Michael Braun (anglicized Brown) emigrated to Philadelphia from the German Palatinate in 1737 and came to the Piedmont where he purchased land in 1758. He was a wheelwright by profession, later becoming a large planter and land owner. He held various political offices and in 1794 established a German-English print shop in Salisbury. Today, there are many of his descendants who live throughout North Carolina.

Known as the oldest and only Colonial building remaining in Rowan County, this massive two-story house features coursed native stone with lined joints on the four bay front and uncoursed stone on the rear and sides. Above and to the right of the front door the names of Michael and his wife, Margareta are inscribed on a stone slab. Then follows a line of lettering, "10 Pe-Me-Be-Mi-Da 1766." This appears to be an abbreviation for a German Biblical phrase, "My undertaking is completed, thanks be to Christ." The numbers refer to October 1766 when the house was completed. From the upstairs room, visitors can see the massive roof trusses.

Inside the house is a splendid example of the Quaker plan so popular in Pennsylvania, Braun's former home. To the left of the entrance are a pair of rooms with corner fireplaces which share the same chimney. To the right is the great room behind which lies a narrow enclosed stairway and a small room furnished as a child's room. Adjoining the great room is the kitchen where the eight foot wide fireplace is braced with a wooden lintel eighteen inches square. From this fireplace the adjoining great room was heated by means of an aperture against a five-plate iron stove into which hot coals were fed.

Notable Collections on Exhibit

The period furnishings include a fine collection of North Carolina and Pennsylvania pieces. A great German kas (wardrobe), a flat back cupboard with a rare pewter collection, German Bibles, fireplace cooking implements, spinning wheels, agricultural tools, are all indicative of the Braun's lifestyle in the 1700s. Of special interest is a weaving loom upstairs that has been in the house as long as anyone can remember.

The Utzman-Chambers House

116 S. Jackson Street
Salisbury, NC 28144
(704) 633-5946

Contact: The Rowan Museum

Open: Thurs.-Sun. 2–5 p.m.

Admission: Adults $1; children $.50. Tours by appointment.

Description of Grounds: An early 19th-century garden, the bird bath in the center is surrounded by brick walks and four geometric beds planted with native flowers

Year House Built: 1815 to 1819

Style of Architecture: Federal

Description of House

The Utzman-Chambers House was built for Lewis Utzman, a cabinet-maker. The building now houses the extensive collections of the Rowan museum in addition to many fine period furnishings.

This handsome two-story building, three bays wide with a Palladian window in the south gable end, is among the few surviving Federal townhouses in Piedmont, North Carolina. From the entrance hall one enters a spacious parlor with the original carved mantel and elaborate wide ornamental plaster cornice. Two 19th-century portraits of Moses and Mary Locke, prominent in the annals of Rowan County history, are exhibited in this room. In the office sits a ladder back chair once owned by Daniel Boone when he lived in this county prior to his migration to Kentucky in 1769. Here may also be seen a stretcher table made in the 1700s, surveyor' instruments, and irons used at the Mansion House Inn. In addition, the upstairs' bedroom contains a handsome Sheraton four poster bed with a Rowan County Bird of Paradise quilt covering the straw tick and feather mattress. A 1759 Queen Anne chest on frame with the original brass hardware and a child's tester bed enhance the elegance of this room. Other rooms of the house contain fine period pieces made between 1760 and 1820.

Notable Collections on Exhibit

Among the many treasured relics on display is a silk ball gown worn by a local young lady during President Washington's visit to Salisbury in 1791. Also on exhibit is a Sheraton knifebox which belonged to John Steele, the first Comptroller of the Currency under Presidents Washington, Adams, and Jefferson. A rare beaded Creek Indian bandolier and the original flag which flew over the Salisbury Confederate prison, later burned by General Stoneman, can also be seen here.

Zebulon B. Vance Birthplace

Route 1, Box 465
Weaverville, NC 28787

Contact: Department of Cultural Resources
Open: April 1-Oct. 31, Mon.-Sat.
9 a.m.–5 p.m., Sun. 1–5 p.m.;
Nov. 1-March 31: Tues.-Sat.
10 a.m.–4 p.m., Sun. 1–4 p.m.
Activities: Tours; Spring and Fall Pioneer
Living Days: costumed staff members
and volunteers demonstrate the skills
and crafts of the early settlers.
Facilities on Premises: Visitor center
Year House Built: c. 1790

Description of House

One of the dominant personalities of the south for nearly half a century, Zebulon Baird Vance, lived in this modest farmhouse. Vance was a popular and beloved figure in North Carolina history, and served the public for thirty years. Though he was a lawyer, his real interest was in politics. Vance was elected to his first public office at the age of twenty-four. He served in the North Carolina House of Commons, the U.S. House of Representatives, and was elected governor three times. In 1879, Vance began the first of three full terms as U.S. State Senator; his death in 1894 interrupted his fourth term.

The homestead, a large two-story structure of hewn yellow pine logs, has been reconstructed around the original chimney with its enormous fireplaces. The furnishings on display are representative of the period from 1790 to 1840 and include a few pieces original to the house. In addition, clustered about the grounds of the house, are six log outbuildings: the corn crib, springhouse, smokehouse, loom house, slave house, and tool house.

Notable Collections on Exhibit

The visitor center/museum houses exhibits portraying the life of Governor Vance.

Additional Information

Each spring and fall the Vance Birthplace recreates Pioneer Living Days with a series of demonstrations by costumed staff and volunteers. During these weeks demonstrations are given on weaving, open hearth cooking, churning, quilting, and woodcrafting and other cherished skills and occupations practiced when Zebulon Vance was living.

Burgwin Wright House and Gardens

224 Market Street
Wilmington, NC 28401
(919) 762-0570

Contact: National Society of the
Colonial Dames of America
Open: Tues.-Sat. 10 a.m.–4 p.m.
Activities: Group tours by
appointment
Description of Grounds: A typical
18th-century parterre garden
Year House Built: 1770
Style of Architecture: Georgian

Description of House

The Brugwin Wright House provides an excellent example of a colonial gentleman's town residence. John Burgwin, treasurer of the colony of Carolina under Arthur Dobbs the Royal Governor, built this stately home in 1770. During the Revolution, Burgwin's business partner Charles Jewkes occupied the house. After his death, his step-son, Joshua Grainger Wright purchased it from Burgwin. The Wright family lived here until after the Civil War. In 1781, when Lord Charles Cornwallis retired to Wilmington, after the battle of Guilford Court House, he established his headquarters here. Eighteen days later he started north toward his final defeat and surrender at Yorktown. The house was purchased in 1937 by the National Society of The Colonial Dames of America in the state of North Carolina.

The house is built on the massive stone foundation of the abandoned town jail. Beneath lies the dungeon where Lord Cornwallis kept his prisoners, and the remains of a tunnel to the Cape Fear River. The Georgian house with its handsome Palladian doorway has double porches on two sides, showing the influence of the West Indies. The finest room in the house is the upstairs drawing room with its elaborate paneling and classic architectural detail. The three-story kitchen building is separated by a paved courtyard.

The house has a fine collection of acquired 18th-century furnishings and decorations.

Hope Plantation

Route 308, P.O. Box 601
Windsor, NC 27983
(919) 794-3140

Contact: Historic Hope Foundation
Open: March-Dec. 23, Mon.-Sat.
10 a.m.–4 p.m., Sun. 2–5 p.m.,
closed Thanksgiving
Admission: Adults $5, students (6-17) $1.75
(admission covers both houses), group
rates available
Description of Grounds: A typical
18th-century parterre garden
Year House Built: 1803
Style of Architecture: Georgian

Description of House

The Hope Plantation offers a view of an agrarian society and an insight into rural domestic life as experienced in the Colonial and Federal periods of northeastern North Carolina. The original owner and builder of Hope Mansion, David Stone, was leading political figure in his state's formative years. He was an attorney, a Superior Court justice, and a member of the state legislature. Later he served as Senator and as governor (1808-1810) of North Carolina.

To build his home, Stone relied on a popular 18th-century pattern book, Abraham Swann's *The British Architect*. This Georgian vernacular home features a handsome drawing room and library located on the second floor. The first floor contains the family parlor and dining room while the above ground basement holds the winter kitchen and several storage rooms. The mansion is filled with period furnishings based on the estate inventory of David Stone and features many outstanding pieces from local and urban cabinetmaker shops.

The Hope estate was a self-sustaining plantation, producing much corn and wheat. In Stone's time, the outbuildings included a grist mill, saw mill, blacksmith's shop, and houses for spinning and weaving. Today, visitors are able to view the reconstructed dairy and meat house as well as a recreated period kitchen garden and orchard.

Additional Information

In order to get a full picture of the progression of plantation life, visitors should start their exploration of Hope Plantation with a visit to the King-Bazemore House (1763). This Georgian-style house was built by a local planter and cooper, William King, and later purchased by Stephen Bazemore in 1840. The house features a Flemish bond brick exterior, a gambrel roof with shed dormers, and a paneled hall and parlor interior, making it an outstanding example of mid 18th-century domestic architecture. To the rear of the house, visitors will find a kitchen with working fireplace and bakeoven, where colonial cooking demonstrations often take place.

Old Salem

Old Salem Road
Winston-Salem, NC 27108
(919) 721-7300

Contact: Old Salem Inc.
Open: Mon.-Sat. 9:30 a.m.–4:30 p.m., Sun. 1:30–4:30 p.m., closed Thanksgiving, Christmas eve, Christmas day
Admission: Adults $10; youths (6-14) $5; family discounts available. Living history demonstrations, self-guided tours, seasonal special events, please contact village for schedule and more information.

Facilities: Visitor's center, gift shop, restaurants
Description of Grounds: Landscaped grounds throughout this historic village
Year House Built: 1766 to 1850
Style of Architecture: Varied

Description of House

The Moravian town of Salem was founded in 1766. Visitors to Old Salem Village will see a faithful reconstruction of this historic town complete with restored houses, shops, schools and other structures important to the community. Careful attention to detail has resulted in an authentic recreation of the buildings, the landscaped grounds and even the lighting which characterized this town of German immigrants.

All tours begin at the Old Salem Visitor's Center where visitors will receive a good introduction to the history of the Moravian community in the United States and their contributions to North Carolina. Some of the more notable buildings open to the public include the John Vogler House, home of the local silversmith. Built in 1819, the house displays many of the original furnishings including a Moravian tile stove. The Miksch Tobacco Shop, built in 1771, is thought to be the oldest tobacco shop still standing in America. The building also served as a residence for the owner, Matthew Miksch. Visitors will also be intrigued by the Single Brothers House where the community's single men used to live. Today the communal house features workshops where artisans practice 18th and 19th-century crafts. The Vierling House is another notable home along the tour. This attractive house, built in 1802, was the home to the local physician, Dr. Benjamin

Vierling, and also includes a recreation of his medical office and an apothecary shop. In addition to the historic houses, Old Salem Village contains a wide range of shops and schools, and living history demonstrations which provide a wonderful view of 19th-century life.

Additional Information

Visitors to the village should not miss the opportunity to the view the Museum of Early Southern Decorative Arts. The museum houses a unique collection of furniture, paintings, textiles, ceramics and silver made in the South from the 1600s to 1820. Admission to the museum is discounted with a combination ticket to Old Salem Village.

Reynolda House– Museum of American Art

Reynolda Road, P.O. Box 11765
Winston-Salem, NC 27116
(919) 725-5325

Contact: Reynolda House
Open: Tues.-Sat. 9:30 a.m.–4:30 p.m., Sun. 1:30–4:30 p.m., closed Thanksgiving, Christmas day, New Year's
Admission: Adults $6; seniors $5; students and children $3; group tours may be arranged by calling or writing in advance
Suggested Time to View House: 1 hour

Facilities: Museum shop
Description of Grounds: Landscaped gardens with weeping cherry trees surround the house and village and are open free to the public
Year House Built: 1917
Style of Architecture: Bungalow
On-Site Parking: Yes **Wheelchair Access:** Yes

Description of House

Reynolda House is a beautiful and distinctive example of a country house built for the wealthy Reynolds family in the early 20th century. Richard Reynolds founded the world's largest tobacco manufacturing business, R.J. Reynolds Tobacco Company, the makers of Prince Albert smoking tobacco and Camel cigarettes. In 1905, he married Katherine Smith, his executive secretary, and she became the motivating force behind the creation of Reynolda as their home. Unfortunately, the couple lived in the house for only a short time; Richard Reynolds died in 1918 and Katherine in 1924. In 1934, the house was acquired by their daughter, Mary, who made substantial renovations to the existing structure.

The house is known for its eclectic combination of architectural styles based on a design by the Philadelphia architect, Charles Barton Keen. The large, two-and-a-half story building appears lower than it actually is due to the horizontal design of the verandas, balconies, and the proportion of the green-tiled roof to the white stuccoed walls. Its exterior and interior feature superb craftsmanship in the ironwork of Samuel Yellin, the ceramic tiles of

Henry Mercer, and the roofing tiles of Lodowici-Celadon. The construction took place between 1912 and 1917, stopping only for interruptions during World War I. During the period that the eldest daughter, Mary, lived here, the front entrance was moved to the east end of the house; the portico was replaced by the terrace and formal garden; and the basement was enlarged to accommodate game rooms, a single-lane bowling alley, and other recreational facilities. Many of the Reynolds's original furnishings are on display, as well as an extensive collection of outstanding pieces of American art. The house has recently been added to the National Register of Historic Places.

Notable Collections on Exhibit

Reynolda House exhibits an impressive collection of paintings, sculpture, and decorative arts by some of America's best known artists. Of note are paintings by Frederick Church, Mary Cassat and Thomas Eakins as well as master prints by Jasper Johns, James Rosenquist, Frank Stella and others. A growing collection of sculpture includes pieces by Paul Manship, Alexander Calder, and David Smith. The balcony houses a beautiful collection of American art pottery and Tiffany glass while the third floor displays the elegant wardrobe of Katherine Reynolds and the clothes and toys of the Reynolds children.

Additional Information

In addition to being a private estate, Reynolda was also planned to be a model farm and village. At one time the estate had 350 acres under cultivation. Today, visitors will enjoy the pastoral landscaping of the surrounding rolling hills, woodland areas, and eighteen springs which were incorporated into the overall landscape design.

South Carolina

1. **Beaufort**
   George Parsons Elliott House
   John Verdier House

2. **Beech Island**
   Redcliffe Plantation

3. **Bennettsville**
   Jennings-Brown House

4. **Camden**
   Historic Camden

5. **Charleston**
   Nathaniel Russell House
   Edmondston-Alston House
   Drayton Hall
   *Middletown Place National
     Historic Landmark*
   Aiken-Rhett House
   Heyward-Washington House
   Joseph Manigault House

6. **Columbia**
   *Hampton-Preston Mansion
     and Garden*
   *Mann-Simons Cottage: Museum
     of African American Culture*
   *Robert Mills Historic House
     and Park*
   Woodrow Wilson Boyhood Home

7. **Edgefield**
   Magnolia Dale
   Oakley Park

8. **Georgetown**
   The Harold Kaminski House
   Hopsewee Plantation

9. **McClellanville**
   Hampton Plantation

10. **McConnells**
    Historic Brattonsville

11. **Mount Pleasant**
    Boone Hall Plantation

12. **Roebuck**
    Walnut Grove Plantation

13. **Woodruff**
    Thomas Price House

George Parsons Elliott House

1001 Bay Street, P.O. Box 11
Beaufort, SC 29901
(803) 524-6334

Contact: Historic Beaufort Foundation
Open: Mon.-Fri. 11 a.m.–3 p.m.;
    closed in Jan.
Activities: Guided tours
Suggested Time to View House:
    30–40 minutes
Facilities on Premises: Gift shop
Description of Grounds: Downtown
    historic district
Best Season to View House: Spring and fall
Number of Yearly Visitors: 11,000
Year House Built: 1845
Style of Architecture: Federal
Number of Rooms: 12

On-Site Parking: Yes **Wheelchair Access:** No

Description of House

Located in picturesque Beaufort, the second oldest town in the state, the Elliot House is a lovely antebellum home which today conveys the refinement of its former occupants. George Parsons Elliott, a planter and politician, built this home overlooking the Beaufort river in 1844.

The interior and exterior proportions of the Elliott House reflect the Greek Revival influence on the traditional "Beaufort Style." Oriented to the south, toward the river, the two-story frame house rests on a raised foundation. Massive columns support the veranda that spans the facade. The furnishings exhibit the changing influences of taste from the mid 19th into the 20th century.

John Verdier House

801 Bay Street, P.O. Box 11
Beaufort, SC 29901
(803) 524-6334

Contact: Historic Beaufort Foundation
Open: Tues.-Sat. 11 a.m.–4 p.m.;
 closed in Jan.
Activities: Guided tours
Suggested Time to View House:
 30–40 minutes
Facilities on Premises: Gift shop
Description of Grounds: Downtown
 historic district
Best Season to View House: Spring and fall
Number of Yearly Visitors: 11,000
Year House Built: 1790
Style of Architecture: Federal
Number of Rooms: 8
On-Site Parking: Yes **Wheelchair Access:** No

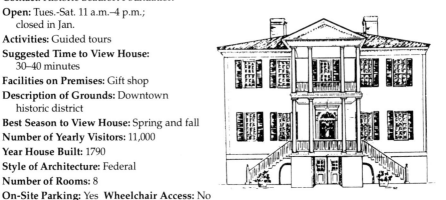

Description of House

This attractive Federal-style residence was built by one of the town's most prosperous merchants and planters, John Mark Verdier. The house has played a significant role in the historical development of Beaufort over the last two centuries. The house was a location for many social gatherings and it is said that the Marquis de Lafayette was entertained here in 1825. In addition, the house served as headquarters for Union troops during the Civil War.

The Verdier house is a fine example of the Adam's style of Federal architecture with its simple white clapboard exterior and graceful interior. There are many excellent period furnishings on display representing the years from 1790 to 1825. Of particular note is a display of silver owned by the Verdier family.

Redcliffe Plantation

181 Redcliffe Road
Beech Island, SC 29841
(803) 827-1473

Contact: Redcliffe Plantation State Park

Open: Thurs.-Sat. and Mon. 10 a.m.–3 p.m.;
Sun. 12–3 p.m.

Admission: Adults $2; students $1.
The mansion may also be opened by
appointment or rented for special
occasions.

Facilities on Premises: Picnic area and
nature trail

Description of Grounds: The house is part
of a 350-acre historical state park.

Year House Built: 1859

Style of Architecture: Antebellum
Plantation

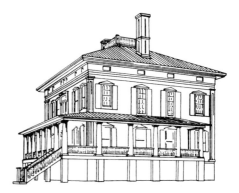

Description of House

Redcliffe was home to a former governor of South Carolina, James H.
Hammond. The house was continually owned and occupied by four generations of the colorful Hammond family until very recently. John Shaw Bill-
ings, former managing editor of *Time* and *Life* magazines and a Hammond
descendant, donated the plantation to the state in 1973 for use as a house
museum.

Located on the banks of the Savannah River, this two-story antebellum
plantation displays much of its original charm and elegance. There are
currently two floors open to the public including the distinguished main
hall and parlor, and the dining room where the Hammond's frequently
entertained many prominent guests. The house is completely furnished
with period furniture including many original pieces and works of art.

Jennings-Brown House

119 S. Marlboro Street
Bennettsville, SC 29512
(803) 479-5624

Contact: Marlborough Historical Society

Open: Mon., Tues. and Thur. 10 a.m.–1 p.m. and 2–5 p.m.; Wed. and Fri. 10 a.m.–1 p.m.; also by appointment

Admission: Adults $1; children $.50. Guided tours, special programs available for local groups

Suggested Time to View House: 1 hour

Number of Yearly Visitors: 250-300

Year House Built: 1826-27

Style of Architecture: Saltbox

Number of Rooms: 8

On-Site Parking: Yes

Wheelchair Access: No

Description of House

Dr. Edward W. Jones, one of the first physicians in the community, built this modest saltbox home in 1826. The house is named for the two families who resided in it the longest, the Jennings and the Browns. Members of both families were widely respected citizens of the community, and, for the most part, stayed out of the limelight of history. The house holds the distinction of having served as headquarters for Major General Frank Blair and his Union troops during Sherman's occupation of Bennetsville in March of 1865. Because of this and its architectural excellence, the Jenning-Brown House has been listed on the National Register of Historic Places.

The house is a two story frame house with a one story kitchen wing at the rear, connected by a rear porch. The exterior is of beaded cypress weatherboarding. The interior features fine architectural details, such as wainscotting, heart pine floors, and Joseph Carpenter locks. The roof is of random width cedar shake shingles. The "crown jewel" of the dwelling is a unique stenciled and hand-painted ceiling in an upstairs bedroom. No date or origin of the ceiling is known at this time. It was discovered under several layers of wallpaper during the restoration. The furnishings have been collected and are appropriate to the period of the restoration (1840 to 1860).

Historic Camden

**Box 710, Highway 521 South
Camden, SC 29020
(803) 432-9841**

Contact: Historic Camden

Open: Tues.-Sat. 10 a.m.– 4 p.m.; Sun.
1–4 p.m.; closed major holidays

Admission: Adults $4.50; students $1.50;
children (under 6) free. Special rates
available for field trips and groups.
Guided tours.

Facilities on Premises: Museum shop

Description of Grounds: Fortified town
site with nature trail and picnic area

Year House Built: Town built between 1733
and 1734

Description of House

Historic Camden consists of a ninety-two acre historical park with many restored buildings of significant historical and architectural interest. Camden, the oldest existing inland town in South Carolina, evolved from instructions issued by King George II in 1730 specifying that a township be located "on the River Watery." As a result, Fredericksburg Township, the first name given the Camden area, was laid out during the winter of 1733 to 1734. Within the two decades following the King's order, a few stalwart families had hacked out homesteads along the Wateree River. Then in 1750 a group of Irish Quakers arrived and named the town Pine Tree Hill. In 1768, the name was changed to honor Lord Camden, a friend of the colonies. During the American Revolution, the town witnessed many battles including the Battle of Camden on August 16, 1780 in which the colonists were defeated. The British occupied the town for a year until May of 1781 when they evacuated and set fire to much of the town.

A small but meaningful segment of our American heritage may be found at Historic Camden. Located immediately south of the partially reconstructed British palisade wall which enclosed the original town, Historic Camden emerged as the result of a project begun in the late 1960s by the Historical Committee of the Camden and Kershaw County Chamber of Commerce. The objectives of this project were to discover, restore, and interpret the significant historical features of 18th and early 19th-century Camden, particularly the period of the British occupation of 1780 to 1781. Today the village features a number of restored houses including the Joseph Kershaw House (1777) where Lord Cornwallis stayed during the Battle of Camden, several log houses built in the early 1800s, and the Craven House, an early frame house built in 1789. The nearby Camden Archives provides a complete history of the town through documents, artifacts, and regional memorabilia.

Nathaniel Russell House

51 Meeting Street
Charleston, SC 29401
(803) 724-8481

Contact: Historic Charleston Foundation
Open: Mon.-Sat. 10 a.m.–5 p.m.;
Sun. 2–5 p.m.
Admission: $5. Guided tours.
Suggested Time to View House: 30 minutes
Facilities on Premises: Museum shop,
book store
Description of Grounds: Formal gardens
Best Season to View House: Spring and fall
Number of Yearly Visitors: 75,000
Year House Built: c. 1808
Style of Architecture: Federal
Number of Rooms: 6
On-Site Parking: No
Wheelchair Access: Yes

Description of House

Nathaniel Russell (1738-1820) was born in Bristol, Rhode Island. Charleston's preeminence among southern ports brought young Nathaniel Russell in search of fortune that would later establish his reputation as "King of the Yankees" among the city's merchant princes.

This handsome example of Federal architecture, a National Trust Landmark, was completed in 1808 for the sum of $80,000, a great sum for the time. Set amid formal gardens, the "main house" is recognized as one of America's most important neo-classical dwellings. The graceful interior features oval drawings with elaborate plasterwork ornamentation and a magnificent "flying staircase". The distinguished rooms are filled with period furnishings, many of Charleston origin.

Notable Collections on Exhibit

The collection contains a large number of furnishings with significant Charleston provenance, not only furniture but also silver, ceramics, metals and needlework, owned and used by Charleston families.

Additional Information

Visitors to Charleston should not miss out on the foundation's other historic house, the Edmondston-Allen House (21 East Battery) with its wonderful view of Charleston Harbor. In addition, each year the historic foundation sponsors the "Festival of Houses and Gardens" which tours privately owned mansions in the Charleston area. Call (803) 723-1623 for more information.

Edmondston-Alston House

21 East Battery
Charleston, SC 29401
(803) 722-7171

Contact: Middleton Place Foundation

Open: Mon.-Sat. 10 a.m.–5 p.m.;
Sun. 1:30-5 p.m.

Admission: Individual or combination tickets and group discounts are available for house museums. Guided tours.

Description of Grounds: The house provides a breathtaking view of the Charleston Harbor.

Year House Built: 1828 to 1838

Description of House

Charles Edmondston, merchant and wharf owner, built this house in 1828, but lived here for only ten years. In 1838, it was bought by Colonel William Alston, celebrated planter and horse-breeder, for his son, Charles, who redecorated it in the fashionable Greek Revival style.

This gracious house was built in a commanding location and still maintains an uninterrupted view across the Charleston River. The interior features elaborate and unconventional woodwork, an outstanding library, and is filled with fine period furnishings, many of which were family-owned.

Notable Collections on Exhibit

The Edmondston-Alston House displays a wide range of documents, portraits, engravings, silver and china, in addition to the excellent collection of 19th-century furniture.

Additional Information

Visitors to Charleston should allow plenty of time to visit the city's other notable historic homes including the John Rutledge House (116 Broad Street) home of a leading South Carolina statesman, and the Nathaniel Russell House (51 Meeting Street). Just a few blocks away stands the lovely, Victorian Calhoun Mansion (16 Meeting Street). This notable structure features elaborate interior design, original floor tiles, and an impressive skylight adorning the extremely high ceilings in the ballroom.

Drayton Hall

3380 Ashley River Road
Charleston, SC 29414
(803) 766-0188

Contact: National Trust for Historic
Preservation

Open: March-Oct., daily 10 a.m.–4 p.m.;
Nov.-Feb., daily 10 a.m.–3 p.m.; closed
Thanksgiving, Christmas and New
Year's Day

Admission: Adults $6; youths (6-18) $3.
Guided tours, video tour (for physically
challenged persons), special events.

Suggested Time to View House: 1 hour

Facilities on Premises: Gift shop

Description of Grounds: The expansive
grounds surrounding the mansion
contain a landscaped lawn with huge
oaks draped with Spanish moss, an old
garden filled with different varieties of
flowers, and nature trails through the
woods and marshes

Best Season to View House: Spring

Number of Yearly Visitors: 60,000

Year House Built: 1738

Style of Architecture: Georgian Palladian

On-Site Parking: Yes **Wheelchair Access:** Yes

Description of House

Settling in Carolina in 1670, the Draytons became one of South
Carolina's most distinguished families. In 1738, John Drayton, a young
planter, purchased land next to his father's plantation, now known as
Magnolia Gardens. After four years of construction, Drayton Hall was
completed and became the center of John's plantation operations.

Built between 1738 and 1742, Drayton Hall is considered one of the finest
examples of Colonial architecture in America. Through seven generations
of Drayton ownership, this National Historic Landmark has remained in
virtually original condition and is the only Ashley River plantation house
to survive the Civil War intact. The house's features closely match architectural concepts sweeping Britain after 1715. The two-story portico is believed
to be the first of its kind in America. Native materials were used freely, while
English limestone and West Indian mahogany enhanced detail. Its unique
state of preservation and rich, handcrafted detail offer visitors a rare glimpse
of a bygone Southern way of life.

In spite of changing tastes, periods of disuse, and occasional repairs, the house has hardly been altered, and approaches the close of the 20th century without running water, electric lighting or central heating. Today, only improvements necessary for the protection of the house are made. Drayton Hall is unfurnished; it provides a fascinating view of architectural design, proportion and detail.

Additional Information

Just a few miles down the road, visitors should also plan a visit to Magnolia Plantation where John Drayton lived while Drayton Hall was under construction. The main house features a fascinating exhibit on life during the Civil War and contains many historic artifacts. Like Drayton Hall, Magnolia Plantation has splendid grounds for walking, and a fifty-acre garden with several hundred varieties of camellias and azaleas.

Middleton Place National Historic Landmark

Ashley River Road
Charleston, SC 29414-7206
(803) 556-6020

Contact: Middleton Place

Open: Daily 9 a.m.–5 p.m.

Admission: Adults $9; seniors $8; children (6-12) $4 (house and gardens); Adults $5 (house only). Tours of gardens, house and stableyards. Special tour group rates and food service functions are available.

Facilities on Premises: Gift shop, restaurant

Description of Grounds: The oldest landscaped gardens in America filled with magnolias, roses, azaleas, and camellias all bloom in different seasons. There is also a restored stableyard with working exhibits.

Best Season to View House: Year-round

Year House Built: 1775

Number of Rooms: 7 open to public

Style of Architecture: Tudor

Description of House

Middleton Place was the home of Henry Middleton, president of the First Continental Congress, and his son, Arthur, a signer of the Declaration of Independence. Several other generations of Middletons lived here including Henry Middleton, former governor of the state and ambassador to Russia, and William Middleton who signed the ordinance calling for South Carolina's secession from the Union.

Middleton Place, on the banks of the Ashley River, is a carefully preserved 18th-century plantation that has survived revolution, Civil War and an earthquake. The house that visitors see today was originally built in 1755 as a gentlemen's guest wing; the house became the family residence after the plantation was burned during the Civil War. Period furnishings, paintings, and silvers and a silk copy of the Declaration of Independence signed by Arthur Middleton are currently on display inside the house.

Notable Collections on Exhibit

Collections include portraits by Benjamin West and Thomas Sully, Charleston rice beds, fine silver, and rare first editions by Catesby and Audubon.

Additional Information

Middleton Place is best known for preserving America's oldest landscaped gardens. These beautiful gardens reflect the elegant symmetry of 17th-century European design. Rare camellias bloom in the winter and azaleas blaze on the hillside above the Rice Mill Pond in the spring. In summer, kalmia, magnolias, crepe myrtle, and roses accent a landscape magnificent throughout the year. In the plantation stables the blacksmith, potter, carpenter, and weaver recreate the activities of a self-sustaining low-country plantation. Agricultural displays, together with horses and mules, hogs and milking cows, sheep, goats and guinea hens, bring to life the rice and cotton eras.

Aiken-Rhett House

87 Church Street
Charleston, SC 29401
(803) 722-0354

Contact: The Charleston Museum

Open: Mon.-Sat. 10 a.m.–5 p.m.;
Sun. 1–5 p.m.

Admission: Adults $5; children (3-12) $3.
Total tour ticket (includes museum and
3 historic houses) $15. Guided tours.

Suggested Time to View House: 30 minutes

Description of Grounds: A carriage house
and garden reproduced from
18th-century English garden; plantings
are contemporary to the house.

Best Season to View House: Spring

Year House Built: 1817

Style of Architecture: Georgian Flemish Bond

Number of Rooms: 12 plus attic and cellar

On-Site Parking: No **Wheelchair Access:** Yes

Description of House

This was the home of Governor William Aiken from 1833 to 1887. Aiken had a long and distinguished political career. He sat in the state legislature from 1838 to 1841, where he was a member of several influential committees. He was also elected state senator in 1842 and governor in 1844. A temporary lull in the nullification and secession controversies enabled him to direct his primary efforts toward economic growth and railroad expansion. A Democrat, he was sent to the U.S. House of Representatives in 1851 and served three terms. Aiken was in retirement when the Civil War began. On a historical note, Jefferson Davis, President of the Confederacy, was a guest in the house during his visit to Charleston in 1863. During the 1864 bombardment, Confederate General Beauregard used this home as his headquarters. The construction of this distinguished brick house began in 1817. Later additions in the Greek Revival style (1833 to 1836) and the Rococco Revival style (1857) created some of the finest rooms in antebellum Charleston. Many of the rooms maintain their original wallpaper and paint colors. The furnishings include original pieces, as well as other items purchased in New York for the 1833 remodeling.

Notable Collections on Exhibit

Collections on display include chandeliers purchased in Paris during the 1830s, a large painting of the governor's wife, and a statuary by American artists.

Heyward-Washington House

87 Church Street
Charleston, SC 29401
(803) 722-2996

Contact: The Charleston Museum

Open: Mon.-Sat. 10 a.m.–5 p.m.; Sun.
1–5 p.m.

Admission: Adults $5; children (3-12) $3.
Total tour ticket (includes Museum and
3 historic houses) $15. Guided tours.

Suggested Time to View House: 30 minutes

Description of Grounds: A formal garden
is planted with the flowers keeping with
the period of the house.

Best Season to View House: Spring

Year House Built: 1772

Style of Architecture: Brick

On-Site Parking: No **Wheelchair Access:** No

Description of House

The Heyward-Washington House was built in 1772 by Daniel Heyward, a prominent rice planter and father of Thomas Heyward, Jr., a signer for South Carolina of the Declaration of Independence. The house is also known for having been leased to George Washington during his visit to Charleston in 1791. The next owner, Judge Grimke purchased the house in 1803 and lived here with his wife and sister-in-law who were both active abolitionists. Over the following years the house was used alternately as a boarding house and a bakery until the Charleston Museum acquired it in 1929 and opened it to the public.

The architectural scale and interior detail of Daniel Heyward's brick double house are a reflection of his family's prosperity and prominence. It is the only 18th-century house open in the city with the original kitchen buildings, carriage house, and necessary in the courtyard. The house is completely furnished with magnificent Charleston-made furniture of the 18th-century period.

Notable Collections on Exhibit

The house contains a valuable collection of 18th-century Charleston-made furniture. The furniture's exceptional quality reflect the wealth and sophistication of the colonial city. The collection includes a rare piece known as the Holmes bookcase, considered one of the finest furnishings in existence.

Additional Information

A visit to the Heyward-Washington House may be combined with visits to the Joseph Manigault and Aiken-Rhett Houses as part of the Charleston Museum's historic houses tour.

Joseph Manigault House

Contact: The Charleston Museum

Open: Mon.-Sat. 10 a.m.–5 p.m.;
Sun. 1–5 p.m.

Admission: Adults $5; children (3-12) $3.
Total tour ticket (includes museum and
3 historic houses) $15. Guided tours

Suggested Time to View House: 30 minutes

Description of Grounds: A garden with a
charming gate temple

Best Season to View House: Spring

Year House Built: 1803

Style of Architecture: Adam style or
Federal

On-Site Parking: No **Wheelchair Access:** Yes

Description of House

The house was designed by gentleman-architect Gabriel Manigault for his brother, Joseph. Both men were wealthy low-country rice planters. A man of independent means, Gabriel was educated in Geneva and London, and owned a valuable library on architecture. He was the first Charleston architect in the modern acceptance of the term, in that he prepared designs which were executed by the builder.

The Joseph Manigault House was built in 1803, and is one of America's most beautiful examples of the graceful Adam style of architecture. The Adam style is also called Federal, and it appealed to many Americans because of its classical associations. In executing designs of Joseph's house, Gabriel Manigault demonstrated a thorough understanding of Adamesque principles as they related to architecture, with their emphasis on delicacy, intimacy, and variety of shape. The curving central stair accentuates the grace of the entrance hall. Well suited to Charleston's climate, the house has high ceilings, many windows, and two-story porches. The house is furnished with an outstanding collection of Charleston, American, English, and French pieces of the period.

Additional Information

For a reduced price, visitors may enter all three of the Charleston Museum's historic houses and the museum itself. The museum houses a wide range of exhibits—from objects found during archeological digs to exhibits pertaining to the region's natural science and cultural history. There is also a unique exhibit of Charleston silver by internationally renowned local silversmiths.

Hampton-Preston Mansion and Garden

1615 Blanding Street
Columbia, SC 29201
(803) 252-7742

Contact: Historic Columbia Foundation

Open: Tues.-Sat 10:15 a.m.–3:15 p.m.;
Sun. 1:15 p.m.-4:15 p.m. Closed
mid-Dec.-Jan.2 and major holidays

Admission: $3. Guided tours.

Suggested Time to View House: 45 minutes

Description of Grounds: Gardens are
being restored using important
horticultural records as
documentation.

Year House Built: 1818 to 1835

Description of House

The Hampton-Preston House has been the home of two of South Carolina's most prominent families, a Union Headquarters during the Civil War, the Governor's mansion during the reconstruction period, and later a fashionable school for young ladies.

The house is restored to its antebellum period (1835-1855) when it was occupied by the Hampton and Preston families. The exterior changed considerably over the years from brick to stucco with a piazza addition. The drawing room reflects the Continental taste of Caroline Hampton. The mantlepiece was carved in Italy by the renowned American sculptor, Hiram Powers, who was the protegé of Mrs. Preston. A handsome spiral staircase leads to the upper floors. The majority of the furnishings on display belonged to the Hampton family.

An elaborate four-acre garden with greenhouses, fountains and statuary surrounded the house until 1947 when the garden was destroyed. Presently, the garden is being recreated as funds become available.

Notable Collections on Exhibit

On display are Hampton family furnishings and the personal possessions and memorabilia of the three famous men who bore the name Wade Hampton.

Mann-Simons Cottage – Museum of African-American Culture

1403 Richland Street
Columbia, SC 29201
(803) 252-7742

Contact: Historic Columbia Foundation

Open: Tues.-Sat 10:15 a.m.–3:15 p.m. Closed mid-Dec.-Jan. 2 and major holidays

Admission: $3. Guided tours; Jubilee Festival in Sept.; special programs during Black History Month; candlelight tour.

Suggested Time to View House: 45 minutes

Facilities on Premises: Gift shop

Description of Grounds: Located in downtown Columbia

Best Season to View House: Summer

Number of Yearly Visitors: 4,000

Year House Built: 1850

Style of Architecture: Antebellum cottage

Number of Rooms: 8

On-Site Parking: Yes **Wheelchair Access:** No

Description of House

The Mann-Simons Cottage represents how free blacks of Columbia's antebellum period lived and worked. The building is the only historic house museum in the Columbia area with roots in the antebellum black community. The movement to preserve and restore the cottage was led by the Richland County Historic Preservation Commission and the Center for Black History, Art and Folklore.

The house's historical importance began when it was bought in 1850 by Celia Mann, a Charleston slave, who purchased her freedom and walked to Columbia. The residence which she established remained in her family for over a hundred years. She was a midwife and an active member of the First Calvary Baptist Church, organized in the basement of her house. After the Civil War, her son-in-law, Bill Simons, a carpenter and prominent musician, lived in the house which passed in time to his brother, Charles Simons. Charles's heirs owned the property until 1970 when it was purchased by the Columbia Housing Authority. Fortunately, this antebellum cottage, located in downtown Columbia, has been able to remain at its original site. The house has been restored to its 1880 appearance with a raised basement, gabled roof and two corbel capped chimneys. The asymmetrical dormers are indicative of a novice builder. The furnishings of the house consist mainly of donated period pieces and a few family-owned pieces.

Notable Collections on Exhibit

The main floor is a house museum containing several family artifacts and furnishings. On the ground floor is a gallery and gift shop displaying art and crafts by black artists.

Robert Mills Historic House and Park

**1616 Blanding Street
Columbia, SC 29201
(803) 252-7742**

Contact: Historic Columbia Foundation
Open: Tues.-Sat 10:15 a.m.–3:15 p.m.; Sun.
1:15 p.m.-4:15 p.m. Closed mid
Dec.-Jan. 2 and major holidays
Admission: $3. Guided tours.
Suggested Time to View House: 45 minutes
Description of Grounds: Formal gardens
Year House Built: c.1823
Style of Architecture: Greek Revival

Description of House

Robert Mills, a native Charlestonian, the first architect for the Federal government and designer of the Washington Monument, planned this house in 1823 for Ainsley Hall, a prominent Columbia merchant. Hall died before the house was completed; the property was purchased by the Presbyterian Theological Seminary and, thereafter, housed religious institutions until 1961 when it was threatened with demolition. An heroic effort by historic preservationists saved the house and, guided by Mills's manuscripts in the South Carolina library and historic American building survey documents in Washington, authentically restored the house, rebuilt the three outbuildings and developed the four-acre grounds.

The elegant principle story with its curved walls, matching drawing rooms and decorative niches are indicative of Mills's style. The marble mantelpieces, silver door knobs and locksets, handsome chandeliers, Venetian windows and plasterwork ornamentation are enhanced by a fine collection of Regency furniture of the fashionable Greek Revival period. Many of the furnishings have been used by former state governors and include 19th-century pieces and reproductions.

Woodrow Wilson Boyhood Home

1705 Hampton Street
Columbia, SC 29201
(803) 252-7742

Contact: Historic Columbia Foundation

Open: Tues.-Sat 10:15 a.m.–3:15 p.m.; Sun. 1:15 p.m.-4:15 p.m. Closed mid-Dec.-Jan. 2 and major holidays

Admission: $3. Guided tours

Suggested Time to View House: 45 minutes

Description of Grounds: In the front gardens a large tea olive plant and several magnolia trees remain from Mrs. Wilson's plantings.

Year House Built: c. 1872

Style of Architecture: Tuscan Villa

Description of House

Thomas Woodrow Wilson, the twenty-eighth President of the United States, lived in Columbia for only four years, but they were important teenage years. Three of those years, from 1872 to 1874, were spent in this house. Wilson's father, Joseph, was a Presbyterian minister and the family was forced to move often. This was the only home that the Wilsons ever owned. Young Tommy witnessed in Columbia a town, still occupied by Federal troops, rebuilding itself after the aftermath of its wartime conflagration. The time the Wilsons spent in Columbia seem to have meant a great deal to the family as the Wilson's parents are buried in the Columbia's First Presbyterian Church yard.

This Tuscan Villa-style house, of the type made popular by Andrew Downing Jackson, was built by Wilson's parents in 1872. The house is an excellent example of a minister's Victorian home. Remnants of gas lighting fixtures remain and the marbleized mantels are original to the house. The late 19th-century furnishings represent the period of the Wilson family occupancy.

Notable Collections on Exhibit

A collection of furniture includes the bed in which the future President was born, his mother's bureau, bedside table, and a four volume set of the Bible, a gift from her husband.

Magnolia Dale

P.O. Box 174, 320 Norris Street
Edgefield, SC 29824
(803) 637-5239

Contact: Edgefield County
Historical Society
Open: Hours by appointment
Admission: $2. Guided tours,
also available for rent for
parties, receptions, and
meetings.
Year House Built: 1837
Style of Architecture: Greek Classic
Revival

Description of House

Magnolia Dale has had a long and varied history of ownership. The mansion was built by Erasmus Youngblood, the grandson of the founder of Edgefield, Arthur Simkins. The house has also been known as the Alfred Norris House, an owner who bought the property in 1873 and made substantial alterations to enlarge the house to its present form. Magnolia Dale was also the home of South Carolina's lieutenant governor James H. Tillman.

The mansion is a fine example of Greek Classic Revival architecture. The house has four spacious rooms with a large center hallway downstairs that has been restored. The main floor has been furnished with pieces of significance to the period and Edgefield County.

Additional Information

The house serves as headquarters for the Edgefield County Historical Society. It is maintained as a museum with reception rooms restored for meetings and social functions of the society and is also available to other groups and organizations. Tours may be arranged by request by contacting (803) 637-3056.

Oakley Park

300 Columbia Road
Edgefield, SC 29824
(803) 637-4027

Contact: The United Daughter of the Confederacy

Open: Thurs. and Sat. 10 a.m.–4 p.m. and by appointment

Activities: Group tours and luncheons by request

Description of Grounds: Oakley Park's original garden of annuals still flourishes in the oval around the driveway.

Year House Built: 1835

Description of House

The beauty of Oakley Park has been well documented in paintings and today it serves as a wonderful museum of the Confederacy. Built by Daniel Bird in 1835, Oakley Park has also been called the "Red Shirt Shrine" because of a famous incident which occurred during Reconstruction. From the balcony of Oakley Park, General Martin Gary rallied the Red Shirts and rode with Douschka Pickens, South Carolina's "Joan of Arc," and led them 1,500 strong to Edgefield Village in 1876. The Red Shirts, led by an invincible trio of General Gary, General M.C. Buster and General Wade Hampton, were successful in the campaign which elected Wade Hampton as governor of South Carolina in 1876, thereby ending the power of the Reconstructionists in South Carolina.

As was local tradition, the home was built on high pillars "to lift it above fevers lurking in the miasma of low mist and fog." The most inviting part of Oakley Park is its large main hall, opening on a front and rear piazza through double doors with fanlights. Hall paneling is hand carved in delicate design on an archway beyond which stairs mount to a second floor having a similar main hall. Four bedrooms open onto this second floor hallway. Many of the furnishings belonged to previous owners, others have been donated as gifts.

Notable Collections on Exhibit

The house exhibits many interesting items of the Confederate period including furniture, an original Red Shirt, Confederate swords and other relics.

The Harold Kaminski House

1003 Front Street
Georgetown, SC 29841

Contact: Historic Georgetown
Open: Mon.-Fri. 10 a.m.–5 p.m.
Admission: $4. Guided tours.

Description of Grounds: Situated on a bluff of land overlooking the Sampit River.
Year House Built: c. 1760
Style of Architecture: Town House

Description of House

The Kaminski House reflects both Georgetown's ancient ties to, and Harold Kaminski's deep love of, the sea. Kaminski was a retired naval officer and former Mayor of Georgetown. He lived here with his wife for many years; the house was bequeathed to the city of Georgetown by Mrs. Kaminski in 1972.

The Kaminski House is one of Georgetown's oldest town houses. This two-story house is typical of so many low-country houses of this era, it sits perpendicular to Front Street on a bluff with a terraced lawn which goes to the edge of the Sampit River. A wide piazza extending the length of the house offers a commanding view of the river. The house is furnished with many heirloom pieces of matchless beauty.

Notable Collections on Exhibit

Of special interest is the magnificent collection of furniture which includes a 15th-century Spanish chest made of oak and walnut, a mahogany grandfather's clock, and a pair of Acajou French Empire side chairs. The dining room displays a mahogany Chippendale design banquet table running almost the entire length of the room with seventeen Duncan Phyfe chairs with carved leaves and pierced slat backs, and an American Empire sideboard. The library contains a Chinese sacrificial table of the Ming Dynasty, where bowls of rice were placed in ancestral worship ceremonies.

Additional Information

Visitors to the historic Georgetown area should also visit the nearby Hopsewee Plantation, a former rice plantation, and Wicklow Hall (Cat Island Road), a restored plantation house where Confederate General Rawlins Lowndes lived.

Hopsewee Plantation

Rt. 2-Box 205
Georgetown, SC 29440
(803) 546-7891

Contact: Hopsewee Plantation

Open: March-Oct.: Tues.-Fri.
10 a.m.–5 p.m.; Nov.-Feb. by
appointment only

Admission: Adults $5; children (6-18) $2.
Tour of house from attic to cellar.

Description of Grounds: The 75-acre
grounds feature wooded trails along the
North Santee River

Year House Built: 1740

Style of Architecture: Clapboard
plantation house

Description of House

Both Thomas Lynch, Sr. and Thomas Jr. were distinguished political figures and were the only father and son of the same family serving in the Continental Congress. Thomas Jr. was a signer of the Declaration of Independence. However, Thomas, Sr. suffered a stroke and could not write his name. There is space left on the document for his signature.

The house is a typical low-country rice plantation dwelling of the early 18th-century, with four rooms opening into a wide center hall on each floor, a full brick cellar and attic rooms. The house has a lovely staircase; there is handcarved molding in each room, and the random-width heart pine floors are almost one-and-one half inches thick. Constructed on a brick foundation that is covered by scored tabby, the house is built of black cypress, which probably accounts for the fact that it is basically the same house the Lynches built over 250 years ago.

Hopsewee, a National Historic Landmark, is a preservation rather than a restoration and has never been allowed to fall into decay as it has always been cherished. Only four families have owned it, although it was built almost forty years before the Revolutionary War. Today, the house contains many fine period furnishings.

Additional Information

Hopsewee Plantation offers visitors a quiet interlude among beautiful surroundings. From the house, there is a impressive vista of the golden river and the green and gray of moss-hung trees.

Hampton Plantation

1950 Rutledge Road
McClellanville, SC 29458
(803) 546-9361

Contact: Hampton Plantation State Park

Open: Year-round, Sat.-Sun. 1–4 p.m.;
April 1-Labor Day, Thurs.-Mon. 1–4 p.m.

Admission: Adults $2; youths (6-16) $1;
South Carolina seniors and children
(under 5) free. Guided tours,
audiovisual programs, special events.

Description of Grounds: Extensive trails
through landscaped gardens, rice fields,
and low country wetlands with rice
fields

Year House Built: 1730s

Style of Architecture: Georgian with
Adam-style portico

Description of House

The halls of the Hampton Plantation have welcomed famous patriots, soldiers, and politicians for two and a half centuries, including George Washington, Lafayette, and Francis Marion. Its owners have included members of South Carolina's most prominent families—the Horrys, Pinckneys, and Rutledges. Its final resident was Archibald Rutledge, beloved author and South Carolina's first poet laureate.

The colossal Adam-style portico at the entrance of the mansion is one of the finest and earliest examples of its kind in North America. The portico is framed with black cyprus and has yellow pine columns. The mansion's interior, purposely left unfurnished, highlights the structure's architectural and construction details. Cutaway sections of the walls and ceilings show the building's evolution from a simple farmhouse to a grand mansion. Exposed timber framing, hand-carved mantels, and delicately wrought hinges and hardware reveal the 18th-century builder's strength. Hampton Plantation has been designated a national historic landmark.

Notable Collections on Exhibit

Hampton exhibits a collection of eighteen first editions Rutledge titles, many of which are autographed. In addition, there is a fine display of Delft tiles.

Additional Information

The grounds surrounding the mansion offer unique opportunities to examine the wildlife of Carolina low country. Cypress swamps, abandoned rice fields and forests of pines and hardwoods are home to a wide variety of flora and fauna. From the massive live oaks to the variety of wild flowers and shrubs, Hampton Plantation is truly a naturalist's and photographer's delight in all seasons of the year.

Historic Brattonsville

1444 Brattonsville Road
McConnells, SC 29726
(803) 684-2327

Contact: York County Historical Commission
Open: March-Nov., Tues. and Thur.
10 a.m.–4 p.m., Sat.-Sun. 2–5 p.m.
Admission: Adults $2; students $1. Guided tours.

Suggested Time to View House: 90 minutes
Facilities on Premises: Museum shop
Best Season to View House: Spring
Number of Yearly Visitors: 20,000
Year House Built: 1776 to 1870s

Description of House

Colonel William Bratton led a rebel force to victory over a British and Tory troops under the command of Captain Christian Huck. Colonel William and Martha Bratton's youngest child, Dr. John Simpson Bratton (1789-1843), significantly increased the acreage, the slave population, and the production of cotton, livestock, and grains on the plantation.

Historic Brattonsville is a restored village of 18th and 19th-century structures developed over several generations by members of the Bratton family. On the tour, visitors will see a replica of a 1750s dirt floor "backwoodsman" cabin, the restored "Scotch Irish" McConnell family cabin, the oldest documented structure in York County, the Ladd's Female Academy, and an authentic antebellum plantation home. There are also many hand-hewn log storage buildings and a brick slave cabin. The restored homes are furnished in period fashion, and collections from the Bratton family are displayed.

Notable Collections on Exhibit

This historic village displays southern pieces of furniture, textiles, and household equipment including a wooden biscuit press, walnut huntboard, tin bath tub, and hundreds of other authentic items.

Boone Hall Plantation

1054 Long Point Road
Mount Pleasant, SC
(803) 884-4371

Contact: Boone Hall Plantation

Open: April-Labor Day, Mon.-Sat.,
8:30 a.m.-6:30 p.m.; Sun. 1–5 p.m., Labor
Day-March, Mon.-Sat. 9 a.m.–5 p.m.,
Sun. 1–4 p.m., closed Thanksgiving day
and Christmas day

Admission: Adults $7.50; children $3;
seniors $6. Guided tours, special events.

Suggested Time to View House: 1 hour

Facilities on Premises: Welcome center

Description of Grounds: Formal gardens
of camellias and azaleas

Best Season to View House: Year round

Number of Yearly Visitors: 20,000

Year House Built: 1750

On-Site Parking: Yes **Wheelchair Access:** Yes

Description of House

This impressive mansion was built on land first acquired John Boone, one of the first settlers of the area. The land was originally run as a cotton plantation. The plantation also produced bricks and tiles, many of which were used in nearby Charleston buildings. A retired Canadian diplomat named Thomas Stone purchased the property in 1935 and built a new main house utilizing as much of the old mansion as possible. In 1939, this classic antebellum mansion played an important role in the film version of *Gone With The Wind.*

The road leading to the entrance of Boone Hall is one of its most striking features. The three-quarter mile long avenue is lined with moss draped oak trees. The 1935 reconstruction maintained many of the original plantation-made bricks and tiles as well as the woodwork and flooring from the earlier house. Many of the original outbuildings are still located on the property. These include the smokehouse, nine slave cabins, and the lime and oyster-shell foundation of the boatdock.

Additional Information

Boone Hall wonderfully evokes the feeling of the old South with its spectacular entranceway and lovely formal gardens surrounding the mansion. The gardens have herringbone-patterned walkways weaving between the flowerbeds for visitors to enjoy after their tour of the mansion.

Walnut Grove Plantation

1200 Ott's Shoal Road
Roebuck, SC 29376
(803) 576-6546

Contact: Spartanburg Co. Historical
Association
Open: April 1–Oct. 31, Tues-Sat.,
11 a.m.–5 p.m.; year round, Sun.
2–5 p.m.; by appointment all year
Admission: Adults $3.50; children $2;
seniors $3; groups $2.50. Guided tours,
family festival, weaving demonstrations.
Suggested Time to View House: 75 minutes
Facilities on Premises: Welcome center
Description of Grounds: Family cemetery,
herb garden, nature trail
Best Season to View House: Year round
Number of Yearly Visitors: 12,000
Year House Built: 1765

On-Site Parking: Yes **Wheelchair Access:** Yes

Description of House

Walnut Grove Plantation is built on land granted to Charles Moore by King George III when this section of South Carolina was the western frontier. His wife, Kate, acted as a scout for General Daniel Morgan during the American Revolution.

The Georgian-style main house has double-shouldered chimneys, clapboard-over-log construction, fielded paneling and Queen Anne mantels. The documented collection of antique furnishings and accessories vividly portrays living conditions in Spartanburg County prior to 1830. The other buildings on the site include the separate kitchen, Rocky Spring Academy, a schoolhouse which signalled the beginning of formal education in the area, the blacksmith's forge, the wheat house, the meat house, the barn sheltering a Conestoga-type wagon, the well house with its dry cooling-cellar, and the office of Dr. Andrew Barry Moore, the county's first doctor.

Notable Collections on Exhibit

The Walnut Grove Plantation houses a fascinating collection of 18th-century gadgets and utensils, old tools, and other artifacts.

Thomas Price House

1200 Oak View Farms
Woodruff, SC 29388
(803) 576-6546

Contact: Spartanburg Co. Historical
Association
Open: April 1-Oct. 31, Tues-Sat.
11 a.m.–5 p.m.; year round, Sun.
2–5 p.m.; by appointment all year
Admission: Adults $2.50; children (6-18)
$1.50; seniors $2; groups (10 or more)
$1.50. Guided tours, spring concert,
Easter egg hunt
Suggested Time to View House: 75 minutes
Facilities on Premises: Rest rooms
Description of Grounds: Double D
boxwood design at front of house with
a view of surrounding valley
Best Season to View House: Year round
Number of Yearly Visitors: 12,000
Year House Built: 1795

On-Site Parking: Yes **Wheelchair Access:** Yes

Description of House

Thomas Price built this house on his 2,000 acre plantation around 1795. Besides farming with his twenty-eight slaves, he also ran the post office, a general store and he had a license to operate a "house of entertainment", that is, to feed and house travelers who came by on the stage coach.

The brick house with its steep gambrel roof and inside end chimneys is most unusual for this section of the country. The bricks for the house were made on the premises, then laid in a Flemish bond pattern which produced walls nearly eighteen inches thick. The kitchen was added around 1820. The Price House exhibits a fine collection of period furniture which has been selected according to a forty-two page inventory found in the Spartanburg County probate judge's office.

Notable Collections on Exhibit

In addition to the period furnishings, the house exhibits several pieces of Thomas Price's artifacts including his original journals.

Tennessee

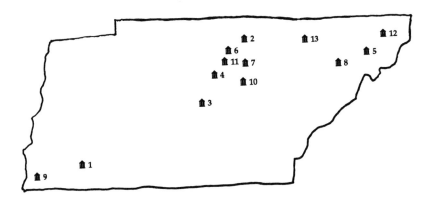

1. **Bolivar**
   The Pillars

2. **Castalian Springs**
   Cragfront
   Wynnewood

3. **Columbia**
   The Athenaeum Rectory
   James K. Polk Ancestral Home

4. **Franklin**
   Carter House
   Carnton Plantation

5. **Greeneville**
   Andrew Johnson National Historic Site

6. **Hendersonville**
   Rock Castle

7. **Hermitage**
   The Hermitage: Home of Andrew Jackson

8. **Knoxville**
   Armstrong-Lockett House
   Ramsey House
   Blount Mansion
   Bleak House (Confederate Memorial Hall)

9. **Memphis**
   Woodruff-Fontaine House

10. **Murfreesboro**
    Oaklands Historic House Museum

11. **Nashville**
    Belle Meade Plantation
    Belmont Mansion

12. **Piney Flats**
    Rocky Mount

13. **Rugby**
    Kingstone Lisle

The Pillars

Washington Street
Bolivar, TN 38008
(615) 658-3600

Contact: Association for the Preservation of
Tennessee Antiquities

Open: By appointment only, contact the
Chamber of Commerce at (901)-658-6554

Admission: Adults $3; children (under 12)
$.50. Guided tours.

Suggested Time to View House: 1 hour

Description of Grounds: Landscaped
grounds with several original
outbuildings

Best Season to View House: Summer-fall

Year House Built: c. 1828

On-Site Parking: Yes

Number of Rooms: 12

Style of Architecture: Federal with Greek
Revival additions

Description of House

The Pillars was home to John Houston Bills, a prosperous businessman who made his fortune in the cotton factoring industry. He married Prudence Polk McNeal in 1823, and the young couple purchased their first home known as the Pillars from a cousin. Today the house is the oldest dwelling still standing in Bolivar. From its beginnings, the home has been host to such notable guests as Andrew Jackson, Davy Crockett, Sam Houston, James K. Polk, and Jefferson Davis.

The original structure was a small, brick Federal home and when Bills bought it, he immediately set about enlarging and aggrandizing it. As one of the richest men in western Tennessee, Bills was well able to afford the improvements and fine furnishings. The home was turned into an elegant dwelling: a one-and-a-half story, L-shaped, six-bay facade, made of brick with a columned veranda and low gable. Whether by design or accident, the eight fluted Doric columns on the veranda were installed upside down.

Additional Information

Bolivar is also the site of the Little Courthouse on East Market Street. Built in 1824, this building is the oldest courthouse still standing in West Tennessee, and is one of three remaining log courthouses in the country.

Cragfront

Route 1, Box 73
Castalian Springs, TN 37031
(615) 452-7070

Contact: Association for the Preservation of
Tennessee Antiquities

Open: April 15-Nov. 1, Tues.-Sat.
10 a.m.–5 p.m., Sun. 1–5 p.m.; Nov.
1-April 15, call for appointment

Admission: Adults $3; children (under 12)
$.50; groups (30 or more) $1.50 per
person. Guided tours.

Suggested Time to View House: 1 hour

Description of Grounds: The grounds
feature a restored garden with a pond
and a gazebo.

Best Season to View House: Summer-fall

Year House Built: 1798-1802

Style of Architecture: Late Georgian

Number of Rooms: 12

On-Site Parking: Yes

Description of House

Started in 1798 and completed in 1802 by General James Winchester, Cragfront was the finest mansion house on the Tennessee frontier. The General named his mansion "Cragfront" because it stood on a rocky bluff with a spring at the base. Winchester was a Revolutionary War officer, Brigadier General in the War of 1812, and a founder of Memphis. Among the notable guests at Cragfront during the General's life were Andrew Jackson, Sam Houston, and the Marquis de Lafayette. Until 1864, the house was occupied by members of the Winchester family, and many members of the family, including the General and his wife, are buried in the cemetery to the rear of the house.

To build his fine home, Winchester brought stone masons, carpenters, and joiners 600 miles through the wilderness from his native Maryland. The T-shaped Cragfront contains a number of unusual architectural details including seven iron stars used as anchor plates for iron rods extending from the front to the rear to strengthen and tie the structure together. Other interesting features include the original stenciling on the parlor walls, a cantilevered staircase with stippled risers, and a large second floor ballroom, the first in Tennessee country. The galleries on each side of the ballroom provide beautiful views of the restored garden and the rolling countryside. The house is furnished with authentic American Federal antiques, some of which are original Winchester pieces.

Notable Collections on Exhibit

In addition to the collection of Federal furniture, the basement contains a typical weaving room, a wine cellar, and a collection of farm and carpentry tools of the early 1800s.

Wynnewood

Castalian Springs, TN 37031
(615) 452-5463

Contact: State of Tennessee

Open: Year round: Mon.-Sat.
10 a.m.–4 p.m., Sun. 1–5 p.m.; closed
Sun. from Nov. 1-April 1

Admission: Adults $3; seniors $2.50;
children (12-18) $1.50; children (under
12) $.50. Tours

Best Season to View House: Year round

Year House Built: 1828

Style of Architecture: Log structure

Description of House

Wynnewood may have been the largest log structure ever erected in Tennessee, and it is by far the largest to survive to this time. The building began in 1828 as a stagecoach stop, and, in 1834, A.R. Wynne purchased the interest of his two partners. He and his family moved into the inn and resided there until his death in 1893. A.R. Wynne received guests at Wynnewood throughout his lifetime. By the 1840s he had built a row of cottages on the lawn east of the inn and set up a race course in the bottom near Lick Creek. Most guests were attracted by the medicinal qualities of the mineral waters but one frequent visitor, Andrew Jackson, was attracted by the race course and he usually brought a favorite thoroughbred to run against one of Wynne's horses. Ownership of Wynnewood remained in the family until 1971 when George Winchester Wynne, grandson of the builder, conveyed it to the state of Tennessee for preservation as a historic site.

The large main house is 142 feet long with an open hallway or dog-trot through the center. Some of the logs composing the walls, which are set firmly on a stone foundation, are thirty-two feet long. Most of them are oak, some walnut and others ash, but none of the original logs are the commonly used poplar. All rooms have outside doors and are entered from the gallery that extends 110 feet across the back of the building. An outside stairway rises to the upstairs rooms from the dog-trot. The furnishings have been collected and are appropriate for the mid 19th century.

Additional Information

Mineral springs at Wynnewood formerly constituted a sulphur lick that was discovered in 1772 by Isaac Bledsoe, a hunter and explorer from southwest Virginia. It immediately became known as Bledsoe's Lick. When Bledsoe discovered the lick, there were so many buffalo in the area of the springs that he was afraid to dismount from his horse for fear of being trampled to death. Long before this time, the Woodland Indians had lived in a fortified village in the flat bottom land immediately north of the lick.

The Athenaeum Rectory

Athenaeum Street, P.O. Box 942
Columbia, TN 38402
(615) 381-4822

Contact: Association for the Preservation of Tennessee Antiquities

Open: May-Aug., Mon.-Fri.
10 a.m.–4:30 p.m., and by appointment

Admission: Adults $2; seniors $1.75; students (6-18) $1; children (under 6) free; groups (10 or more) $1.75. Guided tours, also used for receptions and meetings.

Suggested Time to View House: 1 hour

Description of Grounds: The rectory is part of the 16-acre Athenaeum School complex.

Best Season to View House: Summer

Year House Built: 1835

Style of Architecture: Gothic

Number of Rooms: 6 open to public

On-Site Parking: Yes

Description of House

Although the Athenaeum is best known as one the of South's finest finishing schools for girls, the rectory was first built as a home for Samuel Walker Polk, the nephew of the future President. Polk never lived here as he left for Washington to serve as a secretary to his uncle the year the house was finished. The first occupants of the house were the Reverend Franklin Gillette Smith and his family. Reverend Smith was the founder of the prestigious girls school, and a loyal supporter of the Confederacy. In 1865, he returned from fighting in the war and resumed his work running the school. He died just one year later and his wife, Sarah, continued to run the school. The school remained in the Smith family until 1904, and the rectory remained with the family until 1973.

As the main reception room for the school, the Gothic-style Rectory was decorated in keeping with the prestige of the school and its students. A French marble fountain graces the front lawn as visitors enter the house. In the center reception room the side panels are of "flashed glass" which contained gold and were made in Europe. The house contains three parlors and three bedrooms, but no kitchen as the family always ate at the school. Other notable features in the house include stained glass panes surrounding the rear door, a chandelier made of pewter and copper and other metals, a large Gothic gold-leaf mirror, and beautiful wood floors made of hardrock maple.

Many of the furnishings on display belonged to the Smith family and include a ten-piece parlor set made by Joseph Meeks in Philadelphia in 1840s, and a marble bust of George Washington. The harp in the front parlor is identical to the ones used by the girls at the school.

Notable Collections on Exhibit
The rectory displays fine architectural details and a fine collection of period furniture and portraits. Most of the items on display were gifts of the family or others from the area and all date from the 19th century.

Additional Information
Each year the Athenaeum sponsors the Majestic Middle Tennessee tour with visits to more than ten historic homes including Rippovilla, Rattle and Snap, and Persimmon Ridge, as well as other historic sites in the area. Please contact (615)-381-4822 for more information.

James K. Polk Ancestral Home

301 West 7th Street
Columbia, TN 38401
(615) 388-2354

Contact: James K. Polk Memorial
   Association
Open: Mon.-Sat. 9 a.m.–5 p.m. (April-Oct.),
   9 a.m.–4 p.m. (Nov.-March), Sun.,
   1–5 p.m. (all year); closed Thanksgiving,
   Dec. 24 and 25, New Years Day
Admission: Adults $2.50; students (ages
   6-18) $1; children (under 6) free. Guided
   tours, video programs, special exhibits.
Suggested Time to View House: 45 minutes
Facilities on Premises: Museum shop
Description of Grounds: The grounds
   include a reconstructed kitchen building
   and a formal boxwood garden.
Best Season to View House: Spring
Year House Built: 1816
Number of Rooms: 6

Number of Yearly Visitors: 10,000-12,000
Style of Architecture: Federal
On-Site Parking: Yes **Wheelchair Access:** Yes

Description of House

The two story, painted brick house was the residence of James K. Polk's parents. James lived there from 1818 to 1824 while he began his political and legal career. He went on to become the eleventh President. During his one-term administration from 1845 to 1849, the United States annexed over 800,000 square miles of territory including California and the Oregon Territory.

Today the house exhibits belongings of President Polk from several of his residences including the White House. Though the rooms are representative of the period 1820 to 1850, the home is a Polk museum rather than an exact recreation of a specific house at a specific time. Most of the furnishings were originally Polk possessions. To fully furnish the house, the Polk Association has added other appropriate pieces from the period such as bedclothes and household utensils.

Notable Collections on Exhibit

Original Polk furnishings include matching sofas and chairs made of rosewood and red velvet, a mahogany center table with a marble inlay top, an English pianoforte, a White House day bed, French vases and mantel clocks, Honore and Haviland china, and ormolu Empire chandeliers. Personal belongings include President Polk's trunks and law books, and Mrs. Polk's portable desk, ball gowns, and hand painted inaugural fan. Among the site's documentary artifacts are the Polk family Bible, a White House account book, daguerreotypes of President and Mrs. Polk and of Polk's Cabinet (the earliest known photograph of the White House interior).

Carter House

1140 Columbia Avenue
Franklin, TN 37064
(615) 791-1861

Contact: Association for the Preservation of
Tennessee Antiquities
Open: April-Nov., Mon.-Sat. 9 a.m.–5 p.m.,
Sun. 1—5 p.m.; Nov.-March, Mon.-Sat.
9 a.m.–5 p.m., Sun. 1—4 p.m.
Admission: Adults $3, children (under 13)
$1, group rates available. Guided tours,
museum, video presentation and
battlerama
Suggested Time to View House: 1 hour
Facilities on Premises: Sales desk
Description of Grounds: Located on an
historic battlefield
Best Season to View House: Summer-Fall
Year House Built: 1830
Number of Rooms: 5

Style of Architecture: Brick frame
On-Site Parking: Yes **Wheelchair Access:** Yes

Description of House

The Carter House was built by Fountain Branch Carter, a member of a prominent Virginia family. This simple brick house was used as a Union command post and witnessed one of the bloodiest battles of the Civil War, the Battle of Franklin. The Carter family hid in the cellar while the battle waged overhead. Considered a turning point in a decisive campaign, the battle lead to the rapid downfall of the Confederacy. The heavy casualties totaled 2,326 Union troops and 6,252 Confederates, including twelve generals and Captain Tod Carter, the Carter family's youngest son. The house today still exhibits damage incurred during the bloody battle.

Notable Collections on Exhibit

In addition to the 19th-century furnishings in the house, the adjoining museum holds many treasures and relics of the Civil War as well as a video showing a recreation of the Battle of Franklin.

Additional Information

Visitors to Franklin are also encouraged to visit another home which also witnessed the battle, the Carnation Plantation, located a few miles from the Carter House (just follow the signs). Carnton Plantation served as a hospital for the wounded during the battle; the estate contains a cemetery for Confederate soldiers killed in action.

Carnton Plantation

1345 Carnton Lane
Franklin, TN 37064
(615) 794-0903

Contact: Carton Association, Inc.

Open: Mon.-Sat., 9 a.m.–4 p.m.; Sun.,
1–4 p.m.; closed all major holidays

Admission: Adults, $3; children, $1.50;
seniors, $2.50; groups (20 or more), $2
each. Guided tours

Suggested Time to View House: 1 hour

Description of Grounds: Confederate
cemetery with attached family
cemetery and springhouse

Best Season to View House: Spring

Year House Built: c. 1826

Style of Architecture: Greek Revival

Number of Rooms: 11

On-Site Parking: Yes **Wheelchair Access:** Yes

Description of House

The Carnton Plantation was considered one of the most elegant estates in the area. The mansion was built as a retirement home for an early mayor of Nashville, Randal McGavrock. The McGavock family owned Carnton from 1826 until 1911 when it was sold to Judge Shelton and his family. During the Civil War, the house achieved recognition as the backdrop for the intense Battle of Franklin in November of 1864. The house was used as a field hospital for several days following the battle, and blood stains on the wooden floors are a constant reminder of that brutal time. The family also donated two acres of land to be used as a Confederate cemetery which visitors may see today. The plantation was later owned by four other families until it was acquired by the Carnton Association in 1978.

The house's original architecture was of the Federal style, subsequently, in the late 1840s, it was changed to the Greek revival style with the addition of a front portico and a back veranda extending the full length of the house. Most of the furnishings date from the period from 1830 to 1870. Only a few pieces are original to the house.

Andrew Johnson National Historic Site

P.O. Box 1088
Greeneville, TN 37744

Contact: National Park Service
Open: Daily 9 a.m.–5 p.m., closed on
    Christmas Day

Activities:. Tours; biographical exhibits
Year House Built: Homestead-c. 1850
Number of Rooms: 10

Description of House

On April 15, 1865, following Lincoln's assassination, Andrew Johnson, became the seventeenth President of the United States. Johnson's life was one of extremely humble beginnings; at the age of sixteen he ran away from his home in Raleigh, North Carolina. A self-taught man, Johnson learned to read through his work as a tailor's apprentice. He belonged to a breed of politicians who made their mark by delivering fiery speeches and was known to hold crowds spellbound. President Johnson's administration was shaped by the recurrent theme of his public career—a strong belief in the Constitution. He vetoed the Civil Rights Act, the 14th Amendment, the statehood for Nebraska and Colorado, bills whose constitutionality he questioned. All of these vetoes were overridden with the exception of the Colorado admission. Amid the political turmoil Johnson managed to reopen seaports, federal courts, and post offices in the South. His most far-reaching achievement, the purchase of Alaska from Russia in 1867, remained unappreciated until long after Johnson left office.

Johnson and his wife, Eliza McArdle, lived in this modest homestead beginning in 1851. Today there are ten rooms, furnished with original family possessions, open to visitors. Less than a half a mile away is the national cemetery where Andrew and Eliza Johnson are buried with other family members. A marble memorial has likenesses of the Constitution and the Bible; an American Eagle perches on top. A replica of Johnson's birth home in Raleigh, North Carolina, is located nearby at Tusculum College in Greeneville. The birthplace displays historical objects and documents related to Johnson's time. In addition, the visitor's center houses the tailor shop that Johnson bought in 1831.

Rock Castle

139 Rock Castle Lane
Hendersonville, TN 37075
(615) 824-0502

Contact: Historic Rock Castle

Open: Feb.-Dec., Wed.-sat., 10 a.m.–4 p.m.,
Sun., 1–4 p.m.; closed major holidays

Admission: Adults, $3; seniors, $2.50;
children (6-12), $1.50; under 6, free.
Guided tours, special programs,
lectures, Christmas open house, summer
symphony concerts

Suggested Time to View House: 1 hour

Description of Grounds: Very scenic
grounds overlooking the lake

Best Season to View House: All year
except Jan.

Number of Yearly Visitors: 9,000

Year House Built: c. 1780s

Number of Rooms: 7

Style of Architecture: Modified Federal

On-Site Parking: Yes **Wheelchair Access:** No

Description of House

Five generations of the Smith family have lived in Rock Castle since it was first built in the late 18th century. A Virginia native, Daniel Smith and his wife, Sarah Michie, settled upon the "western waters" of Virginia where he was appointed deputy surveyor of Augusta County in 1773. In 1774, he became a captain in the company militia in Fincastle County and aided in defending the frontier during the American Revolution. He assisted in drawing up the "resolutions of liberty" in 1775 and, after serving in the Revolutionary War in a variety of different military and political offices, emigrated with his family to the Cumberland settlement. There he became a prominent figure in the development of America's newest frontier.

Rock Castle was the first house of masonry constructed in the Middle Tennessee area and probably took ten to twelve years to complete. The Federal-style architecture is typical of houses built in Virginia during the 1700s. The structure uses a variety of woods: the joints and rafters are oak and cedar; the interior woodwork is black walnut; the floors are oak and yellow pine; while the window frames and sills are poplar. The front porch columns and back porch (both later additions) are cedar. The house has been substantially altered over the years, but the essential character of the house has been maintained through the period furnishings, some from the original residents, and the interior decor.

Notable Collections on Exhibit

The attractive collection of period furnishings features a walnut blanket chest, a needlepoint picture of red roses, a cotton-hooked rug, slat-back arm chair, poplar one drawer table, overshot coverlet, cherry two-drawer table, a pair of metal candlesticks, handmade rug, a pair of Queen Anne brass andirons, Windsor spindle chairs, a cannonball rope bed, and a walnut trundle bed.

The Hermitage–
Home of Andrew Jackson

4580 Rachel's Lane
Hermitage, TN 37076
(615) 889-2941

Contact: Ladies' Hermitage Association

Open: Daily, 9 a.m.–5 p.m.; closed Thanksgiving, Christmas and the third week in Jan.

Admission: Adults $7; seniors $6.50; children (6-18), $3.50; under 6, free; group rates available. Orientation film, changing museum gallery, guided tours with audio cassette machine and interpreters.

Suggested Time to View House: 2–3 hours

Facilities on Premises: Restaurant and museum store

Description of Grounds: 625 acres of original pastores with 200-year old nature toup poplars, original drive (1838)

Best Season to View House: All seasons

Number of Yearly Visitors: 300,000

Year House Built: 1821, wings 1831; rebuilt after fire of 1834 in 1835-36

Style of Architecture: Greek Revival

Number of Rooms: 17

On-Site Parking: Yes **Wheelchair Access:** Yes

Description of House

The Hermitage, Andrew Jackson's beloved homestead, saw this man through the most important years of his life, from his troubled marriage to Rachel Donelson Robards through his celebrated military and political career. When his years at the White House as the seventh President of the United States were over, he returned to spend the rest of his life at his beloved Hermitage. Best remembered for his years as President, Andrew Jackson was also known as the "Hero of New Orleans" for his military victories during the War of 1812. In fact, he preferred the title of General best and General Jackson was what he remained during his years in Washington.

The Hermitage Mansion, built between 1819 and 1821, was a simple brick home in the Federal style, a conservative choice for this time. In a major remodeling undertaken in 1831, library and dining room wings were added, and a one story colonnade of ten columns with a two-story pedimented section in the center completed the facade in the Palladian style. Fire ravaged the Hermitage in 1834, destroying the upper story and seriously damaging the ground floor rooms. Although many Federal features remain in the rebuilt house completed in 1836, on the whole, the new Hermitage was a strong statement of the fashionable Greek Revival style. Inside, the mansion an outstanding collection of original French wallpapers (1835) *in situ* considered among the most important in the nation. Nearly all furnishings in the house are original to President Jackson residency after his years in the White House from 1837 to 1845.

Notable Collections on Exhibit

The house boasts one of the largest, most complete and original collections of decorative and fine arts of the Greek Revival period in the United States. The collection includes furniture and silver from Philadelphia, original glass from Bakewell & Co. of Pittsburgh, original French porcelain, original George Healy and Ralph Earl, Jr. portraits of President and Mrs. Jackson and family members, original Argand, Sinumbra and solar lamps, and the Brewster carriage which carried Jackson from Nashville to Washington.

Additional Information

Spread across the grounds behind the Hermitage are extensive grounds for visitor's enjoyment. Rachel's Garden, designed by English gardener William Front, was created in 1819 and today displays a wide variety of shrubs and planting. The cemetery holds the tombs of Andrew and Rachel Jackson as well as the graves of family members. In addition, a short distance from the house stands the original cabins where the Jackson's lived until their beautiful mansion was completed.

Armstrong-Lockett House

2728 Kingston Pike
Knoxville, TN 37919
(615) 637-3163

Contact: Armstrong-Lockett House
Open: March-Dec.: Tues.-Sat. 10 a.m.–4 p.m.,
Sun. 1–4 p.m.
Admission: Adults $2.50, youths (12-18)
$1.50. Tours.

Description of Grounds: The W.P. Memorial
Gardens are a series of seven terraces
leading to the river's edge.
Year House Built: 1834

Description of House

The Armstrong-Lockett House is one of the oldest, continuously lived in houses in Knoxville. The dwelling was built in 1834 by Drury Paine Armstrong as the main house for his 600-acre estate. At the time the house was known as Crescent Bend. The building was restored and renovated in 1977 to house the Toms Collection of 18th-century English and American furniture, decorative arts and an outstanding collection of English silver.

Additional Information

Visitors to Knoxville will not want to miss James White's Fort, built by the founder of Knoxville (205 East Hill Avenue). This log cabin features extensive exhibits devoted to local history. The property also contains a guest house, blacksmith shop, and loom house with period furniture and tools and artifacts of the period.

Ramsey House

2614 Thorngrove Pike
Knoxville, TN 37914
(615) 546-0745

Contact: Association for the Preservation of Tennessee Antiquities

Open: March-Nov., Tues.-Sat. 10 a.m.–5 p.m.; Sun. 1—4 p.m.; Nov.-March, by advance appointment only

Admission: Adults $2,50, children (6-12) $1, group rates available. Guided tours with costumed docents, slide show, special exhibits, lectures, workshops, and demonstrations, annual September Country Market, call for information

Suggested Time to View House: 1 hour

Description of Grounds: The 100-acre grounds are on a peninsula surrounded by a lake

Facilities on Premises: Visitor's center

Best Season to View House: Spring-fall

Style of Architecture: Georgian

On-Site Parking: Yes

Year House Built: 1797

Number of Rooms: 6

Wheelchair Access: Partial

Description of House

This stately stone home was built for Colonel Francis Alexander Ramsey, an early pioneer to the Tennessee frontier. Trained in mathematics and surveying, Ramsey came to the western North Carolina frontier from Pennsylvania in 1783. He explored and surveyed the countryside and claimed land overlooking a shallow lake called Swan Pond. Here he built this fine stone house which became a center of social, political, and religious life in early Tennessee. Ramsey's children also played prominent roles in Tennessee history; the eldest son, Dr. James Gettys Ramsey, promoted early railroads to join Knoxville to the east coast while the second son, William Blaine Ramsey was the first popularly elected mayor of Ramsey.

Ramsey employed Thomas Hope, an English-born master carpenter and cabinetmaker, to design and construct a fine house with notable architectural features. These include the quoins, belt course and keystone arches over the windows and doors, which tie the house to the classic architecture of the Georgian period. Also, the house's exterior makes a striking impression with its use of blue limestone to trim the pink marble. The consoles under the cornice are fine examples of late 18th-century architectural carving. The interior features other notable details including hall doors with raised panels in the "cross and open bible" design. In addition, the house was the first in the area to have an attached kitchen. Most of the furnishings have been collected to represent the detailed inventory made at the time of Colonel Ramsey's death. There are, however, some family-owned items including a pair of Chippendale chairs, a drop leaf table, a silver tea pot, and two needlepoint samplers made by one of the Ramsey daughters.

Blount Mansion

200 West Hill Avenue
Knoxville, TN 37901
(615) 525-2375

Contact: Blount Mansion
Open: March-Oct.: Tues.-Sat.
9:30 a.m.–4:30 p.m., Sun. 2-4:30 p.m.;
Nov.-Feb.: Tues.-Fri. 9:30 a.m.–4:30 p.m.
Admission: Adults $3, seniors $2.50,
children $1.50. Nov.-Feb. open on
weekends for pre-arranged groups; tours;
audiovisual orientation; exhibits

Facilities on Premises: Museum shop
Description of Grounds: Colonial Revival
gardens
Year House Built: 1792

Description of House

This attractive house was one of the first frame houses to be built west of the Allegheny mountains and served an important function as the Executive Mansion for the area before it became the state of Tennessee. Governor William Blount was the first and only governor of the Southwest Territory from 1790 to 1796. Following his term as governor, he became the first United States Senator from Tennessee serving from 1796 to 1798. In addition, this influential political figure was a signer of the United States Constitution.

This gracious frame dwelling is a complete departure from other early Knoxville dwellings. Despite its unpretentious exterior, frontiersmen and settlers referred to it as "the Blount Mansion." The governor's office, located behind the mansion, served as the capitol of the Southwest Territory from 1792 to 1796. This is the site where the Tennessee State Constitution was drafted. The Blount Mansion is Knoxville's only registered National Historic Landmark.

Additional Information

The surrounding gardens, governor's office building, and detached kitchen for the mansion provide an intriguing picture of this frontier capitol. The nearby visitor's center located in the Craighead Jackson House also displays exhibits related to this historic site.

Bleak House –
Confederate Memorial Hall

3148 Kingston Pike
Knoxville, TN 37919
(615) 522-2371

Contact: United Daughters of the
Confederacy

Open: April-Sept., Tues.-Fri. 2–5 p.m.;
Oct.-March, Tues.-Fri. 1–-4 p.m.

Admission: Adults $2, children (under 12)
$.50. Tours, annual Dogwood Arts
Festival, organizational and bus tours by
appointment, available for receptions and
meetings

Suggested Time to View House: 45 minutes

Facilities on Premises: Sales desk

Description of Grounds: Lovely
Mediterranean gardens included in tours

Best Season to View House: Spring and fall

Number of Yearly Visitors: 1,000

Year House Built: 1858

Style of Architecture: Italianate

Number of Rooms: 15

On-Site Parking: Yes **Wheelchair Access:** No

Description of House

This lovely antebellum mansion was built by Robert Houston
Armstrong shortly after his marriage to Louisa Franklin. The young couple
named their stately home "Bleak House" after Charles Dickens's novel
which was popular at the time. The house was called into service during the
siege of Knoxville from November 17 to December 2, 1863 when it served
as headquarters for Confederate General James Longstreet and his staff. The
house suffered considerable damage during this time and lost part of a wall
when a cannonball shot from inside failed to explode and tore the brick work
in the front room. Bleak House remained in the Armstrong family until 1906
when it was sold to the Brown family. The United Daughters of the Confederacy obtained the mansion in 1959 for preservation.

Bleak House has been restored to its former grandeur and elegance.
Each room contains a fine collection of period furniture and artifacts as well
as many notable architectural details. The blue room on the first floor
features a hand-carved sandstone mantelpiece, a hand-blown glass chandelier, and painted ceilings. The pink room contains a crystal chandelier, an
Italian marble mantel, and a pilaster ceiling with molding by European
artisans. Visitors to the tower, where much of the action occurred during the
siege, can still see blood stains on the walls and bullet holes in the window
sills as well as crude pictures of Confederate sharp-shooters on the walls.

The furnishings are an eclectic mix of Empire, Victorian, and early
Colonial pieces and include a hand-carved bed, a Lincoln rocker, and an
Empire sideboard with a ripple front.

Notable Collections on Exhibit

The mansion exhibits a distinctive collection of historic furnishings
including the banquet table owned by the attorney general of Tennessee,
and love seats hidden from Sherman's army during the burning of Atlanta.
In addition, many fine portraits adorn the wall including ones of Robert
Armstrong, the builder of the house, and Jefferson Davis, the President of
the Confederacy. The house also displays Confederate flags, a lithograph of
the Confederate seal, and a picture of the last meeting of Stonewall Jackson
and Robert E. Lee.

Woodruff-Fontaine House

680 Adams Avenue
Memphis, TN 38105
(901) 526-1469

Contact: Assoc. for the Preservation of
Tennessee Antiquities

Open: Daily, Mon.-Fri., 10 a.m.–4 p.m.;
Sun., 1–4 p.m.; closed Christmas Eve
and Day, Thanksgiving, July 4th

Admission: Adults $4; seniors $3; students
$2; group rates available. Guided tours,
dinner and luncheon group tours.

Suggested Time to View House: 60 minutes

Facilities on Premises: Victorian shop

Description of Grounds: Gingerbread
house museum shop, playhouse, garden
with fountain

Best Season to View House: Spring-fall

Number of Yearly Visitors: 15,000

Year House Built: 1870

Number of Rooms: 16

Style of Architecture: French Victorian

On-Site Parking: Yes **Wheelchair Access:** Yes

Description of House

Two prominent Memphis families called this beautiful Victorian mansion home. Amos Woodruff, a native of New Jersey, moved to Memphis to expand his carriage making trade and became successful in the area of banking, real estate and railroading. He had the house constructed in 1870 and later sold it to Noland and Virginia Fontaine in 1883. Mr. Fontaine was a wealthy cotton factor in the city of Memphis. John Phillip Sousa and Grover Cleveland were both entertained by the Fontaines as well as other well-known figures of the turn-of-the-century. The Fontaines remained in the house until Mrs. Fontaine's death in 1928. Later, the dwelling became an art school before it was restored and opened to the public in 1964.

The house stands three stories high with a central tower, mansard roof, and terra cotta lintels. Surrounding the property is wrought iron fence and a garden with a three tiered fountain lies adjacent to mansion. Several outbuildings will intrigue visitors: a restored carriage house behind the property and a gingerbread dollhouse which now houses the museum shop.

The mansion's furnishings are by the finest of Southern cabinet makers such as Mallard, Hunzunger and Belter; there are also decorative pieces by Sevres, Mary Gregory and Aubusson. The majority of the furnishings were donated by generous citizens of Memphis and the surrounding area; all are appropriate for the period.

Notable Collections on Exhibit

In addition to the exquisite furnishings, the mansion houses a large collection of antique clothing and accessories. This clothing is displayed on mannequins throughout the house in vignette settings. Exhibits on various aspects of Victorian life are on view throughout the year. Past exhibits have included "Victorian Brides" and "Victorian Mourning Customs."

Oaklands Historic House Museum

900 N. Maney Avenue
Murfreesboro, TN 37130
(615) 893-0022

Contact: Oaklands
Open: Tues.-Sat. 10 a.m.–4 p.m.,
 Sun. 1 p.m.-4 p.m.
Admission: Adults $3; seniors $2.50;
 children $1.50. Guided tours; special
 programs; presentations
Suggested Time to View House: 45 minutes
Facilities on Premises: Museum shop
Description of Grounds: The mansion sits
 on ten acres of land.
Number of Yearly Visitors: 15,000
Year House Built: 1815-1860
Style of Architecture: Italianate
Number of Rooms: 20

On-Site Parking: Yes **Wheelchair Access:** Yes

Description of House

This gracious antebellum home has changed considerably over the years, and today reflects the architecture and lifestyle of a mid Victorian planter family. The house was built by Dr. James Maney and his wife, Sally Hardy Murfree. Sally inherited the property from her father, Lt. Colonel Hardy Murfree, for whom Murfreesboro is named. The house was then passed to their Major Lewis Maney and his wife, Rachel Adeline Cannon, daughter of Newton Cannon, Tennessee's governor from 1835 to 1839. During the Civil War, both Confederate and Union troops camped on the plantation. In 1862, a daring raid resulted in the surrender of Union General William Duffield to Confederate forces. Later that year, General Jefferson Davis stayed at the mansion while visiting troops in the area.

Oaklands started as a simple one-and-a-half story house, but as the Maney family prospered, the house was enlarged in the early 1820s with an addition in the Federal style. With continued growth, further additions were made in the 1830s. At its peak, Oaklands was the center of a 1500-acre plantation and considered one of the most elegant homes in Middle Tennessee. The distinctive Italianate style facade was the last addition to the mansion, adding four rooms, a spacious hallway, the semicircular staircase, and the gracefully arched veranda. The interpretive period of Oaklands is 1860 to 1865. The furnishings are local pieces appropriate to the period and approximately ten percent are original to the mansion.

Notable Collections on Exhibit

The mansion showcases decorative arts of the antebellum period from approximately 1830 to 1865 including furnishings, portraits, and textiles.

Belle Meade Plantation

5025 Harding Road
Nashville, TN 37205
(615) 356-0501

Contact: Assoc. for the Preservation of Tennessee Antiquities

Open: Mon.-Sat. 9 a.m.–5 p.m.; Sun. 1–5 p.m.

Admission: Adults $5; seniors $4.50; students (13-18) $3.50; children (6-12) $2; groups (15 or more) $4. Guided tours, video initiation.

Suggested Time to View House: 1 hour

Facilities on Premises: Gift shop

Description of Grounds: The beautiful grounds feature gardens, an aboreteum with 37 varieties of trees and numerous outbuildings

Best Season to View House: Spring and summer

Number of Yearly Visitors: 110,000

Year House Built: 1820, remodeled and expanded in 1853

Style of Architecture: Greek Revival

Number of Rooms: 12

On-Site Parking: Yes **Wheelchair Access:** Yes

Description of House

Once a frontier outpost and a successful thoroughbred farm, Belle Meade Plantation continues to convey the elegance and charm of the Old South. The main house was built by John Harding in 1807. The building and plantation was further expanded and developed by his son, William Giles Harding, and son-in-law, William Hicks Jackson. The plantation eventually reached 5,400 acres and became a world renowned thoroughbred race horse nursery and stud farm. Presidents Grover Cleveland and William Howard Taft were both entertained here.

The two-story Greek Revival stucco mansion features limestone columns made from limestone quarried on the plantation. An enclosed breezeway connects the mansion with the former kitchen house, now the gift shop. Inside the house is being restored to the 1880 period which was the heyday of the plantation. Painted wood grain woodwork may be seen throughout the downstairs and on the outside of the house. The downstairs paint schemes have been restored to the original colors of the 1880s. The entry hall features a cantilevered staircase and portraits of the famous horses who lived here. Some of the furnishings are original to the house, especially in the library. Other pieces date from the period of 1830 to 1900.

Notable Collections on Exhibit

A collection of paintings of the family and the horses who lived here. The furniture consists of pieces by Belter and Meeks as well as a marvelous half tester bed by Prudent Mallard. Another full canopy bed, original to the house, was once slept in by President Grover Cleveland when he visited the mansion in the 1880s. Mannequins in vintage clothing showcase the costume collection. The carriage house contains one of the largest collection of carriages in the South.

Additional Information

In addition to the carriage house, Belle Meade features a remarkably complete series of outbuildings such as the smoke house, garden house, creamery and log cabin, one of the oldest houses in the state.

Belmont Mansion

Belmont University
1900 Belmont Blvd.
Nashville, TN 37212
(615) 269-9537

Contact: Belmont Mansion Association

Open: Summer, Mon.-Sat., 10 a.m.–4 p.m.;
Winter, Tues.-Sat., 10 a.m.–4 p.m.

Admission: Adults $4; children (6-12), $1;
group (15 or more), $3.50. Guided tours

Suggested Time to View House: 1 hour

Facilities on Premises: Gift shop

Description of Grounds: University
campus

Best Season to View House: Spring-Fall

Number of Yearly Visitors: 15,860

Year House Built: 1850

Style of Architecture: Italian style villa

Number of Rooms: 14

On-Site Parking: Yes **Wheelchair Access:** Yes

Description of House

This ornate Italian-style villa was built for Joseph and Adelicia Acklen; Mrs. Acklen was one of the wealthiest women in America and held one of the largest slave populations in 1860. The two-story villa was designed by Adolphus Heimen.

Belmont features a central block with an octagonal cupola. The recessed one-story flanking wings are surrounded by cast iron balconies. The interior is equally impressive with its free flying staircase leading to the cupola, a ballroom with an arched ceiling, a European-style state room, and decorative marble mantels. The furnishings are of the same period as house; some have been collected and some belonged to the Acklen family.

Notable Collections on Exhibit

Belmont exhibits five major marble statues by expatriate American sculptors and the largest collection of mid 19th-century cast-iron garden ornaments in the country.

Rocky Mount

Rocky Mount Parkway and
200 Hyder Hill Road
Piney Flats, TN 37686-4630
(615) 538-7396

Contact: Rocky Mount Historical Association
Open: March-Dec., Mon.-Fri. 10 a.m.–5 p.m.,
  Sun. 2–6 p.m., rest of year, Mon.-Fri.
  10 a.m.–5 p.m., closed major holidays

Admission: Adults $4, students $2.50. Tours
  by costumed guides, living history
  demonstrations.
Year House Built: 1770-1772
On-Site Parking: Yes
Wheelchair Access: Yes

Description of House

Rocky Mount was built by William Cobb from 1770 to 1772. This was the site of the oldest original territorial capital in the United States when Governor William Blount was guest. This simple log structure was the center for the state's affairs until the new capitol was built in Knoxville in 1792.

The original log cabin has been restored to its original appearance during this historic period with period furnishings and artifacts. The rest of the Rocky Mount complex provides a fascinating view of life and crafts in 18th-century Tennessee. Costumed interpreters guide visitors through the main house, and other dwellings, as well as the blacksmith shop, the barn and the carpentry shop. In the kitchen, open hearth cooking demonstrations take place while in the kitchen shed, visitors may see the practice of dyeing and other household functions in action. The demonstrations also extend to the yard and gardens where herbs and vegetables are grown. In addition, the grounds feature a weaving cabin, a blacksmith shop and a barn, where the animals are housed and blacksmithing, pewter casting, and woodworking take place.

Kingstone Lisle

P.O. Box 8
Rugby, TN 37733
(615) 628-2430

Contact: Historic Rugby, Inc.
Open: Feb. 1-Dec. 31, Mon.-Sat.
  10 a.m.–4:30 p.m., Sun. 12–4:30 p.m.
Activities: Visitors Center, orientation,
  guided tours
Suggested Time to View House: 1 hour
Facilities on Premises: Gift shop, book store

Description of Grounds: Small garden
Best Season to View House: Spring
Number of Yearly Visitors: 70,000
Year House Built: 1884
Style of Architecture: English rural Gothic
Number of Rooms: 7
On-Site Parking: Yes **Wheelchair Access:** Yes

Description of House

The British tradition lives on in historic Rugby, and Kingstone Lisle conveys this history well. The house was built but never occupied by Thomas Hughes, a British social reformer, lawyer, judge, politician, writer and the founder of Rugby. Instead, the house served as the rectory for Christ Church for many years. Father Joseph Blacklock lived here as did several other priests. In the 1930s and 1940s, sisters Lola and Nona Smith, lived here and operated the Rugby post office in the parlor. Another resident, Patricia G. Whichman lived in the house as a child, and returned in the 1950s, purchased the building, and worked for the local library and nearby Christ Church. She also wrote reminiscences of her life in Rugby and Kingstone Lisle.

This Queen Anne-style Gothic cottage features architectural details influenced by writings A.J. Downing. The one-and-a-half story structure is painted brown on the exterior with darker brown and deep rust trim. The furnishings are original to the Rugby settlement, either factory made in or crafted in the village, during the 1880s and 1890s.

Notable Collections on Exhibit

Kingstone Lisle displays a fine collection of period furnishings including a limited edition portrait of Queen Victoria, hand painted on silk, and mounted on silk string Union Jack. Also displayed are the following items: an ornate Eastlake shelf unit, a Weber square grand piano with rosewood veneer, a Gothic-style writing table, made in Rugby for Hughes, used to write biography of David Livingstone, a large, Rugby-made, chestnut china cabinet, and a balanced angle lamp, still in working order, and used at current special events.

Additional Information

Visitors to Rugby may also want to see the Hughes Public Library with its 7,000 volumes of Victorian literature, and The Newbury House, a bed and breakfast inn (c.1880), furnished with original antiques. An annual pilgrimage allows visitors to see many other Victorian homes not usually open to the public, contact Historic Rugby for more information.

Virginia

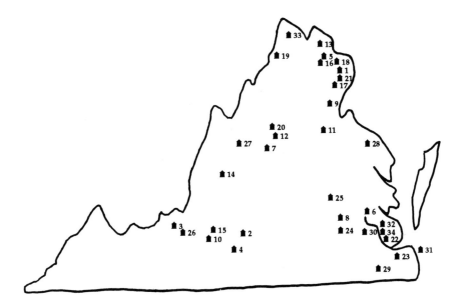

1. Alexandria
  Lloyd House
  Ramsay House
  Gadsby's Tavern
  Boyhood Home of Robert E. Lee
  Carlyle House
  Lee-Fendall House

2. Appomattox
  McClean House-
    19th Century Village

3. Blacksburg
  Smithfield Plantation

4. Brookneal
  Red Hill

5. Chantilly
  Historic Sully

6. Charles City
  Berkeley Plantation
  Evelynton
  Sherwood Forest Plantation

7. Charlottesville
  Ash Lawn-Highland
  Historic Michie Tavern
  Monticello

8. **Chesterfield**
   Magnolia Grange

9. **Dumfries**
   Weems-Botts Museum

10. **Forest**
    Poplar Forest

11. **Fredericksburg**
    Kenmore
    Mary Washington House

12. **Gordonsville**
    The Exchange Hotel

13. **Leesburg**
    Oatlands

14. **Lexington**
    Stonewall Jackson House

15. **Lynchburg**
    Point of Honor

16. **Manassas**
    Stone House

17. **Mason Neck**
    Gunston Hall

18. **McLean**
    Arlington House–
       Robert E. Lee Memorial
    The Claude Moore Colonial Farm

19. **Middletown**
    Belle Grove Plantation

20. **Montpelier Station**
    Montpelier

21. **Mount Vernon**
    Mount Vernon
    Pope-Leighey House
    Woodlawn Plantation

22. **Newport News**
    The Newsome House

23. **Norfolk**
    Hunter House Victorian Museum
    Moses Myers House
    The Willoughby-Baylor House

24. **Petersburg**
    Centre Hill Mansion

25. **Richmond**
    Agecroft Hall
    White House of the Confederacy
    Maymont
    Wickham House
    Wilton House Museum

26. **Roanoke**
    Buena Vista

27. **Staunton**
    Woodrow Wilson Birthplace

28. **Stratford**
    Stratford Hall Plantation

29. **Suffolk**
    Riddick's Folly

30. **Surry**
    Bacon's Castle
    Jones-Stewart Mansion

31. **Virginia Beach**
    Upper Wolfsnare
    Francis Land House
    Adam Thoroughgood House

32. **Williamsburg**
    Colonial Williamsburg
    Governor's Palace
    Bassett Hall

33. **Winchester**
    Abrams' Delight Museum
    Stonewall Jackson's Headquarters

34. **Yorktown**
    Carter's Grove Plantation
    Moore House

Lloyd House

220 N. Washington Street
Alexandria, VA 22314
(703) 838-4577

Contact: Alexandria Historical Restoration
and Preservation Commission

Open: Mon.-Sat. 9 a.m.–5 p.m.

Description of Grounds: A large garden
and brick patio are located behind the
house.

Year House Built: 1797

Style of Architecture: Georgian

Description of House

This fine example of Georgian architecture was designed by John Wise who also built Gadsby's Tavern. In the early 1800s, Charles Lee, attorney general under the Washington and Adams administrations, lived here as did Jacob Hoffman, the mayor of Alexandria. Benjamin Hallowell, tutor of Robert E. Lee, moved his school into the home's large rooms in 1826. The house was owned by the Lloyd family until 1918, when it was purchased by William Albert Smoot, a lumber dealer and a mayor of Alexandria. The Smoot family owned Lloyd House until 1942. During World War II it became a boarding house. This beautiful house has been scheduled for demolition on several occasions, but fortunately was rescued through individual and community efforts.

The classic facade of the building has been carefully preserved and the interior has been adaptively restored for use by the Alexandria Library. Furnishings, objects, and paintings belonging to former residents of the house and city are on display.

Notable Collections on Exhibit

The first floor is a museum with 18th and 19th-century books from Alexandria Library Company, a subscription library formed in 1794.

Additional Information

Lloyd House is a branch of the Alexandria Library which includes not only books, but photographs, maps, microforms, and manuscripts pertaining to Alexandria and Virginia history and genealogy. Lloyd House serves genealogists, students, local historians and archaeologists, and delights Civil War buffs with a fine collection on that subject. Professional librarians and a research historian are on hand to assist people with the collection.

Ramsay House

221 King Street
Alexandria, VA 22314-3209
(703) 838-4200

Contact: City of Alexandria

Open: Daily 9 a.m.–5 p.m.; closed Thanksgiving, Christmas and New Year's Day

Activities: Ramsay House is Alexandria's official visitors center. Brochures on the city's historical attractions, special events, and other information are available.

Year House Built: c. 1724

Style of Architecture: Georgian

On-Site Parking: Yes

Wheelchair Access: Yes

Description of House

The house is named for one of Alexandria's most distinguished founders, William Ramsay, a Scottish merchant and esteemed friend of George Washington. Ramsay was a hardworking, resourceful Scotsman who became very involved in trade and civic affairs. He served as town trustee, census taker, postmaster, member of the Committee of Safety, and, according to tradition, colonel of the militia regiment. He was highly respected by his fellow citizens and received many honors during his lifetime. His wife, Anne, was also a patriot and is reported to have been praised by Thomas Jefferson for having raised over $75,000 in funds to support the American Revolution.

The gambrel-roof design on the Ramsay House is rarely found today in the Alexandria region, but it is not unlike roofs used between 1675 and 1725 on Colonial homes in parts of Maryland, Delaware, New England, and the Virginia Tidewater region. The original house contains only one room on each floor but was expanded to two rooms per floor before it was moved to its present site. Some major alterations were made during the late 18th century, including an addition of new siding, windows, moldings, and paneling. None of the early materials are visible today, except the old weatherboard facing the porch, because a fire in 1924 partially damaged the house. During the 19th and 20th centuries, the house changed ownership many times and was used for various purposes including a tavern, grocery store, rooming house and cigar factory.

Additional Information

This historic house now serves as the visitor's center for Alexandria and contains a wealth of information on other houses open to the public and a lovely walking tour of this picturesque city.

Gadsby's Tavern

134 North Royal Street
Alexandria, VA 22314
(703) 838-4242

Contact: Gadsby's Tavern Museum
Open: Tues.-Sat. 10 a.m.–5 p.m.,
Sun. 1–5 p.m.
Admission: Adults $3; children (11-17) $1;
children (under 11 with adult) free;
special senior and group rates. Guided
tours, costume interpretive tours,
18th-century entertainments (fairs, balls,
children's programs).
Suggested Time to View House: 30 minutes
Facilities on Premises: Small gift shop
Description of Grounds: There is a small
courtyard associated with the restaurant.
Best Season to View House: Spring-fall
Number of Yearly Visitors: 18,000
Year House Built: c. 1770
Number of Rooms: 12

Style of Architecture: Georgian/Federal

Description of House

Although not a private dwelling, many patrons felt at home here due to
the generous hospitality provided by tavern keepers Mary Hawkins, John
Wise and John Gadsby. The buildings are named for the Englishman John
Gadsby who operated them as a tavern from 1796 to 1808. Mr. Gadsby's
establishment was a center of political, business and social life in early
Alexandria. George Washington was a frequent guest here, and he and his
wife twice attended the annual Birthnight Ball in his honor. Other prominent
individuals who entertained at the tavern included John Adams, Thomas
Jefferson, James Madison, and the Marquis de Lafayette.

Gadsby's Tavern consists of two tavern buildings, the 1770 Georgian
Tavern and the 1792 City Tavern and Hotel. The historic rooms of both
buildings have been restored to their original 18th-century appearance
complete with period furnishings. There are two documented articles in the
museum that are original to the tavern. The remainder of the collected
furnishings represent the years from 1770 to 1810. The tavern also features
an unusual hanging musician's balcony.

Notable Collections on Exhibit

Gadsby's Tavern Museum exhibits period furniture and clothing appropriate to Tavern visitors and workers.

Boyhood Home of Robert E. Lee

607 Oronoco Street
Alexandria, VA 22314
(703) 548-8454

Contact: Lee-Jackson Foundation

Open: Mon.-Sat. 10 a.m.–4 p.m., Sun.
1–4 p.m.; closed Easter, Thanksgiving
and Dec. 15-Feb. 1

Admission: Adults $3; youths (11-17) $1;
groups (10 or more) $2; 10 years and
under free. Guided tours.

Suggested Time to View House: 30 minutes

Description of Grounds: A large boxwood
garden adjoins the house.

Best Season to View House: All year

Number of Yearly Visitors: 10,000

Year House Built: 1795

Style of Architecture: Late Georgian/
early Federal

Number of Rooms: 7

On-Site Parking: No **Wheelchair Access:** No

Description of House

Robert E. Lee lived in the house as a child from 1812 to 1816 and from 1821 to 1825. In 1825, Lee left to enter West Point and begin his illustrious military career. This attractive townhouse was originally built by John Potts, and later sold to William Fitzhugh; both were business associates of George Washington. Fitzhugh's daughter married Washington's adoptive grandson in the house. The Lee family never owned the house, instead they rented it for an extended period of time.

This two-and-a-half story Georgian mansion features a well-preserved brick facade. The interior features woodwork done in the Adams style which decorates the central hall and stairway. The rooms are furnished to represent the period of Lee's occupancy during the early 19th century.

Additional Information

The house sponsors a series of annual programs which commemorate historic dates and events related to the house. These include Robert E. Lee's birthday on January 19th, the Fitzhugh wedding in mid October, and the anniversary of Lafayette's visit to the house. Contact the foundation for more information.

Carlyle House

Contact: Northern Virginia Regional
Park Authority
Open: Tues.-Sat. 10 a.m.–5 p.m.,
Sun. 12–5 p.m.
Admission: Group rates available.
Tours; special events.
Year House Built: 1752
Style of Architecture: Georgian

Description of House

When Scottish merchant John Carlyle built this riverfront mansion in 1752, it was considered one of the grandest homes in Alexandria. Business and social ties made John Carlyle a leading citizen in the area. His marriage to Sarah Fairfax allied him with one of the most prestigious and powerful families in the colony. His partnership in two merchant firms and his business acumen brought him outstanding wealth for those times and his numerous appointments to public office brought him considerable recognition. The Carlyle House gained its place in history when British Edward Braddock used it for his headquarters in 1755. It was here that Braddock summoned five colonial governors to what John Carlyle called "...the Grandest Congress ever known on this Continent...," a council held to discuss the strategy and funding of the French and Indian War.

With its stone construction and manor-house design, the Carlyle House was unique to Alexandria. The design is believed to have been inspired by an engraving of Craigiehall, an elaborate Scottish country house illustrated in *Vitruvius Scoticus*, a popular architectural patternbook at the time. The elegance of the stone cornice which graces the facade, a rare feature in colonial Virginia, is matched by the superbly carved woodwork of the formal parlor. Originally, the house stood on an acre lot overlooking the Potomac River, but as the shoreline filled in, other buildings were erected around it.

Additional Information

In 1801, John Carlyle's son-in-law, William Herbert, constructed the bank building which still stands on the corner of the property. Also, one of the most popular features of the house is the unplastered room that illustrates, layer by layer, the construction and restoration history of the structure.

Lee-Fendall House

614 Oronoco Street
Alexandria, VA 22314
(703) 548-1789

Contact: Virginia Trust for Historic
Preservation

Open: Tues.-Sat. 10 a.m.–4 p.m.; Sun.
12–4 p.m.; weekend hours may vary;
closed major holidays

Admission: Adults $3; students (11-17) $1;
groups (10 or more) $2. Guided tours,
and a rental program for private use.

Suggested Time to View House: 40 minutes

Description of Grounds: Large public
garden adjoins the historic house

Best Season to View House: Spring-fall

Number of Yearly Visitors: 8,000-11,000

Year House Built: 1785

Style of Architecture: Remodeled
1850-Greek Revival

Number of Rooms: 12 open

On-Site Parking: Yes **Wheelchair Access:** No

Description of House

The gracious house was built in 1785 by Philip Fendall, a Lee family descendant. He was an attorney, bank president, director of the Potomac Canal Company and an active Alexandria leader. Both "Light Horse Harry" Lee and George Washington were frequent visitors, and it was in this home that Lee wrote the farewell address from the citizens of Alexandria when Washington left to become our first President. In 1799, Lee prepared and delivered Washington's funeral oration in which he coined the historic phrase "First in war, first in peace, and first in the hearts of his countrymen." The house was home to thirty-seven Lees during the period from 1785 to 1903; the last private owner was labor leader John L. Lewis (from 1937 to 1969).

This large, clapboard house contains many family furnishings and possessions which give visitors a sense of the famed "Lees of Virginia". In addition, guided tours interpret the 1850 to 1900 period, based on ar-cheological and historic research, and household inventory records from 1850. The Lee-Fendall House is listed on the National Register of Historic Places.

Notable Collections on Exhibit

The large collection of original antique furnishings is complemented by a permanent exhibit of dollhouses and miniature architecture. There are also special changing exhibitions on a regular basis.

Additional Information

The house is enhanced by a lovely garden with magnolias, roses, and boxwood paths which provide a colorful oasis in the center of Old Town, Alexandria.

McClean House – "19th-Century Village"

P.O. Box 218
Appomattox, VA 24522
(804) 352-8987

Contact: Appomattox Court House National Historical Park

Open: Daily 9 a.m.–5 p.m.; closed Federal holidays

Admission: $2. Slide programs; living history discussions; and ranger programs in the summer.

Suggested Time to View House: 2 hours

Facilities on Premises: Book store

Description of Grounds: 1,300 plus acres for self-guided tours along a 6 mile trail

Best Season to View House: Year round

Number of Yearly Visitors: 120,000

Year House Built: 1819 to 1870

Number of Rooms: 6

On-Site Parking: Yes

Style of Architecture: Georgian/Federalist

Description of House

The site of Robert E. Lee's surrender of the Confederate Army of north Virginia to Ulysses S. Grant has been wonderfully preserved in this 19th-century village. The surrender of April 9, 1865, which ended the bloody Civil War, took place in the McLean House which has been accurately reconstructed for exhibition. The house's owner, a local merchant named Wilmer McLean lived in the three-story brick house with his wife and five children. The house was originally built 1848, and dismantled in 1893; the present reconstruction was completed in the 1940s. This historic dwelling features original furnishings, reproductions, and collected period pieces. Near the house are reproductions of the original outbuildings—the separate kitchen, the servants' quarters, and the icehouse.

Visitors will also enjoy the many other historic buildings in this typical, rural 19th-century village. These include the Clover Hill Tavern, the oldest structure in the village, where travellers would stay and be entertained for the night, a general store, the famous courthouse (completely reconstructed), and several other historic homes, some of which are currently under renovation. The "Surrender Triangle" is located a few minutes from the McClean House. It was here that over 28,000 Confederate soldiers laid down their weapons and furled their flags; the fighting had stopped, the war was over.

Notable Collections on Exhibit

The visitor's center has a museum with numerous exhibits showing artifacts related to soldiers at the surrender and on the final campaign.

Smithfield Plantation

1000 Smithfield Plantation Road
Blacksburg, VA 24060
(703) 951-2060

Contact: Association for the Preservation of
Virginia Antiquities

Open: April 1-Nov. 1, Wed., Sat.-Sun.
1–5 p.m.

Admission: Adults $4; children $1.50;
children on school tours $1.
Guided tours.

Description of Grounds: Enclosed garden
with plants authentic to period and
vegetable garden

Year House Built: 1772

Style of Architecture: Colonial

Description of House

This well-preserved plantation house is one of the oldest in this part of western Virginia. Smithfield Plantation was part of a crown grant of 120,000 acres in 1745 to James Patton, who later died in the frontier Indian massacre of 1755. His nephew, Colonel William Preston, built this Colonial-style house in 1772 and named it for his wife, Susannah Smith. Preston turned the house into a Revolutionary stronghold as well as headquarters for the family's business operations in Virginia, West Virginia, and Kentucky. Smithfield Plantation is also notable as the birthplace of two Virginia Governors, James Patton Preston and John Buchanan Floyd. The plantation was also briefly the home of a third governor, John Floyd, Jr.

This white clapboard, story-and-a-half house is considered by the National Trust for Historic Preservation to be of considerable statewide interest, as well as a nationally recognized historic site. Several noted architects have called Smithfield "the best Colonial house west of the Blue Ridge." The building's long L-shape is of fine Georgian proportions, similar to those found in Williamsburg and Yorktown. The interior woodwork of the house has been returned to its original colors. The cook's cabin has also been restored along with the smoke house. The house features a fine collection of Colonial and Federal furnishings which have been collected and are appropriate for the period.

Red Hill

Route 2, Box 127
Brookneal, VA 24528
(804) 376-2044

Contact: Patrick Henry Memorial
Foundation
Open: April-Oct., daily 9 a.m.–5 p.m.;
Nov.-March 9 a.m.–4 p.m.
Admission: Adults $3; children $1.
Audiovisual presentation, self-guided
tours, Henry family cemetery.
Suggested Time to View House: 45 minutes
Facilities on Premises: Museum gift shop
Description of Grounds: A colonial garden
with a boxwood maze surrounds the
historic buildings, picnic tables on site
Best Season to View House: Spring and fall
Number of Yearly Visitors: 7,000
Year House Built: Main house is a replica
of the original built ca. 1765
Style of Architecture: Southside Virginia
Colonial

Number of Rooms: 3 rooms open to public

Description of House

Patrick Henry embodied the spirit of American courage and patriotism. He is recognized as the "The Voice of the Revolution" with his famous call for "give me liberty or give me death". Henry was the first governor of Virginia and served five terms. Perhaps his greatest contribution to the nation was his work towards the adoption of the Bill of Rights. While desiring a more effective federal government, he was adamant in demanding protection of basic individual civil liberties.

The favorite of Patrick Henry's many homes was Red Hill, which he called "one of the garden spots of the world." The plantation consisted of 2,920 acres, a modest frame home, and several dependencies, including an overseer's cottage which Henry used as his law office. Henry is buried in the cemetery located on the grounds. The furnishings are almost all late 18th-century originals or reproductions; they also include a few pieces which belonged to Patrick Henry.

Notable Collections on Exhibit

Notable items on display include Patrick Henry's writing desk, an original oil painting "Patrick Henry before the Virginia House of Burgesses" by Peter Rothermel, and the statesman's letters and documents. Personal possessions such as one of his fiddles, a letter opener, and salt dishes and spoons are also on display.

Additional Information

The giant osage orange tree in the Henry house's front yard has been declared the national champion of its species by the Society of American Foresters.

Historic Sully

3601 Sully Road (Route 28)
Chantilly, VA 22030
(703) 437-1794

Contact: Fairfax County Park Authority
Open: March-Dec., Wed.-Mon.
   11 a.m.–4 p.m.; Jan.-Feb., Sat.-Sun.
   11 a.m.–3:30 p.m.; closed Thanksgiving,
   Christmas and New Year
Admission: Adults $3; children $1. Guided
   tours; specialized tours for children,
   scouts, and other groups; special events.
Suggested Time to View House: 45 minutes
Facilities on Premises: Gift shop

Description of Grounds: Spacious open
   field grounds surround historic house
   area; sample vegetable and formal flower
   gardens
Best Season to View House: Year round
Number of Yearly Visitors: 33,000
Year House Built: 1794
Style of Architecture: Rural frame house
   with Federal and Georgian influences
Number of Rooms: 9
On-Site Parking: Yes **Wheelchair Access:** Yes

Description of House

Richard Bland Lee, the uncle of Robert E. Lee, resided on the tract of land he called "Sully" for thirty years. He had a plantation of over 700 acres and used the labor of more than thirty slaves. In addition to farming, he was involved with the land development and elected and appointed offices. As a member of the first Congress, he was recognized for his role in establishing the location of the Capital on the Potomac. He was married to the former Elizabeth Collins of Philadelphia and they raised four children.

Sully Plantation has been restored to its 1794 to 1799 appearance along with four original outbuildings—a kitchen-laundry, a smokehouse, a dairy, and a small office. The main house has original bead siding and contains a two-and-a-half story main section, and a one-and-a-half story wing. A wide, high-ceilinged hall separates the two sections. The house maintains the original moldings, window and door frames. The wainscotting and fireplace mantels are traditional Georgian in design while the scale and proportions of interior spaces, windows, and doors are Federal. Two massive exterior chimneys serve the main section; a single interior chimney serves the wing with a double fireplace on the first floor.

One genuinely unique feature of the house is the Chippendale-style curved trim along the length of the piazza or porch. Other distinctive elements can be seen in the covered way connecting the main house to the separate kitchen/laundry, and a garret-level lodging room with a "borrowed light" window. The furnishings of the house are a combination of original furnishings and period furnishings appropriate to the first occupancy from 1795 to 1811. In addition, carefully chosen reproductions augment the overall interpretation of the time period.

Notable Collections on Exhibit

Furnishings with a tradition of Richard Bland Lee ownership include dining, card, and sewing tables, a pair of all American Hepplewhite dining chairs, and other various pieces.

Additional Information

The first floor wing holds an exhibit illustrating a 250-year period in the history of the property with photographs, objects, drawings, and personal narratives.

Berkeley Plantation

Route 5
Charles City, VA 23030
(804) 829-6018

Contact: Berkeley Plantation
Activities: Guided tours with costumed docents
Facilities on Premises: Gift shop
Number of Rooms: 11

Open: 8 a.m.–5 p.m.
Description of Grounds: Formal gardens with a gazebo
Year House Built: 1726
Style of Architecture: Georgian

Description of House

Berkeley Plantation has been called one of the most beautiful plantations in Virginia, and is certain to impress visitors with an interest in the antebellum South. The plantation was associated with the influential Harrison family. Benjamin Harrison, son of the builder of Berkeley and its second owner, was a signer of the Declaration of Independence. His son, William Henry Harrison, and grandson, Benjamin Harrison, both served as Presidents of the United States. Berkeley also played an important role in the Civil War; Lincoln reviewed Union troops led by General McClellan here and legend says that "Taps" was composed here during the 1862 encampment.

The three-story brick house is said to be the oldest in Virginia that can prove its date (due to a datestone over a side door) and the first with a pediment roof. The interior is noted for its handsome Adam-style woodwork; the double arches of the "great rooms" in the mansion were installed by Benjamin Harrison VI under the direction of Thomas Jefferson. The rooms are furnished with a magnificent collection of 18th-century furnishings.

Additional Information

Visitors to Berkeley will also want to see the Gothic-style Edgewood House, built in 1849 by New Jersey native Spencer Rowland. Once a part of Berkeley Plantation, Edgewood has served in various capacities throughout its colorful history. The Civil War's tragic history is literally etched into one of Edgewood's window panes. Elizabeth "Lizzie" Rowland, wrote her name on an upstairs bedroom window. She died of a broken heart after waiting in vain for her lover to return from the war. Many believe she still waits for him, watching from the upstairs from window. It was also during the Civil War years that the third floor was used as a lookout for Confederate generals to spy on McClellan's troop when they were camped at Berkeley. In subsequent years the house has served as a church, a post office, telephone exchange, restaurant, and a nursing home.

Evelynton

Route 2, Box 145
Charles City, VA 23030
(804) 829-5075

Contact: Evelynton

Open: Daily 9 a.m.–5 p.m.; closed Thanksgiving, Christmas and New Year's Day

Admission: Adults $6; seniors $5; youths (7-12) $3; group rates (25 or more). Tours of main house, gardens and grounds.

Description of Grounds: A delightful English boxwood gardens and landscaped grounds

Year House Built: 1935

Style of Architecture: Georgian

Description of House

Evelynton was part of William Byrd's expansive Westover Plantation, and named after his daughter Evelyn. Evelyn is believed to have died from a broken heart before she reached the age of 30. Legend insists she haunts over Westover to this day, although many claim to have seen her ghost at Evelynton as well. Since 1847, Evelynton has been home to the Ruffian family. Its fertile soil has known the fruits of prosperity, the blood-shed of battle and the agony of reconstruction. The plantation's original 860 acres were purchased at auction by Edmund Ruffian, Jr. His father, Edmund Ruffian, was credited with firing the first shot of the Civil War at Fort Sumter. The senior Ruffian is also renowned for his agricultural advances.

During the Colonial period, Evelynton was part of Westover Plantation. In 1862 during the Battle of Evelynton Heights, the original house and slave quarters were burned, fields sown with salt and the oldest trees girdled. In the 1930s, noted architect, Duncan Lee, who was responsible for the restoration of Carter's Grove, was commissioned to design a Georgian Revival manor house atop the original foundation. Constructed of 250-year old brick, the house is considered a brilliant interpretation of the style.

The house has been lovingly restored and furnished with American, English and continental antiques, many of them family heirlooms.

Additional Information

In addition to the lovely gardens, the grounds also feature historical markers indicating where Civil War skirmishes took place.

Sherwood Forest Plantation

P.O. Box 8
Charles City, VA 23030
(804) 829-5377

Contact: Historic Sherwood Forest
Plantation

Open: Daily 9 a.m.–5 p.m. (by appointment)

Admission: 1 to 4 persons $30 minimum;
seniors $6.25; students $6. Guided tours
(an additional $2 per person and by
appointment).

Suggested Time to View House: 45 minutes

Description of Grounds: 50 acres—
80 variety of trees, all over 200 years old

Best Season to View House: Any season

Number of Yearly Visitors: 2,500

Year House Built: 1732 Main house

Style of Architecture: Federal

Number of Rooms: 12

On-Site Parking: Yes

Wheelchair Access: No

Description of House

Sherwood has been a working plantation for over 350 years. This gracious estate has the notable distinction of having been owned by two U.S. Presidents: John Tyler and William H. Harrison. Tyler spent the last twenty years of his life in these beautiful surroundings. Currently, a grandson of President Tyler lives in the main house of this still-working plantation.

This National Historic Landmark has a number of remarkable architectural characteristics. As long as a football field, the main house is considered the longest frame house in America. Many of the original outbuildings are still standing on the property including a separate kitchen, laundry, law office, slave quarters, the overseer's house, a smoke house, wine house, and the milk house. The main house displays a fine collection of original furniture, silver, and portraits which belonged to the many generations of Tylers over the years.

Notable Collections on Exhibit

Visitors will be impressed by the original artifacts on display; there are numerous oil paintings, several miniatures, wonderful 18th-and 19th-century Oriental rugs and porcelains, 19th-century French, English, and American china, President Tyler's French china, and a series of other notable furnishings.

Additional Information

The extensive grounds contain over eighty different varieties of trees, many of which are a century old, as well as beautiful gardens.

Ash Lawn-Highland

Route. 6, Box 37
Charlottesville, VA 22902
(804) 293-9539

Contact: Ash Lawn-Highland
Open: Closed Thanksgiving, Christmas, New Year's Day
Admission: Adults $6; youths (6-11) $2; seniors $5.50; groups $5.50. Guided tours, seasonal craft demonstrations.
Suggested Time to View House: 60–90 minutes
Facilities on Premises: Gift store (includes books)

Description of Grounds: Boxwood gardens, floral and culinary gardens
Best Season to View House: Spring-fall
Number of Yearly Visitors: 97,000
Year House Built: 1799, additions 1816, 1880
Style of Architecture: Vernacular Federal, Victorian addition
Number of Rooms: 10 open to the public
On-Site Parking: Yes **Wheelchair Access:** Yes

Description of House

Ash Lawn-Highland was home to James Monroe, fifth President of the United States, and his wife, Elizabeth Kortright Monroe of New York City, from 1799 to 1823. The Monroes moved to this area in 1789 upon the request of Thomas Jefferson who was living at Monticello. Jefferson invited several statesmen like Monroe to help him create a "society to our taste". The Monroes owned this gracious home during the period of Monroe's Presidency from 1817 to 1825, years which were optimistically called "the era of good feelings." During his years as President, Monroe resolved grievances with the British, acquired Florida from the Spanish in 1819, and proclaimed the Monroe doctrine in 1823.

The Monroes repeatedly altered and extended the original Highland House, a simple frame structure to which they added a one-and-a-half story wooden wing which in turn was altered. By the time the Monroes sold the Highland in 1826, they had a home of nearly 4,400 square feet. The simplicity of the house is in striking contrast to Mount Vernon or Monticello. This comfortable house reflects Monroe's less prosperous upbringing, the debts and cost of many years of government service, and his professed belief in the simple life of the country farmer.

Ash Lawn-Highland features a remarkable collection of Monroe artifacts and furnishings in its beautiful period rooms. The dining room holds the largest collection of Monroe furnishings including a Hepplewhite dining room table and handcarved American Federal chairs. The children's room contains the family crib and an antique French Aubusson carpet. The bedroom features the Monroes's elegant highpost bed and a Sheraton cabinet and writing desk which belonged to President James Madison. The drawing room, with its French Zuber wallpaper and French gilt mantel clock, reflects the interest in French culture that was shared by many Americans immediately after the revolutionary period.

Notable Collections on Exhibit

Visitors will be impressed by the extensive collection of original Monroe furnishings, paintings, and artifacts decorating the rooms. Temporary exhibits feature collections of textiles, archaeological artifacts, and photographs.

Historic Michie Tavern

Thomas Jefferson Parkway
Charlottesville, VA 22902
(804) 977-1234

Contact: Historic Michie Tavern

Open: Daily 9 a.m.–5 p.m.

Admission: Adults $5.50; seniors $5; children (6-11) $1.50.
Guided tours of Historic Michie Tavern Museum consists of 1784 Tavern-Museum, its dependent outbuildings and Meadow Run Grist Mill; living history and craft demonstrations.

Suggested Time to View House: 45 minutes

Facilities on Premises: Gift shop; lunch in "The Ordinary" 11:30 a.m.–3:30 p.m.

Year House Built: 1784

Style of Architecture: Georgian

Description of House

William Michie, a young Scotsman, whose father came to Virginia as an indentured servant, owned the original homestead. To accommodate the many travelers seeking food and shelter at his home, Michie opened his dwelling as an "Ordinary" in 1784. Descendants owned and operated this historic meeting place for more than 150 years.

Historic Michie Tavern is one of the oldest homesteads remaining in Virginia and was originally located on a well-travelled stagecoach route some seventeen miles northwest of the present site. The tavern forms part of a settlement of authentic rural Virginia structures. These date from a 1790 single-room log cabin to a larger clapboard-sided dwelling from the Civil War. An 18th-century barn, critical to a functioning tavern, will also be included.

The tavern contains one of the largest and finest collections of 18th-century furniture and artifacts. Rare, southern pieces are highlighted throughout the old tavern and its dependent outbuildings. Once completed, this architectural time capsule will provide visitors with an accurate representation of a Virginia landowner's way of life and offer a setting for 18th-century living history and craft demonstrations.

Notable Collections on Exhibit

The tavern displays an excellent collection of period furnishings and an unusual collection of household inventions such as a cheese press and a folding Murphy bed. The Wine Cellar now houses the Virginia Wine Museum.

Additional Information

In 1927, the Colonial inn was dismantled piece by piece, relocated and painstakingly reconstructed. The move itself was a historic event and ultimately served as a prime example of the 1920s preservation movement.

Monticello

P.O. Box 316
Charlottesville, VA 22903
(804) 295-8181

Contact: Thomas Jefferson Memorial
Foundation, Inc.

Open: Nov.-Feb., 9 a.m.–4:30 p.m.;
March-Oct., 8 a.m.–5 p.m.; closed
Christmas Day

Admission: Adults $7; seniors $6; children
(6-11) $3; groups (over 25) $6 per person;
student groups $1. Guided tours, film.

Suggested Time to View House: 30 minutes

Facilities on Premises: Museum shop

Description of Grounds: The expansive
grounds contain many gardens (flower
and vegetable), vineyards, orchards, and
rare trees. There is also a picnic area
available.

Best Season to View House: Spring-fall

Number of Yearly Visitors: 500,000 plus

Year House Built: 1769 and fully completed
in 1809

Style of Architecture: Neo-classical

Number of Rooms: 33

On-Site Parking: Yes **Wheelchair Access:** Yes

Description of House

Few house's in America reflect the personality of their owner than does
Jefferson's Monticello. Built over a period of forty years, Monticello was
Jefferson's home when he travelled to Philadelphia to write the Declaration
of Independence as well as when he served as President. After Jefferson died
in 1826, the house and all its contents were sold to pay debts. After a brief
period of ownership by James T. Barclay, the house was purchased by the
Levy family of New York. Uriah P. Levy retained the house through the 19th
century, and eventually his nephew Jefferson Monroe Levy offered it up for
sale in the 1920s. At that time, a group of citizens rallied together to raise
the money for a mortgage and the Thomas Jefferson Memorial Foundation
was formed to operate the house as a museum.

Architecture endured as one of Jefferson's chief delights. The house was
built and subsequently remodeled over a period of forty years, reflecting the
pleasure he found in "putting up and pulling down." In 1789, after a period
of service in France, he withdrew himself from public service and devoted
his time to redesigning the mansion. He enlarged the house from eight
rooms to twenty-one by removing the upper story and demolishing the east
walls. He constructed a dome, the first built in America, based on the design
of the ancient temple of Vesta in Rome. Throughout the rooms are reminders
of Jefferson's thoughtful mind and keen interest in the scientific. The house
is equipped with dumbwaiters, disappearing beds, and a revolving serving
door in the dining room. Visitors are surprised to find that the entrance hall

functioned as a museum containing fossil bones, a buffalo head, elk antlers, and a seven-day clock which indicated the day in addition to the hour.

The majority of the furnishings in the house belonged to Thomas Jefferson; the remainder are from the same period. However, the collection represents only about a fraction of what Jefferson owned during his lifetime.

Notable Collections on Exhibit

Monticello exhibits a rich assortment of personal and family memorabilia, in addition to artifacts discovered during recent archaeological excavations on the Monticello grounds, architectural models and drawings, and two audiovisual presentations. In total, nearly 400 objects and artifacts are on display, many for the first time.

Additional Information

Because Jefferson was also an avid gardener, the grounds to Monticello comprise a good part of most visitors's tour. A full day could be spent wandering among the many beautiful gardens, orchards, and flower beds with their splendid assortment of tulips, sweet williams, and Maltese crosses, among other varieties.

Magnolia Grange

10021 Iron Bridge Road
Chesterfield, VA 23832
(804) 748-1026

Contact: Chesterfield Historical Society
Open: Mon.-Fri. 10 a.m.–4 p.m.,
 Sun. 1–4 p.m.
Admission: Adults $2; seniors $1.50;
 students $1. Walking tour.
Year House Built: 1822
Style of Architecture: Federal

Description of House

The families who have called Magnolia Grange home—the Winfrees, and later the Du Vals and the Cogbills—all have made important contributions to life in Chesterfield County and the Commonwealth of Virginia.

Built in 1822, Magnolia Grange is a handsome Federal-style plantation house named after the circle of magnolia trees that once graced its front lawn. Noted for its distinctive architecture, Magnolia Grange contains elaborate ceiling medallions as well as sophisticated carving mantels, doorways, and window enframements. Careful paint restoration has been executed through wood graining and marbleizing. Scenic wallpaper by Zuber and carpeting of the period combine with authentic furnishings to return the house to its 1820s appearance.

Today, Magnolia Grange continues to contribute to the lives of its visitors, welcoming them to an interpretation of life in a country mansion of the early 19th century.

Additional Information

Fast-growing Chesterfield County has preserved its charming turn-of-the-century government complex. Visitors are invited to wander through these fine, old structures and absorb the texture of early self-government in Virginia. The early 1900s courthouse, the old jail, the old clerk's office built in 1889, and an earlier clerk's office used in the latter part of the century as the treasurer's office are located in the complex surrounding a replica of the first courthouse built in 1750.

Weems-Botts Museum

300 Duke Street, P.O. Box 26
Dumfries, VA 22026
(703) 221-3346

Contact: Historic Dumfries Virginia, Inc.
Open: April-Oct. 31, Mon.-Sat.
10 a.m.–5 p.m., Sun. 2–5 p.m.;
Nov.-March 31, Mon.-Sat.
10 a.m.–4 p.m., Sun. 1–4 p.m.
Admission: Donations accepted.
Guided tours.
Suggested Time to View House: 45 minutes
Facilities on Premises: Gift shop and
book store
Description of Grounds: Adjacent to a
public park, with available picnic table
and rest rooms.
Best Season to View House: Spring and
summer
Number of Yearly Visitors: 9,500
Year House Built: Late 18th century
Number of Rooms: 6

On-Site Parking: Yes **Wheelchair Access:** Yes

Description of House

Parson Mason Locke Weems purchased this building at 300 Duke Street in 1798 to be used as a bookstore. Weems was the first biographer of George Washington. He will be remembered as the man who invented the now-famous story of George chopping down a cherry tree. In 1802, Weems sold the house to Benjamin Botts, a prominent lawyer. Botts was the youngest defense attorney involved in the Aaron Burr treason trial.

The building now housing Weems-Botts Museum has a venerable and checkered history. While documentation has not been fully completed, it is conjectured, on the basis of evidence uncovered during restoration, that the small section of the house, comprising the Weems bookstore and garret, predated its purchase by Parson Weems in 1798. This part of the building is one of the oldest extant structures in the town. The house is furnished with period pieces which have been collected to represent the years of Weems's ownership.

Notable Collections on Exhibit

A large number of Parson Weems books are on display, as well as a collection of artifacts.

Poplar Forest

P.O. Box 419
Forest, VA 24551-0419
(804) 525-1806

Contact: The Corporation for Jefferson's Poplar Forest

Open: April-Oct., Wed.-Sun. 10 a.m.–4 p.m.

Admission: Adults $5; children $1. Tours, group tours available year round by appointment, persons requiring special assistance are encouraged to contact the property before visiting.

Facilities on Premises: Gift shop

Year House Built: 1806

Style of Architecture: Greek Revival

Description of House

Thomas Jefferson, the author of the Declaration of Independence built only two homes for his own use—Monticello and Poplar Forest. Overwhelmed by an almost perpetual round of visitors at Monticello, Jefferson escaped several times a year to find at Poplar Forest what he called the "solitude of a hermit." During the building of the retreat Jefferson also stated, "When finished, it will be the best dwelling in the state, except that of Monticello; perhaps preferable to that, as more proportioned to the facilities of a private citizen."

Poplar Forest is the home which Thomas Jefferson designed and used as his personal retreat. In 1806 while President, Jefferson himself assisted the masons in laying the foundation for the dwelling which today is considered one of his most creative and original designs. He chose to build his retreat at the Bedford County plantation which he called "the most valuable of my possessions." There he created an extraordinary octagonal house with accompanying dependencies and landscaping.

At Poplar Forest you can see the restoration of a national landmark as it happens. Poplar Forest opened to the public for the first time recently to afford visitors an opportunity to see it before it is restored. Restoration of the buildings and landscape is just beginning. Architects and archaeologists are exploring the buildings and grounds for clues about Poplar Forest's past. Currently a work-in-progress, a visit to the restoration of Poplar Forest would be a worthy complement to Jefferson's completely furnished home, Monticello.

Kenmore

**1201 Washington Avenue
Fredericksburg, VA 22401
(703) 373-3381**

Contact: Kenmore Association, Inc.

Open: March-Nov. 30, daily 9 a.m.–5 p.m.;
Dec.-Feb. 29, daily 10 a.m.–4 p.m.;
closed on holidays.

Admission: Adults $5; students $2.50;
group rates available. Guided tours and
children's tours with hands-on activities.

Suggested Time to View House: 30 minutes

Facilities on Premises: Gift shop

Description of Grounds: Colonial-style
flower garden

Best Season to View House: Spring,
summer and fall

Number of Yearly Visitors: 43,000

Year House Built: early 1770s

Style of Architecture: Georgian

Number of Rooms: 8

On-Site Parking: Yes **Wheelchair Access:** Yes

Description of House

This home of George Washington's only sister witnessed the birth of the nation. Just before the American Revolution, Colonel Fielding Lewis began construction of Kenmore for his wife, Betty. Colonel Lewis, truly an unsung hero of the Revolution, led in establishing a gunnery in Fredericksburg which supplied arms to the American troops.

The first impression of Kenmore, seen through the dogwood and oaks from Washington Avenue, or rising above walks and terraces from the garden front, is a of classical simplicity. Massive brick walls contain subtle details—a curved brick water table, a belt line defining the upper floor. On three sides are entrance stoops; on the fourth, a small portico overlooks the gardens. Yet within the simple exterior is a series of perhaps the richest and most elaborate rooms of Colonial America. The splendid work seen today is a rare example of the artistry of two centuries, combined in great beauty and harmony. Kenmore is renowned for its extraordinary decorative plaster-work which graces the walls. Legend says that George Washington, a frequent visitor to the house, even helped to design the plaster decorations.

Notable Collections on Exhibit

Kenmore is also known for its excellent collection of 18th-century furnishings, many of them made in Virginia, and displays of period English creamware, figurines, and glassware. The first floor of the house features a modern gallery with changing exhibits and a diorama of early Fredericksburg.

Additional Information

In very recent years an unexploded cannonball was discovered wedged between floors in the mansion.

Mary Washington House

1200 Charles Street
Fredericksburg, VA 22401
(703) 373-1569

Contact: Mary Washington Branch of Assoc. for the Preservation of Virginia Antiquities

Open: March-Nov., 9 a.m.–5 p.m.; Dec.-Feb., 10 a.m.–4 p.m.

Admission: Adults $3; children (6-18) $1; children (under 6) free. Guided tour by costumed docents.

Suggested Time to View House: 30 minutes

Facilities on Premises: Gift shop

Description of Grounds: The grounds have been restored by the Garden Club of Virginia with a vegetable garden behind the kitchen.

Best Season to View House: Spring, summer and fall

Number of Yearly Visitors: 25,000

Year House Built: 1750s

Number of Rooms: 5

Style of Architecture: Colonial

On-Site Parking: Yes **Wheelchair Access:** No

Description of House

Mary Ball Washington spent her last seventeen years in this comfortable home, bought for her by her son, George Washington. This modest house was the last home she was to have before her death in 1789. He purchased it in 1772 so that Mary could live near her only daughter, Betty Lewis, and be better protected during the oncoming Revolution. Washington came to this house to receive a blessing from his mother before his inauguration as the country's first President in 1789.

The original house was a three-room cottage. George had a wing built with two additional rooms as well as a foyer. The house has retained all of the original moldings on the fireplaces, ceilings and chairrails. The detailing is still very crisp and in excellent condition and the original paint colors have been restored. There are many original furnishings on exhibit as well as collected pieces appropriate to the period.

Notable Collections on Exhibit

In the house, visitors will find many of Mrs. Washington's favored possessions including the mirror she called her "best dressing glass." There is also a 16th-century Bible box on display in her bedroom, a grandfather clock made by a local clockmaker in the parlor. In the garden, the same sundial still marks the passing time, as when Mrs. Washington passed the hours among her beloved plants. The large boxwoods she planted line a brick walkway that separates a well-tended vegetable garden from the picturesque English-style flower garden.

The Exchange Hotel

400 South Main Street
Gordonsville, VA 22942
(703) 832-2944

Contact: Historic Gordonsville, Inc.
Open: March 15-Dec. 31, Tues.-Sat.
10 a.m.–4 p.m.; open Sun. from
June-Aug., 12:30-4:30 p.m.
Admission: Adults $3.50; seniors $2.50;
children $1. Guided tours, audiovisual
introduction, special programs.
Suggested Time to View House: 45 minutes
Facilities on Premises: Small gift shop
Description of Grounds: Simple grounds
with picnic areas
Best Season to View House: Summer
Number of Yearly Visitors: 5,000
Year House Built: 1860
Number of Rooms: 12

Style of Architecture: Greek Revival
On-Site Parking: Yes **Wheelchair Access:** Yes

Description of House

In the mid 19th century, Gordonsville, Virginia's Exchange Hotel was a welcome stopping place for weary passengers on the Virginia Central Railway. This beautifully-restored antebellum building once housed many elegant guests during the years before the Civil War. After the War started, the hotel was transformed into a as a Confederate military receiving hospital. In one year alone, 23,000 men were treated at the Exchange; 6,000 of these were admitted in one single month—a result of the Wilderness campaign of 1864. By the war's end, the hotel was nearly destroyed and the field behind the building became a cemetery for more than 700 soldiers.

The hotel is partially furnished with antiques of the Civil War era which represent its status as a hotel during this period; the other rooms house a Civil War museum.

Notable Collections on Exhibit

On display are the weapons, uniforms, and personal effects of the Union and Confederate cavalryman, artilleryman, and infantryman. Of particular note are many medical artifacts and surgeons's implements, some of which were used in the very room where they are currently displayed.

Oatlands

Route. 2, Box 352
Leesburg, VA 22075
(703) 777-3174

Contact: Oatlands, Inc.

Open: April-late Dec., Mon.-Sat.
10 a.m.–4:30 p.m., Sun. 1–4:30 p.m.;
closed Thanksgiving

Admission: Adults $5; seniors, students
and group tour (15 or more) $4; under 12
free. Guided tours, audiovisual
presentations.

Suggested Time to View House: 40 minutes

Facilities on Premises: Gift shop (with
books)

Description of Grounds: 4½ acre garden

Best Season to View House: April-Oct.

Number of Yearly Visitors: 50,000

Year House Built: 1803

Number of Rooms: 18

Style of Architecture: Classical Revival

On-Site Parking: Yes **Wheelchair Access:** No

Description of House

The mansion's original owner, George Carter, great-grandson of Virginia's famed grower Robert "King" Carter, built Oatlands in 1803 from bricks molded and fired on the property and from wood brought from the surrounding forests. By 1816, Carter had constructed a gristmill on nearby Goose Creek, supplying ground flour for President Monroe's nearby Oak Hill estate and other area farms. Soon Oatland Mill became the center of a thriving community that included the miller's residence, a blacksmith shop, a school, and a store. Following the war, the Carter fortune declined steadily. In 1897, Oatlands was sold to Stilson Hutchins, the founder of *The Washington Post*. He never lived at Oatlands, however, and the property deteriorated. In spite of its condition, in 1903, Mr. and Mrs. William Corcoran Eustis fell in love with and purchased Oatlands. The grandson of William Corcoran, the Washington banker and philanthropist, and the daughter of Levi P. Morton, Vice President under Benjamin Harrison, together they returned the house and garden to its original beauty.

Between the nation's Capitol and the Shenandoah Valley, in hills that America's early Presidents called home, Oatlands reigns as a prime example of the classic Virginia lifestyle. Oatlands, built in the early 1800s, carefully balances the formality of its architecture with the genuine warmth of the families who once lived there.

Notable Collections on Exhibit

The house is decorated with an excellent collection of pieces ranging from the 18th through the 19th centuries of American, English and French origin. Much of the setting conveys the feeling of the traditional English-style country house of the 1920s and 1930s, when the Eustises were in residence.

Stonewall Jackson House

8 East Washington Street
Lexington, VA 24450
(703) 463-2552

Contact: Historic Lexington Foundation
Open: Mon.-Sat. 9 a.m.–5 p.m. (June-Aug., open until 6 p.m.)
Admission: Group rates available with reservation. Guided tours, introductory slide show, in-school programs.
Suggested Time to View House: 45 minutes
Facilities on Premises: Museum store
Description of Grounds: Restored garden and carriage house
Best Season to View House: Spring-early summer
Number of Yearly Visitors: 35,000 plus
Year House Built: 1801, with a mid 19th-century addition
Number of Rooms: 7 open to the public

Style of Architecture: Federal-style townhouse
On-Site Parking: No **Wheelchair Access:** Yes

Description of House

This former home of Confederate general, Stonewall Jackson, was originally built by the county jailer, Cornelius Dorman, in 1801. A later resident, Dr. Archibald Graham, a town physician, probably built the six-room addition in the 1840s. The house's most famous resident, Thomas Jonathan Jackson, known to the world as "Stonewall" Jackson, was the Confederate general who earned his nickname for his stand at First Manassas and who is best known for his brilliant leadership in the valley campaign of 1862. Jackson lived and taught in Lexington for ten years before the Civil War. A graduate of West Point and a career military officer, Jackson came to Lexington in 1851 to embark on a new career as Professor of Natural Philosophy at the Virginia Military Institute. He and his wife, Mary Anna Morrison, moved to the house early in 1859 and shared two years here before he rode off to war on April 21, 1861.

The brick portion of the house was constructed in 1801 as a two-story, four-bay Federal-style townhouse. The mid 19th-century alterations provided only three bays and an exposed English basement. A mid 19th-century stone addition more than doubled the size. After Jackson died, Mrs. Jackson rented the house for forty years. In 1906 the house became Lexington's only hospital and remained so for nearly fifty years. In 1954, the house was opened as a museum and in 1976, the foundation began a fundraising drive to restore the house to the Jackson period. The restoration was completed in 1979 and the house was opened to the public for guided tours.

Notable Collections on Exhibit

The house is furnished with many of Jackson's own possessions, as well as appropriate period pieces. A rocking chair, mahogany sofa, and an American Bible Society Bible said to have been Jackson's, six original canebottomed chairs and many other personal effects are now on exhibit.

Point of Honor

112 Cabell Street, P.O. Box 60
Lynchburg, VA 24505
(804) 847-1459

Contact: Lynchburg Museum System

Open: Daily 1–4 p.m.; closed Christmas Eve and Day, Thanksgiving and New Year's Day

Admission: Adults $1; students $.50; under 12 free. Guided tours, Christmas open house; Garden Day tour and tea.

Suggested Time to View House: 40 minutes

Description of Grounds: Lawn and grounds

Best Season to View House: Spring-fall

Number of Yearly Visitors: 5,130

Year House Built: c. 1815

Style of Architecture: Federal

Number of Rooms: 7 plus hallways

On-Site Parking: Yes **Wheelchair Access:** No

Description of House

Dr. George Cabell, first resident, was an eminent physician in the area whose most notable patient was statesman Patrick Henry. He established his medical practice in Lynchburg in 1790. A tobacco grower, he also built a tobacco warehouse on his 1000-acre tract and sought to establish a town there. Later residents were all prominent in Lynchburg history.

The mansion is a magnificent example of Federal style residential architecture and includes the distinctive motifs, furnishings, and rich, contrasting colors of the period. The structure is made of Flemish bond brick over a rubble stone basement. The main structure has first and second floor porches. The building is one of few surviving Federal period homes with semi-octagonal bay structures, which flank the central hallway. The interior is made up of finely crafted woodwork which is almost completely original to the house. The furnishings are collected to represent the period of the Cabell family occupancy and include several noteworthy examples of Virginia-made furniture.

Notable Collections on Exhibit

The well-preserved furnishings include a Clementi pianoforte, a fine Virginia dining table which belonged to John Warwick, a Baltimore sideboard, an 18th-century mahogany drop leaf table, and a Virginia china press and chest of drawers. Other outstanding items on display include a drawing of Judge William Daniels, Sr. by St. Memin, a Barr & Barr tea service, and a collection of old Parisian porcelain.

Additional Information

The house has been authentically decorated using wallpaper, paint colors, and methods which would be correct for 1815 and the status of the Cabell family.

Stone House

6511 Sudley Road
Manassas, VA 22110

Contact: Manassas National Park Service

Open: June-Sept., 1–5 p.m.

Admission: $1; family rate $3 (for access to entire battle field and visitors center)

Description of Grounds: The house is on the grounds of the Manassas National Battlefield Park.

Year House Built: c. 1820s

Style of Architecture: Georgian

Description of House

The Stone House remains one of the most notable landmarks on the Manassas battlefield. Even in its heyday the Stone House was never a fancy hotel noted for fine food. The place sold hard liquor to hard men. Its success was short lived, however, as railroads in the 1850s replaced wagons as the principle means of transportation. As the turnpike era ended, the Stone House and its owners, Henry P. and Jane Matthews, seemed to slip into obscurity. But it was not to be. Twice the determined armies of a divided nation would clash on the fields near Bull Run and each time the Stone House would be brought into the mainstream of battle, its significance marked in blood. In this house and others like it, many soldiers's dreams of heroism and valor were forgotten in the nightmare of pain and agony experienced within its walls. For those men the glory of battle was replaced by the grim realities of war.

The house is one of only two surviving Civil War era houses remaining within the park. Built in the 1820s as an inn serving teamsters who drove wagons along the turnpike, the house today stands as a vivid reminder of the past. Much of the structure appears to be original, including the stone walls, windows, and door frames, and several of the upstairs floor boards. Today the house is furnished to resemble its appearance of 1861. Inside the house, two soldiers from the Fifth New York Volunteer Infantry left behind tangible marks of their stay at the house. Private Eugene P. Geer and Charles E. Brehm were wounded on August 30, 1862 in a futile attempt to halt Longstreet's counterattack. Somehow the men found their way to one of the rooms upstairs and carved their initials on the floorboards. Charles Brehm recovered from his wounds and survived the war. Unfortunately, Eugene Geer died of his wounds on September 30, 1862 at the age of seventeen. Their initials are visible today.

Gunston Hall

10709 Gunston Road
Mason Neck, VA 22079
(703) 550-9220

Contact: Board of Regents of Gunston Hall

Open: 9:30 a.m.–5 p.m.; closed New Year's Day, Thanksgiving, Christmas

Admission: Adults $5; seniors and groups $3.50; students $1. Guided tours, orientation video, special seminars.

Suggested Time to View House: 60–90 minutes

Facilities on Premises: Gift shop, picnic area, nature trail

Description of Grounds: Boxwood gardens and other areas of 500 acres open to the public

Number of Yearly Visitors: 45,000-50,000

Year House Built: 1755-59

Number of Rooms: 12

Style of Architecture: Georgian

On-Site Parking: Yes **Wheelchair Access:** Yes

Description of House

The first owner and builder of this impressive mansion was George Mason (1725-1792) a statesman and political thinker whose writings and council played an important role in the founding of our country. He seldom left Gunston Hall and his family; his longest absence was the summer of 1787 when he stayed in Philadelphia to help write the Constitution. Mason helped draft key documents fundamental to American government, the most important being the Virginia Declaration of Rights which became the model for our federal Bill of Rights. Mason's statement, "That all men are by nature equally free and independent and have certain inherent rights... namely, the enjoyment of life and liberty, with the means of acquiring and possessing property, and pursuing and obtaining happiness and safety," was written before Jefferson's Declaration of Independence.

This outstanding example of Colonial Virginia stands on land overlooking the Potomac River near Mount Vernon. The one-and-a-half-story Gunston Hall features a brick exterior with stone quoins, a Palladian portico on landfront, and a Gothic portico on riverfront. Mason began construction of the house before bringing William Buckland from England to complete the building and design the superb carving. The house features a few Mason family pieces; all other furnishings predate 1792, the year of George Mason's death.

Additional Information

Gunston Hall has an exceptionally beautiful formal garden restored by the Garden Club of Virginia. The original boxwood *allee* was planted by George Mason. In addition, the grounds feature several reconstructed outbuildings: the kitchen, laundry, dairy, and smokehouse.

Arlington House—
Robert E. Lee Memorial

George Washington
Memorial Parkway
McLean, VA 22101

Contact: National Park Service
Open: April-Sept. 9:30 a.m.–6 p.m.;
Oct.-March 9:30 a.m.–4:40 p.m.
On-Site Parking: Yes

Activities: Guided tours by appointment;
tourmobiles operate April-Sept.
8 a.m.–7 p.m. and Oct.-March
8 a.m.–5 p.m.
Year House Built: 1807-1817
Style of Architecture: Greek Revival

Description of House

Arlington House is uniquely associated with the families of Washington, Custis, and Lee. This impressive Greek Revival mansion was built by George Washington Parke Custis. He was the grandson of Martha Washington by her first marriage to Daniel Parke Custis. After his father died, young Custis was raised by his grandmother and her second husband, George Washington at Mount Vernon. In 1804, Custis married and had a daughter, Mary Anna Randolph Custis. Young Robert E. Lee, whose mother was a cousin of Mrs. Custis, frequently visited Arlington. Two years after graduating from West Point, Lieutenant Lee married Mary Custis at Arlington on June 30. The couple shared this home with Mary's parents. When Mary's father died, he left the estate to his wife and later to his daughter and husband, Robert E. Lee.

The Arlington House, overlooking the Potomac River and Washington D.C., was built on a 1,100-acre estate. The house was designed by George Hadfield, a young English architect who was for a time in charge of the construction of the Capitol. The north and south wings were completed between 1802 and 1804. The large center section and the portico, presenting an imposing front over 100 feet in length, were finished thirteen years later. Robert E. Lee described the house, situated on a hill high above the Potomac as one "anyone might see with half an eye." The furnished rooms feature several pieces which belonged to family members china, silver, glassware, and twin serving tables in the dining room, and a small cupboard in the dressing room.

Additional Information

A wartime law required that property owners in areas occupied by Federal troops appear in person to pay their taxes. Unable to comply with this rule, Mrs. Lee saw her estate confiscated in 1864. An 200-acre section was set aside as a military cemetery, the beginning of today's Arlington National Cemetery. In 1882, George Custis Lee's suit against the Federal Government for the return of his property was successful. By then, hundreds of graves covered the hills of Arlington and he accepted the Government's offer of $150,000 for the property.

The Claude Moore Colonial Farm

6310 Georgetown Pike
McLean, VA 22101
(703) 442-7557

Contact: The Claude Moore Colonial Farm

Open: April 1-Dec. 20, Wed.-Sun.
10 a.m.–4:30 p.m.

Admission: Adults $2; seniors and children (3-12) $1. Group visits must be scheduled; special events; environmental living program; 18th-century skills course, special access for physically challenged people may be made by calling the office in advance.

Description of Grounds: A 100-acre cultivated farm complete with all necessary outbuildings

Year House Built: c. 1800

Style of Architecture: Farmhouse

Description of House

The Claude Moore Colonial Farm at Turkey Run is a living history museum which demonstrates the life of a poor family living on a small farm in northern Virginia during the late colonial period. The farmhouse and related buildings stand in stark contrast to the antebellum mansions in the area, yet a visit will give visitors real insight to how the "other half" lived in 18th-century Virginia. The farm includes approximately 100 acres of land, twelve of which are farmed with corn, tobacco, wheat, kitchen gardens and an orchard. The fields are tilled, planted and cultivated by hand, applying basic principles of hoe agriculture. The small log house is used as the family dwelling, where meals are prepared over the hearth fire from food raised on the farm. Clothing, furniture, tools and equipment used by the farm family are reproductions of 18th-century artifacts.

Additional Information

The farm hosts a series of special events which range from corn and wheat planting to candle making and a pig roast. Each year at harvest time there is a week-long Autumn Market Fair in which the farm's produce and crafts are sold.

Belle Grove Plantation

P.O. Box 137
Middletown, VA 22645
(703) 869-2028

Contact: National Trust for Historic
Preservation

Open: Mid March-mid Nov., Mon.-Sat.
10 a.m.–4 p.m., Sun. 1 p.m.-5 p.m.

Admission: Adults $3.50; senior citizens $3;
children (6-12) $2. Guided tours by
volunteer docents.

Suggested Time to View House: 60 minutes

Facilities on Premises: Gift shop, book
shop and quilt shop

Description of Grounds: A small
demonstration garden with old
varieties of plants and flowers

Style of Architecture: Neo-Classical
(Jefferson's design influence)

Best Season to View House: Spring

Number of Yearly Visitors: 60,000

Number of Rooms: 7 open to public

Year House Built: 1794

On-Site Parking: Yes **Wheelchair Access:** No

Description of House

Belle Grove was the home of Major Isaac Hite, Jr. and his family for more than seventy years. Major Hite was the grandson of Joist Hite, one of the first permanent settlers in the Shenandoah Valley. Much of Belle Grove's architectural importance derives from the active involvement of Thomas Jefferson in its design. Jefferson's considerable talent was enlisted by his close friend, James Madison. Madison had become Major Hite's brother-in-law in 1783 when his sister, Nelly Conway Madison, of Montpelier married Hite. Belle Grove also witnessed action during the Civil War when it served as headquarters for Union General Philip Sheridan in 1864.

Surrounded by the fertile farmland of the northern Shenandoah Valley, Belle Grove is at once an 18th-century plantation, a working farm, and a center for the study of traditional rural crafts. Early in the 19th century, the dwelling was described as "a most spacious and elegant building." The building's architectural value has not lessened over the years, and its dressed limestone south facade makes it one of the most imposing structures of the late 18th century remaining in the Shenandoah Valley. The house is furnished appropriately to the period, and includes some original pieces.

Additional Information

Following James Madison's marriage to Dolley Payne Todd in 1794, the newlywed couple spent part of their honeymoon visiting the Hites at Belle Grove.

Montpelier

P.O. Box 67
Montpelier Station, VA 22957
(703) 672-2728

Contact: National Trust for Historic
Preservation

Open: Daily 10 a.m.–4 p.m.; closed
Thanksgiving, Christmas, New
Year's Day

Admission: Adults $6; seniors $5; children
(6-12) $1; group rates available. Guided
tours, slide show.

Suggested Time to View House: 90 minutes

Description of Grounds: Tree walk, James
Madison family cemetery

Best Season to View House: Spring-fall

Year House Built: Original portions in
1760, additions in 1797, 1809, 1901

Number of Rooms: 55

Number of Yearly Visitors: 40,000

Style of Architecture: Georgian (original
1760 structure)

On-Site Parking: Yes **Wheelchair Access:** Yes

Description of House

Three generations of the Madison family built this homestead and made it a center of renowned hospitality. James Madison, Jr., the fourth President of the United States, was raised by a family that had prospered in Virginia since 1653. Montpelier was first settled in 1723 by his grandparents. Born March 15, 1751, James, Jr. was the first of twelve children. As the eldest son, he was given the best education, eventually concentrating in law and religion and settling on a political career. Madison's most far reaching contributions were made between 1785 and 1789. As his title "Father of the Constitution" indicates, he was the primary author of that document as well as one of the authors of the Federalist Papers. His participation was also a key factor in the passage of the Bill of Rights. Montpelier later passed into the hands of the Dupont family, wealthy industrialists from Delaware.

Madison's father built the original portion of the home in 1760. James Madison added onto the house twice in his lifetime, the first time to provide living quarters for himself and his bride, Dolley Payne Todd, a young Quaker widow. In addition to the main floor of the rambling, fifty-five room mansion, more than 100 other structures and features may be viewed, including houses and barns, stables, a bowling alley, and the garden temple Madison built over his ice house. Spacious panoramas reveal vast lawns, steeplechase and race courses, and a formal garden. Very few original furnishings remain in the house as most were sold at auction by Dolley Madison. The family furniture on display includes three Windsor chairs, a bookcase, and a small table. Two rooms are partially furnished with Dupont family furniture.

Additional Information

The spacious lawns and grounds are the perfect setting for the annual Montpelier Hunt Races, sponsored by the steeplechase association. Contact the house for schedule information.

Mount Vernon

Mount Vernon, VA 22121
(703) 780-2000

Contact: Mount Vernon Ladies' Association
Open: March-Oct. 9 a.m.–5 p.m.; Nov.-Feb. 9 a.m.–4 p.m.
Admission: Adults $7; seniors $6; children (6-11) $3; group rates available (20 or more) please inquire. Guided tours, special holiday programs, after hours tours by special arrangement, please inquire for schedule.
Suggested Time to View House: 2 hours

Facilities on Premises: Gift shop, snack bar, restaurant, post office
Description of Grounds: More than 30 acres of gardens and wooded grounds including a botanical garden used by George Washington
Best Season to View House: Year round
Year House Built: 1735 (original structure)
Style of Architecture: Georgian
Number of Rooms: 14 open to public
On-Site Parking: Yes **Wheelchair Access:** Yes

Description of House

Considered the most popular historic home in the country, Mount Vernon, the plantation home of George and Martha Washington, continues to impress visitors with its meticulously restored appearance and beautiful grounds. It is not hard to imagine the elegant entertaining of politicians and dignitaries that went on in these beautifully decorated and furnished rooms. Mount Vernon is an outstanding example of Colonial architecture which Washington himself appears to have designed. The house shows influences of the Governor's Palace in Williamsburg, and other design elements, such as the large Palladian window, from 18th-century English books on the design of country houses.

The exterior is unusual in its use of rusticated boards (a term used by Washington) meaning that the siding was beveled to give an appearance of stone, then sand was applied to the freshly painted surface. The most striking architectural feature of the mansion is the high-columned piazza extending the full length of the house. This seems to have been an innovation introduced by Washington which would later be copied by others. The interior is equally remarkable; the paint has been restored to the original colors favored by Washington at the end of his life. A vivid green decorates the dining room while a bright blue enlivens the west parlor. The original wallpaper has also been carefully restored.

The room settings are based on a 1799 inventory prepared after Washington's death. Each object—from the English liquor cabinet to Martha's French desk—has been carefully arranged in their original locations.

Notable Collections on Exhibit

The period furnishings and artifacts include many outstanding and historic items such as Washington's Presidential chair, a plaster profile of Washington by artist Joseph Wright, rare mezzotints of Washington, Franklin, and Lafayette, Washington's brass telescope, and a series of portraits and paintings by the well-known artists Charles Willson Peale, Gilbert Stuart, and James Sharples, among others.

Additional Information

The Mount Vernon complex features a full complement of outbuildings typical for Colonial plantations. Visitors are able to see a separate kitchen where all food was prepared, the smokehouse where hams and other meats were stored, the spinning house, a reconstructed greenhouse and slave-quarters, a 19th-century ice house, as well as the period gardens. Washington's design for the plantation included three gardens: an upper garden for a variety of flowers, vegetables and trees; the lower garden which supplied fresh produce for the house, and the botanical garden used by Washington to experiment with seeds and plants not native to Virginia soil.

Pope-Leighey House

P.O. Box 37
Mount Vernon, VA 22121
(703) 780-4000

Contact: National Trust for Historic
Preservation

Open: 9:30 a.m.–4:30 p.m.; closed
Thanksgiving, Christmas Day. Open
weekends only Jan.-Feb.

Admission: Adults $4; students and seniors
$3. Guided tours.

Description of Grounds: On the
landscaped grounds of Woodlawn
Plantation

Year House Built: 1940

Style of Architecture: Modern

Description of House

Originally located in Falls Church, Virginia, this distinctive house was built by one of the most celebrated architects of the 20th century, Frank Lloyd Wright. He designed the house for Loren Pope, a man of moderate means.

Constructed of cypress, brick, and glass, the Pope-Leighey House exhibits many of the significant contributions that Wright made to contemporary architecture—concepts of organic unity, free and fluid space and the relation of the building and its construction materials to their natural setting. The house contains many architectural features, which, although familiar today, were uncommon when the house was built. These include a flat roof, recessed lighting, a carport, heated concrete slab floors and windows designed as an integral part of the wall. Even by today's standards, the Pope-Leighey House, built more than a half-century ago, seems surprisingly modern. The house features many interior furnishings especially designed or selected by Wright.

Although designed by a famous architect, this house was not built for a wealthy man. The structure reflects Wright's belief that people of moderate means were entitled to well-designed homes. In 1938, Wright said, "The house of moderate cost is not only America's major architectural problem, but the problem most difficult for her major architects... I would rather solve it...than build anything I can think of..." This concept, which Wright described as Usonian architecture, had a major impact on the architecture of this century.

Additional Information

The house stands in striking contrast to the nearby Georgian plantation house, Woodlawn. Visitors will have a unique architectural experience in visiting these two buildings maintained by the National Trust for Historic Preservation.

Woodlawn Plantation

P.O. Box 37
Mount Vernon, VA 22121
(703) 780-4000

Contact: National Trust for Historic
Preservation
Open: Daily 9:30 a.m.–4:30 p.m.; closed
Thanksgiving, Christmas, New
Year's Day. Open weekends only
Jan.-Feb.
Admission: Adults $5; seniors and students
$3.50. Guided tours.
Suggested Time to View House: 40 minutes
Facilities on Premises: Gift shop, book store
Description of Grounds: Formal gardens,
herb garden, orchards
Best Season to View House: Spring-fall
Year House Built: 1800-1805

Style of Architecture: Late Georgian
On-Site Parking: Yes **Wheelchair Access:** Yes

Description of House

Once part of George Washington's land holdings, Woodlawn Plantation provides a fascinating view of plantation life in northern Virginia between 1800 and 1840. The retired president bequeathed the estate to his adopted daughter, Eleanor Park Custis ("Nelly") and his nephew, Lawrence Lewis. The couple commissioned Dr. William Thornton, architect of the U.S. Capitol, to design the mansion. Lawrence and Nelly Lewis were actively involved in the business and social life of Alexandria, Washington D.C., and Georgetown, and Woodlawn was the site of much of their entertaining. Later occupants included Quaker and Baptist settlers, a playwright, and Senator Oscar Underwood and his wife.

This impressive Georgian brick mansion stands on a hill overlooking Mount Vernon and the Potomac River. Construction began in 1800; the Lewises moved to the property once the north wing was completed in 1802. It took another four years to finish the entire mansion. Despite long periods when the house remained unoccupied, Woodlawn today showcases a splendid interior with fine period furnishings and paintings dating from the Federal period; many of the furnishings are family owned. Woodlawn's elegant proportions and gracious interiors make it one of the major Potomac River plantation homes.

Additional Information

The grounds feature extensive lawns, large trees, boxwood planting and a Colonial Revival garden based on a design by the house's architect, William Thornton. The Pope-Leighey House, designed by Frank Lloyd Wright, also stands on the grounds.

The Newsome House

2803 Oak Avenue
Newport News, VA 23607
(804) 247-2360

Contact: The Newsome House Museum
and Cultural Center

Open: By appointment

Admission: Rates vary. Free admission for
special events. Guided tours,
audiovisual presentations, special
programs and exhibits.

Suggested Time to View House: 30 minutes

Description of Grounds: Small landscaped
yard enclosed by wrought iron fence

Best Season to View House: Year round

Year House Built: 1899

Number of Rooms: 15

Style of Architecture: Modified Queen Anne

On-Site Parking: Yes **Wheelchair Access:** Yes

Description of House

This beautiful Queen Anne-style house was home to J.T. Newsome, a prominent local black attorney. Newsome was the sixteenth of seventeen children born to former slaves. He transcended his poor rural environment to become one of the first black lawyers to argue before the Virginia Supreme Court. He was also a civil rights activist, the editor of a weekly black newspaper, a churchman, and an orator. He and his wife, Mary, welcomed important guests such as Booker T. Washington to their home, and also offered refuge to troubled individuals. They hosted meetings to organize the Warwick County Colored Voters League and the creation of the city's first high school for black students. Newsome was appointed sergeant-at-arms at the 1920 National Republican Convention in Chicago. At the time of his death, he was president of the Old Dominion Bar Association.

This elegant structure features a wrap-around porch, a Palladian window and a graceful turret with bay windows. The home's interior features gleaming oak floors, exquisite Victorian woodwork and stained glass. Family-owned furnishings are on display throughout much of the dwelling. The house also functions as a repository and research facility for archival items and objects relating to the Newsome family and the rich black cultural heritage of Newport News.

Notable Collections on Exhibit

The period furnishings include a Steinway piano, grandfather clock, tiger maple sideboard, upholstered wine chairs, framed bevelled mirrors and prints that belonged to the Newsome family. The master bedroom features a permanent installation called "The Life and Times of Joseph Thomas Newsome". The museum collection consists of several thousand pieces, including archival materials, artifacts, and books.

Additional Information

The facility offers a variety of programs including meeting space for seminars and receptions, educational activities, and exhibits on black culture.

Hunter House Victorian Museum

240 W. Freemason Street
Norfolk, VA 23510
(804) 623-9814

Contact: Hunter Foundation

Open: April-Dec., Wed.-Sat.
10 a.m.–3:30 p.m., Sun. 12–3:30 p.m.

Activities: Guided tours, teas, ice cream socials, Christmas open house

Suggested Time to View House: 1 hour

Facilities on Premises: Gift shop

Description of Grounds: Townhouse garden and garden benches

Best Season to View House: May-Aug.

Number of Yearly Visitors: 4,000

Year House Built: 1894

Style of Architecture: Richardsonian Romanesque

Number of Rooms: 15, 9 open to public

On-Site Parking: Yes

Wheelchair Access: No

Description of House

This imposing Victorian house was built for the prominent merchant and banker, James Wilson Hunter. Mr. Hunter and his wife, Lizzie, moved into their new home on the cobblestoned Freemason Street with their family of one son, James Wilson, Jr., and two daughters, Harriet and Cornelia. As the children never married, the house became their family home.

Rich in architectural details, the house displays the family's collection of Victorian furnishings and decorative pieces, including stained glass windows, a Renaissance Revival bedchamber suite, a nursery of children's playthings, an inglenook, and an elaborately embroidered crazy quilt.

Notable Collections on Exhibit

The collections are complemented with lavish period reproduction floor coverings, wall coverings, lighting fixtures and drapery treatments. Also exhibited is a collection of early 20th-century medical memorabilia, including an electrocardiograph machine, belonging to the late Dr. James Wilson Hunter, Jr.

Additional Information

The Hunter House forms part of the Freemason Historic District walking tour which takes visitors past many other beautiful Victorian homes in the neighborhood. As part of the tour, visitors will see the Allmand-Archer House, the oldest house in the city.

Moses Myers House

323 East Freemason Street
Norfolk, VA 23510
(804) 622-1211

Contact: The Chrysler Museum

Open: Jan.-March 31, Tues.-Sat. 12–5 p.m.;
   April 1-Dec. 31, Tues.-Sat.
   10 a.m.–5 p.m., Sun. 12–5 p.m.

Admission: Adults $2; seniors and
   children $1. Guided tours.

Suggested Time to View House: 40 minutes

Facilities on Premises: Gift shop

Description of Grounds: 18th-century
   garden including cutting, herb and
   formal sections

Year House Built: 1792

Best Season to View House:
   Spring-summer

Number of Rooms: 9

Style of Architecture: Federal-Georgian
   townhouse

On-Site Parking: Yes

Description of House

Moses Myers and his wife came to Norfolk in 1787 from New York. They were one of the first Jewish families to settle in Norfolk. Myers was a merchant and traded both domestically and internationally. Five generations of the family lived in the house between 1792 and 1930. In 1931, the house was sold to a preservation group and was soon opened for public tours.

The Myers House was one of the first brick homes built after the Revolution. The red Flemish bond brick masonry alternates stretchers, or long bricks, with the shorter header bricks to create this Federal-style townhouse. The arched fanlight attic window, white classical pediment and slim-columned porches contrast against the building's brick facade, accentuating the home's late Georgian/early Federal style. In 1797, the Myers added a two-story octagonal wing to the rear of their house to accommodate their growing family and the couple's social obligations. The wing consisted of two bedrooms and a long dining room. A separate kitchen was constructed on the side of the house.

Approximately seventy percent of the furnishings owned by the first generation of the family now decorate the house. The remaining portion of the collection is drawn from the Chrysler Museum's decorative arts collection and represents the Federal period.

Notable Collections on Exhibit

The collections include the tall case clock and pier mirrors in the passage below which actually came to Norfolk with Moses and Eliza in 1787. Two Gilbert Stuart companion portraits depicting Mr. and Mrs. Myers hang in the drawing room. The collection also boasts artworks by Thomas Sully, John Wesley Jarvis, Charles Bird King, William Dunlap and many other noted American artists.

The Willoughby-Baylor House

601 East Freemason Street
Norfolk, VA 23510
(804) 622-1211

Contact: The Chrysler Museum
Open: Admission by appointment only
Admission: Adults $2; children (6-18)
$1. Guided tours, holiday events, living history performances, decprating seminars, horse drawn carriage rides.
Suggested Time to View House: 1 hour
Description of Grounds: 18th-century garden
Best Season to View House: March-Oct.
Number of Yearly Visitors: 5,000
Year House Built: 1794
Style of Architecture: Federal/Georgian
Number of Rooms: 6 on view

Description of House

Owner of a construction business, William Willougby's company prospered during Norfolk's reconstruction following the American Revolution. Willoughby only lived in the house for a few short years before he died in 1800 at age forty-two. Upon his death, the house went to his daughter Margaret Willoughby Sharp who bequeathed it in 1845 to her daughter Elizabeth Frances, wife of Dr. Baynham Baylor. The house served as home to the Baylor family until 1890. During the early to mid 20th century, the house fell into ruin as a boarding house.

The popular Georgian and Federal styles are reflected in the construction of the Willoughby-Baylor House. The Georgian style is evident in the home's symmetrically placed windows and baseboard to chair-rail paneling inside. During a later renovation, the family added a true Federal-style porch with slender white columns which contrast with the Flemish bond brick. The furnishings are on loan from The Chrysler Museum's extensive decorative arts collection. Selection was based on the estate inventory made after William Willoughby's death.

Notable Collections on Exhibit

The collections showcase some very fine examples of traditional Federal furnishings. One notable item is an early 19th-century American tall case clock. In addition to telling the time and date, it also shows the phases of the moon, an important indicator of the changing tides which allowed merchant ships to travel into and out of Hampton Roads. The front hall contains two exquisite amethyst globe sconces. There is also a Virginia black walnut chest with Virginia soft pine bracing (visitors can see where the cabinet makers practiced on the pine before inscribing the final pattern into the black walnut). Silver serving spoons made by Jeremiah Andrews, one of Norfolk silversmiths active in the late 17th century, are also on display.

Centre Hill Mansion

1 Centre Hill Court
Petersburg, VA 23803
(804) 733-2400

Contact: Petersburg Museums
Open: April-Oct., Mon.-Sat. 9 a.m.–5 p.m.,
Sun. 12:30–5 p.m.; Nov.-March, Mon.
Sat. 10 a.m.–4 p.m., Sun. 12:30–4 p.m.
Activities: Guided tours; lecture series;
changing exhibitions
Suggested Time to View House: 45 minutes
Facilities on Premises: Museum shop
Description of Grounds: Gardens restored
by the Garden Club of Virginia
Best Season to View House: Spring
Number of Yearly Visitors: 11,000
Year House Built: 1823
Style of Architecture: Federal with Greek
Revival additions

On-Site Parking: Yes **Wheelchair Access:** No

Description of House

The house was built in by Robert Bolling IV, a prominent Virginian merchant and property owner. The mansion is one of the oldest and most historic in the city. During its finest hours, the house received three U.S. Presidents as guests: President John Tyler, President Abraham Lincoln and President William Howard Taft. Bolling's son, Robert Buckner Bolling, inherited the property and remodeled it in the late 1840s in the Greek Revival Style. In 1901, Charles David Hall made additional Colonial Revival changes.

The furnishings have been collected and are appropriate to the period of the house. One of the more notable items on display is a rare 1886 Knabe Art piano.

Notable Collections on Exhibit

The mansion displays various 19th-century decorative arts as well as an exhibit of Civil War memorabilia. There is also an exhibit on the early history of Petersburg.

Additional Information

Visitors to Petersburg should make an effort to see the Trapezium House (North Market Street). This unusually shaped house has no right angles and no parallel sides because the owner was convinced that evil spirits and ghosts inhabited them.

Agecroft Hall

4305 Sulgrave Road
Richmond, VA 23226
(804) 353-4241

Contact: Agecroft Association

Open: Tues.-Sat. 10 a.m.–4 p.m., Sun. 2–5 p.m.; closed July 4th, Christmas Eve and Day, Thanksgiving, New Year's Day

Admission: $3 per person; special rates for children and groups. Guided tours, audiovisual presentation, lectures, living history events.

Suggested Time to View House: 1 hour

Description of Grounds: Herb garden, knot garden, formal garden, and numerous boxwood walks

Best Season to View House: April-Sept.

Year House Built: 1925 in US, 1485 in England

Number of Yearly Visitors: 21,000

Style of Architecture: Tudor

Number of Rooms: 9

On-Site Parking: Yes **Wheelchair Access:** Yes

Description of House

While many historic houses have been moved from their original locations, few have travelled as far as Agecroft Hall. The mansion originally stood in Lancashire, England and was built in the 15th century. In England, the house was lived in by the Langley family and then the Dauntesey family until the early 1900s. In 1925, the house was purchased by Mr. Thomas C. Williams and brought to Richmond. It was lived in as a private home until 1967, and became a house museum in 1969.

This country manor house was originally built in 1425 and is an excellent example of Tudor architecture. The interior features rich oak paneling and leaded glass windows. The mansion is now decorated with furnishings of the Tudor and early Stuart period; all of the pieces are authentic with the exception of the library which features 20th-century items.

Notable Collections on Exhibit

The manor's furnishings recreate the English lifestyle through the period furnishings, many paintings, and extensive array of decorative arts including silver, stoneware, and tapestries.

The White House of the Confederacy

1201 East Clay Street
Richmond, VA 23219
(804) 649-1861

Contact: Confederate Memorial Literary Society

Open: Mon.-Sat. 10 a.m.–5 p.m., Sun. 12–5 p.m.; closed Thanksgiving Day, Christmas Day, and New Year's Day

Admission: Adults $4; seniors $3.50; children (7-12) $2.25; children (under 7) free. Guided tours; specialized tours focusing on domestic life and decorative arts; and costumed tours for the visually and hearing impaired.

Suggested Time to View House: 90 minutes

Facilities on Premises: Modern Civil War Museum, museum store, research library

Description of Grounds: Formal garden behind the White House and brick patio with military artifacts to the east of the House

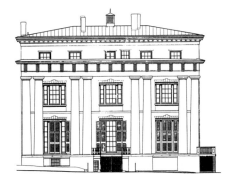

Best Season to View House: Spring

Year House Built: 1818

Number of Rooms: 11 period rooms

Number of Yearly Visitors: 90,000

Style of Architecture: Neo-classical

On-Site Parking: Yes **Wheelchair Access:** No

Description of House

The White House of the Confederacy was the executive mansion of Jefferson Davis during the Civil War and was the Confederacy's center of state and social activity. After the Civil War, the house served as headquarters for occupying Federal troops during Reconstruction. The house has been a museum since 1896. In 1988 it was re-opened as a restored historic house.

The White House has been restored to its Civil War appearance and is decorated in the Southern Victorian and Roccoco Revival styles. A majority of the furnishings have Davis family provenance. The house maintains the original gasoliers while the wallpapers and carpets match those in the house from 1861 to 1865. The majority of the furnishings on display were in the house during the Civil War. Those remaining are appropriate to the region for this period.

Notable Collections on Exhibit

The eleven period rooms showcase over 1,000 objects including paintings, sculpture, furniture and decorative objects. The Museum of the Confederacy, next door to the White House, maintains the world's most comprehensive collection of Confederate art and artifacts.

Maymont

1700 Hampton Street
Richmond, VA 23220
(804) 358-7166

Contact: Maymont Foundation
Open: Tues.-Sun. 12–5 p.m.
Admission: Donations are
  encouraged. Guided tours (by
  reservation), estate walk
Suggested Time to View House: 30 minutes
Description of Grounds: 105 acres with
  Italian and Japanese gardens
Best Season to View House: April-Sept.
Year House Built: 1893
Number of Rooms: 33 (16 on display)

Number of Yearly Visitors: 300,000
Style of Architecture: Romanesque Revival
On-Site Parking: Yes **Wheelchair Access:** No

Description of House

Maymont was the estate of a wealthy entrepreneur, Major James Henry Dooley (1841-1922). He named it Maymont after his wife, the former Sallie May (1846-1925). After serving in the Army of Northern Virginia during the War between the States. Major Dooley began a law practice in his native Richmond and contributed to the rebuilding of Virginia by serving for six years in the state legislature, and offering his time and financial support to a variety of philanthropies.

The mansion was designed by Edgerton S. Rogers in the neo-Romanesque style, with a massive sandstone facade accented by pink granite columns. The architectural details of the formal rooms recall various historical styles—most notably the two drawing rooms in 18th-century French styles. Stained glass transoms, woodwork, ceilings, and mantels vary in design from room to room of this opulent home. All of the objects in the house were owned by the Dooleys; the furnishings include Revival-style pieces, art nouveau objects, porcelain, tapestries, sculpture, rugs, and other items reflecting the ornate tastes of the turn of the century.

Notable Collections on Exhibit

The Maymont House Collection showcases decorative and fine arts acquired in Europe and the U.S. at the turn of the century by the Dooleys to furnish their ornate mansion. The collection includes a unique Tiffany silver and ivory dressing table, a 17th-century Italian marble group by sculptor Grassia, and a monumental Rococo-Revival cabinet exhibited at the 1855 Paris Universal exposition. The Bocock Carriage Collection includes twenty-three vehicles and other antique equestrian equipment.

Additional Information

The grounds feature over 200 species of native and exotic trees and shrubs ranging from a Persian Parrotia to a White Enkianthus. There is also an award-winning Japanese garden and a carefully restored Italian garden for visitors's enjoyment. For the younger set, Maymont features a children's farm with a wide variety of animals including domestic animals as well as rare and endangered breeds.

Wickham House

1015 East Clay Street
Richmond, VA 23219
(804) 649-0711

Contact: The Valentine Museum
Open: Mon.-Sat. 10 a.m.–5 p.m.;
   Sun. 12–5 p.m.
Admission: Adults $3.50; seniors $3;
   students $2.75; children $1.50; group
   rates available. Guided tours,
   workshops, lunch facilities.
Suggested Time to View House: 1 hour
Facilities: Museum and gift shop
Description of Grounds: Garden
Best Season to View House: April-Oct.
Year House Built: 1812
Number of Rooms: 12

Number of Yearly Visitors: 102,000
Style of Architecture: Neo-Classical
On-Site Parking: Yes   **Wheelchair Access:** Yes

Description of House

Wickham House was built by Richmond lawyer John Wickham, who lived here with his wife, Elizabeth, her father-in-law, and fourteen of their future family of seventeen children from 1815 to 1820. Wickham gained national fame when he was on the defense team for the treason trial of Aaron Burr. He was originally from Long Island and came to Virginia as a young man and as a Tory. He attended William and Mary Law school, and lived in Richmond from 1791 until his death in 1839. Later the house was home to John Ballard (1854-1858), owner of the Exchange Hotel, James Brooks (1858 to 1882), a prominent businessman, and Mann S. Valentine (1882 to 1892), inventor of the automatic bottle corker and other unusual items; Valentine left $50,000 to endow the house as a museum.

Designed by Massachusetts architect Alexander Parris, this Neo-Classical structure features ten rooms and a basement complete with a wine cellar and slave quarters. The interior features a remarkable series of wall paintings which have been attributed to George Bridport, an English decorative painter working out of Philadelphia. The patterns feature illustrations drawn from the book *Costumes of the Ancients* including figures involved in bacchanalian rites. The stucco work and many of the details from the woodwork are from Asher Benjamin's *American Builders Companion*. The curving staircase in the entryway is one of the most photographed in the city. The furnishings feature four pieces owned by the original owners: two New York cardtables made by Charles Honore Lannuier and two locally-made bookcases. The rest of the furniture has been borrowed from other museums such as the Met, Henry Ford, Museum of the City of New York, and the Maryland Historical Society.

Additional Information

The house is currently undergoing restoration, but visitors are able to see the remarkable paneling, Neo-Classical wall paintings, and *trompe l'oeil* ceiling paintings when visiting.

Wilton House Museum

215 South Wilton Road
Richmond, VA 23226
(804) 282-5936

Contact: National Society of Colonial
Dames in America

Open: Tues.-Sat. 10 a.m.–4:30 p.m.,
Sun. 1:30–4:30

Admission: Adults $3.50; group rate $2;
students, seniors and AAA members $3;
children under 6 free. Guided tours.

Suggested Time to View House:
45–60 minutes

Facilities on Premises: Small gift shop

Description of Grounds: Landscaped in a
terraced colonial revival garden with a
spectacular view of the James River

Best Season to View House: Spring

Year House Built: 1750-53

Number of Rooms: 10

Number of Yearly Visitors: 3,600

Style of Architecture: Early Georgian

On-Site Parking: Yes **Wheelchair Access:** Yes

Description of House

William Randolph III and his wife Anne Carter Harrison Randolph were part of the Colonial tobacco aristocracy which developed along the James River. Connected by birth and marriage to every important family in the region, they hosted several important visitors in their house including George Washington and the Marquis de Lafayette. The men in the family participated in Virginia politics and all served in the House of Burgesses.

Wilton is an important early Georgian-style double pile plantation house with Neo-Classical detailing and full heart pine paneling in every room. The house clearly demonstrates the social aspirations and restrained conservative taste of Virginia Colonial aristocracy who patterned their houses and lifestyles after the English gentry of whom they considered themselves to be a part. The full, early Georgian paneling is used throughout the entire house including the small alcoves on each side of the eight chimneys. Wilton is probably the only house in the U.S. with such complete architectural interior paneling. Paint research is revealing the original colors as they are being replaced. The house is completely furnished with American and English decorative arts from the late 18th and early 19th centuries. Many pieces are Southern in origin.

Notable Collections on Exhibit

The strongest collection is the American 18th-century furniture which includes an important Simon Willard tall case clock, a Southern sideboard, Newport chairs, bed and tall chest, as well as fine examples of 18th-century glass, and ten original family portraits.

Buena Vista

Penmar Avenue and 9th Street S.E.
Roanoke, VA 23219
(804) 786-3143

Contact: City of Roanoke
Open: Call for schedule
Admission: Donations. Guided tours.
Suggested Time to View House: 30 minutes
Description of Grounds: Landscaped
  grounds
Best Season to View House:
  Spring-summer
Number of Yearly Visitors: 300,000
Year House Built: c. 1840
Style of Architecture: Greek Revival

On-Site Parking: Yes **Wheelchair Access:** No

Description of House

This lovely antebellum mansion was built for George Tayloe (1804-1897). He was born and raised at the well-known Mount Airy plantation in nearby Richmond county. Tayloe was prominent figure in both state and local affairs. He represented Roanoke county in the state legislature, and was a signer of the Ordinance of Secession, although he was originally opposed to secession. Tayloe is chiefly remembered in the Roanoke area for his support of Hollins College.

Buena Vista is a notable example of the type of Greek Revival architecture constructed in the Roanoke area by master builders who acquired their knowledge of Greek detail through reading architectural handbooks. The name Buena Vista refers to the prominent setting of the mansion which overlooks the surrounding countryside. The exterior of the two-story brick dwelling features a combination of American bond and Flemish bond patterns. There is a massive Greek Doric portico on the front facade and a central entrance with simple pilasters and entablature. The interior features much of the original wood and plasterwork and exhibits a collection of period furnishings.

Additional Information

In addition to the main house, the grounds feature a log meat house, one of the few remaining log structures in the city. In later years, the simple structure was used as a garage.

Woodrow Wilson Birthplace

24 North Coalter Street
Staunton, VA 24401
(703) 885-0897

Contact: Woodrow Wilson Birthplace
Foundation, Inc.
Open: Daily 9 a.m.–5 p.m. (Sun. in Jan. and
Feb., 1–5 p.m.); closed Thanksgiving,
Christmas and New Year's Day
Admission: Adult groups (10 or more) $4;
children (6-12) $1; seniors $4.50. Guided
tour, seven exhibit galleries.
Suggested Time to View House: 30 minutes
Facilities on Premises: Gift shop
Description of Grounds: Formal Victorian
bowknot garden created in 1933 by the
Garden Club of Virginia
Best Season to View House: April-Oct.
Number of Yearly Visitors: 32,000
Year House Built: 1846
Number of Rooms: 12

Style of Architecture: Greek Revival

Description of House

Woodrow Wilson served two terms as President of the United States. During those early years of the 20th century, from 1913 to 1921, our nation entered World War I and experienced vast changes in industry and government at home—all of them shaped by the minister's son born in the Presbyterian Manse in Staunton, Virginia. As President, Wilson was our first international leader. His vision for world peace and collective security among nations is stronger than ever as the 20th century fades into history.

Built by the Presbyterians as a manse for their ministers, the handsome house is restored to its appearance at the time the Reverend Joseph Ruggles Wilson and his family lived there. The twelve recreated rooms contain many items that belonged to the Wilsons. Wilson was born into these unpretentious surroundings on December 28, 1856. The house is one of few birthplaces of a President still in existence in its original form. The furnishings are a combination of mid 19th-century period pieces and items which belonged to President Woodrow Wilson and his family.

Notable Collections on Exhibit

The Wilson artifacts feature the crib where Woodrow Wilson was placed as an infant after birth, and his mother's rocking chair. Also on display are his mother's guitar, her flower vase, her side saddle, some of the family china and silver, his father's books, rocker, and walking stick as well as the Wilson family Bible. The most prized possession on display is the 1919 Pierce-Arrow limousine Wilson used in the White House and bought for his personal use after retirement; the car is in running condition and completely restored.

Stratford Hall Plantation

Stratford, VA 22558
(804) 493-8038

Contact: Stratford Hall Plantation

Open: Daily 9 a.m.–4:40 p.m., closed on
Christmas Day

Activities: Tour of the "Great House,"
special furniture and garden tours are
available; plantation lunch during
summer months

Description of Grounds: The plantation is
still managed as a working farm on 1600
of its original acres.

Year House Built: Late 1730s

Style of Architecture: Colonial

Description of House

Perhaps no other family in American history has produced as many men who have served their country with such distinction as the Lee family. Thomas Lee was justice, burgess, commander of the militia and finally acting governor of the Colony. Of his six sons, five played major roles in the creation of a new nation. Richard Henry Lee made the motion for independence in the Continental Congress in 1776, and Arthur and William were diplomats securing European assistance for the Revolution. Four were elected burgesses and two became members of the Congress of the United States. The last Lee child born in Stratford to survive to maturity was the most famous: General Robert E. Lee. His father, "Light Horse Harry," was a hero of the Revolution and a favorite of George Washington. In his son the virtues of a great inheritance seem to have gathered; a nobility of courage, kindness, wisdom and devotion to duty.

Stratford Hall is one of the great houses of American history. Its magnificent setting on a high bluff above the Potomac River and its bold architectural style set it apart from any other Colonial house. Built in the late 1730s, using brick made on the site and timber cut from virgin forest, builders and craftsmen constructed the H-shaped manor house, its four dependencies, coach house and stable. The Great Hall in the center of the house, twenty-nine feet square with an inverted tray ceiling seventeen feet high, is elaborately panelled. The hall is considered one of the most architecturally significant rooms to survive from Colonial America.

The period furnishings, which include some Lee family items, date from the years 1730 to 1810.

Additional Information

For visitors's enjoyment, a formal garden outlined in boxwood invites a stroll to the east of the Great House. To the west, eighteenth century vegetable and flowers flourish in orderly patterns. There is also a log cabin dining room at the edge of the woods which serves a plantation lunch from April through October.

Riddick's Folly

510 North Main Street
Suffolk, VA 23434
(804) 934-1390

Contact: Riddick's Folly, Inc.

Open: Tues.-Fri. 10 a.m.–5 p.m.;
Sun. 1–5 p.m.

Admission: Free. Changing exhibits, long term exhibits, house tours, films, workshops, lectures, preservations and demonstrations.

Facilities on Premises: Gift shop featuring local arts and crafts, historical archives

Suggested Time to View House: 1 hour

Number of Yearly Visitors: 5,000

Year House Built: 1837

Style of Architecture: Greek Revival

On-Site Parking: Yes

Number of Rooms: 20 plus

Wheelchair Access: Partial

Description of House

Six generations of the Riddick family, a very old Suffolk family, called this attractive dwelling home. Riddick's Folly was built over a two year period beginning in 1837 by Mills Riddick, III, after his former home, which had stood on the same site, was consumed in the fire which leveled much of Suffolk on June 3, 1837. During the Civil War, the house served as headquarters for Union Major General John Peck and as a field hospital during the Siege of Suffolk. The brick house was built in a version of the Greek Revival style which was not common in Virginia at the time. The rectangular two-and-a-half story house is raised above an English basement to create a total of four floors. This large house is five bays wide and four bays deep. Prior to the additions made onto the house after the turn of the century, the building was radically symmetrical from the exterior. Inside, the carved cypress woodwork survives and decorative medallions crown the fourteen-foot ceilings. There are several pieces of original Riddick furnishings on display; the rest have been collected and are appropriate for the period.

Notable Collections on Exhibit

The house features permanent historical exhibitions as well as regularly changing special exhibits.

Bacon's Castle

Route 10
Surry, VA 23883
(804) 357-5976

Contact: Assoc. for the Pres. of Virginia
Antiquities

Open: Tues.-Sat. 10 a.m.–4 p.m., Sun.
12–4 p.m.

Admission: Adults $4; students $1. Guided
tours.

Suggested Time to View House: 1 hour

Facilities on Premises: Gift shop

Description of Grounds: The grounds
include the best preserved, sophisticated
Colonial garden in America.

Best Season to View House: Summer-fall

Year House Built: 1665

Style of Architecture: Jacobean

On-Site Parking: Yes

Description of House

Bacon's Castle was built in 1665 by immigrant Arthur Allen, and is the oldest documented brick house in English North America. The castle's name comes from the 1676 Bacon's Rebellion in which the colony of Virginia rebelled against the tyrannical rule of Royal Governor William Berkeley. Young Nathaniel Bacon assumed the role of leader of the rebels and directed his aggressive actions first against the Indians and then toward Berkeley's government. Together with his rebel forces, he besieged the home of Major Arthur Allen and from this point ruled the county of Surry for four months.

Bacon's Castle possesses several architectural features that have, over the centuries, become all but extinct in this country. The castle is the earliest Virginia house to be constructed in cruciform design, with the main body of the house joined by a porch tower on the front and a stair tower to the rear. The handsome curvilinear or Flemish gables are accented by robust offset triple chimney stacks which augments the feeling of the period that surrounds this unusual plantation setting. The house is furnished with English and Southern antiques of the late 17th and early 18th centuries as reflected in the inventory records of the Allen home.

Additional Information

Outside Bacon's Castle, visitors are treated to a rare view of Virginia's oldest garden and one of the most impressive Colonial gardens in America. The gardens have been reconstructed according to archeological and historic research and are filled with period flowers, vegetables, ornamental shrubs, benches, and walkways.

Jones-Stewart Mansion

Route 1, Box 213
Surry, VA 23883-9728
(804) 294-3625

Contact: Chippokes Plantation State Park
Open: Memorial Day-Labor Day,
Wed.-Sun. 1–4 p.m.
Admission: Adults (13 and over) $2; children
(6-12) $1; group (10 or more) $1 per
person. Slide programs, annual events
such as the Christmas open house in Dec.,
Garden Week (April), and the Pork,
Peanut and Pine festival (July).
Suggested Time to View House:
35–40 minutes

Facilities on Premises: Gift shop
Description of Grounds: Picnic area and
hiking and biking trails along the
shoreline of the James River
Best Season to View House: Year round
Number of Yearly Visitors: 100,000
Year House Built: 1854 to 1860
Style of Architecture: Italianate
Number of Rooms: 8
On-Site Parking: Yes **Wheelchair Access:** Yes

Description of House

During the first decades of English occupation the property changed
hands frequently, always serving as a secondary plantation managed by
overseers or farmed by tenants. Even during the 130 year tenure of the
prominent Ludwell family and their descendants, beginning around 1684,
the plantation continued to be run by overseers. Not until its purchase in
1837 by Albert C. Jones of neighboring Isle of Wight County did Chippokes
become an owner-occupied plantation seat.

The mansion is constructed of brick and clad with stucco on the main,
or northeast, facade. This impressive building rises a full two stories over a
low-pitched hipped roof capped by a square belvedere. The floor plan
follows a standard central passage, double pile configuration, with four
interior end chimneys flush with the exterior walls. The one-story, single-
bay porches offer differing forms of shelter to the main doors at front and
rear. The only addition to the house is a brick wing (c. 1955) on the southwest
end. The mansion also features attractive ornamental plasterwork in several
of the rooms and extremely high ceilings. All of the furnishings have been
collected to represent the 19th-century period of occupancy.

Additional Information

Surrounded by mulberry trees, the Jones-Stewart Mansion stands in a
beautiful state park with many recreational facilities. Nearby, there is a Farm
and Forestry Museum where visitors may learn about the agricultural
history of the area.

Upper Wolfsnare

2040 Potters Road
Virginia Beach, VA 23454
(804) 491–0127

Contact: Princess Anne County Historical
Society
Open: Summer months, Wed.-Thur.
10 a.m.–4 p.m.
Admission: Adults $2; children $1;
groups (20 or more) $1 each.
Lectures, workshops, special events.
Suggested Time to View House: 45 minutes
Description of Grounds: Herb garden,
country setting
Best Season to View House: Summer
Number of Yearly Visitors: 6,000
Year House Built: 1759
Style of Architecture: Georgian
Number of Rooms: 9
On-Site Parking: Yes
Wheelchair Access: No

Description of House

This fine 18th-century home has remained virtually unaltered since it was first constructed. Upper Wolfsnare was built in 1759 by Thomas Walke III. His grandfather, Thomas Walke, reportedly came to the area from Barbados about 1660 and quickly became prominent in the social, political, and economic life of the community. His will, and those of his son, Thomas II and his grandson, Thomas III, show extensive lands, many slaves, a herd of cattle, fine furnishings, and large shipping interests. Thomas Walke IV, one of the two representatives from the county on the ratification committee for the Constitution, died at an early age and left no direct heirs; the house passed out of the Walke family at that time.

The furnishings have all been donated over the years and include both period pieces and reproductions. There are also several portraits of Walke family members hanging on the walls.

Notable Collections on Exhibit

The house features exhibits illustrating the lifestyle of 18th-century Princess Anne County with a special emphasis on the role of women.

Francis Land House

3131 Virginia Beach Boulevard
Virginia Beach, VA 23452
(804) 340-1732

Contact: Francis Land Historic Site and Gardens

Open: Tues.-Sat. 9 a.m.–5 p.m., Sun. 12–5 p.m., closed Mon.

Admission: Free. Tours with costumed guides, living history demonstrations of flax spinning and other crafts.

Suggested Time to View House: 30 minutes

Facilities on Premises: Gift shop

Description of Grounds: An herb garden and a garden with heirloom varieties of corn and other vegetables

Best Season to View House: Summer-fall

Year House Built: 1732

Style of Architecture: Georgian

On-Site Parking: Yes

Description of House

Francis Land was a member of a wealthy Virginia family and built this attractive brick house in the early 18th century. Visitors will learn about the history of the Land family from costumed guides, as well as see a remarkably well-preserved example of coastal Virginia architecture. At the entrance of the house lies the remains of a very old well, thought to be an early one because it is constructed from materials the family would have used on the plantation. From the cellar one can examine the hand-hewn beams and joists, the twenty-inch thick walls and even a brick arch support for the chimney. The house also maintains the original pine flooring and pine paneling with wood cut from nearby forests.

In the midst of modern-day Virginia Beach, the Francis Land House provides a refreshing experience of the past.

Notable Collections on Exhibit

The first floor features changing exhibits depicting the comfortable lifestyle of the Land family. Each of the rooms is arranged to portray everything from afternoon tea to holiday celebrations.

Adam Thoroughgood House

**1636 Parish Road
Virginia Beach, VA 23455
(804) 622-1211**

Contact: The Chrysler Museum
Open: Jan.-March 31, Tues.-Sat. 12–5 p.m.;
April 1-Dec. 31, Tues.-Sat.
10 a.m.–5 p.m., Sun. 12–5 p.m.
Admission: Adults $2; seniors and
children $1. Guided tours.
Suggested Time to View House: 40 minutes
Facilities on Premises: Gift shop
Description of Grounds: Restored
17th-century pleasure garden
Best Season to View House: Spring
Year House Built: 1680
Style of Architecture: English Country
On-Site Parking: Yes

Description of House

Captain Adam Thoroughgood arrived in the Virginia Colony in 1621 as an indentured servant. Prospering in the New World and serving as one of Virginia's first burgesses, he married Sarah Offley and recruited 105 settlers to the colony. In 1635, Thoroughgood was awarded 5350 acres of land along the western shore of the Lynnhaven River. It was on this inherited land that a descendant of Adam Thoroughgood built the house that today bears his name.

The Thoroughgood House is a modified hall and parlor, one-and-a-half story structure. Made of local brick and oyster shell mortar, this house's exterior on the east, north, and south sides features bricks laid in an English bond pattern, and on the west side in Flemish bond. Glazed headers can be found at the gable ends and on the west side of the house. The south end of the structure has an exterior pyramid chimney while the the chimney at the north end is interior. The leaded glass casement windows are true to 17th-century fashion. The house contains a spectacular collection of late 17th-century and early 18th-century English furniture.

Notable Collections on Exhibit

The collection of furniture contains a fine selection of ornately carved and inlaid court cupboards along with many fine armchairs. The collection of unusual lighting devices include rush, phoebe, and betty lamps.

Additional Information

The Adam Thoroughgood House one of three historic houses administered by The Chrysler Museum. The 17th-century garden was a gift of the Garden Club of Virginia.

Colonial Williamsburg

P.O. Box 1776
Williamsburg, VA 23187-1776
(804) 229-1000

Contact: The Colonial Williamsburg Foundation

Open: March-Dec. 8:30 a.m.–8 p.m.; Jan.-Feb. 9 a.m.–5 p.m.

Admission: Adults $22.50; youths (6-12) $13.50 (basic admission provides admission to any 12 buildings with the exception of selected sites); other passes available, inquire for rates. Costumed interpreters, many special events.

Suggested Time to View House: At least 1 day

Description of Grounds: Colonial Williamsburg is a historic town with landscaped grounds, many gardens, and a village green.

Best Season to View House: Year-round

Number of Yearly Visitors: 950,000

Year House Built: Varies, most c. 18th century

Style of Architecture: Varied

On-Site Parking: Yes **Wheelchair Access:** Yes

Description of House

A visit to Colonial Williamsburg is a rendezvous with an important chapter of America's history and with an entire community that existed two centuries ago. Often cited as the most visited historic site in the country, Colonial Williamsburg provides a unique experience for lovers of historic homes. This historic village covers almost 130 acres and contains more than 450 structures ranging from the elaborate Governor's Palace to the simple silversmith's home. Originally known as Middle Plantation, the town served as the capital of Virginia for eighty years from 1699 to 1769. The town was renamed Williamsburg after King William III, and as the capital features many fine government buildings and homes which housed politicians and diplomats. Colonial Williamsburg has been meticulously restored to its 18th-century appearance and more than eighty buildings are original to the site. Other buildings which have been destroyed over the years have been accurately recreated on the sites of the original structures.

In the central colonial area of the city, there are many representative houses for visitors to see to start their tour. The Peyton Randolph House was home to one of the most prominent families in Virginia. Randolph was the speaker of the House of Burgesses and president of the first Continental Congress. One of the oldest houses in Williamsburg, this white-frame structure was constructed in 1715; other members of the family built an addition in 1725. The Randolph House is considered to have one of the best series of original paneled rooms in the village and is completely furnished with English and American antiques, including several pieces of Randolph family silver.

Another notable house was home to George Wythe, a friend of Peyton Randolph and one of the most influential Americans of his era. Wythe was a prominent lawyer who had a distinguished career in public service. In addition, he was extremely important as Thomas Jefferson's teacher and advisor. The Georgian-style brick Wythe House features a symmetrical floor plan with four rooms on each floor opening onto a central hallway. This attractive home has many outbuildings, including a smokehouse, kitchen, laundry, and stable, where demonstrations of crafts and open-hearth cooking take place seasonally.

The Brush-Everard House provides another fascinating stop along the walk through Williamsburg. Thomas Everard was a wealthy civic leader who owned the house from 1755 to 1781. A later occupant, William Dering, was a dancing master and painter. This simple wood-frame house was typical of the houses built here in the early 18th century. The interior is distinguished by fine paneling and rich carving, probably executed by the joiner who worked at nearby Carter's Grove Plantation.

In addition to the many houses, Williamsburg offers a wide variety of shops, museums, and taverns to complete the experience of this truly extraordinary historic village.

Notable Collections on Exhibit

Each house offers a fine collection of period furnishings and decorative arts, many of which were owned by the original residents. In addition, Williamsburg has several excellent museums such as the Dewitt Wallace Decorative Arts Gallery which displays more than 8,000 decorative objects, and Rockefeller Folk Art Center with one of the most distinctive folk art collections in America. Separate admission fees are charged for the museums.

Governor's Palace

Palace Green
Williamsburg, VA 23187-1776
(804) 229-1000

Contact: The Colonial Williamsburg
Foundation

Open: March-Dec. 8:30 a.m.–8 p.m.,
Jan.-Feb. 9 a.m.–5 p.m.

Admission: Adults $13 (free with Patriot's
pass or Royal Governor's pass)

Suggested Time to View House: 2 hours

Description of Grounds: The palace has a
lovely courtyard and formal gardens

Best Season to View House: Year-round

Number of Yearly Visitors: 950,000

Year House Built: 1720 (reconstruction of
original structure)

Style of Architecture: Georgian-style palace

On-Site Parking: Yes **Wheelchair Access:** Yes

Description of House

At the time of its completion in 1722, this residence of Virginia's royal governor was considered one of the finest such buildings in British America. Seven royal governors and the first two governors of the Commonwealth of Virginia—Patrick Henry and Thomas Jefferson—lived within this elegant building. The original building was begun in 1706 and finally completed in 1722. However, the palace which visitors see today is actually a meticulous reconstruction on the original site of the palace which burned to the ground in 1781.

The Governor's Palace features beautifully furnished rooms ranging from the grand entrance hall to the fashionable ballroom and supper room. The formal dining room is arranged as if royal guests were about to step through the door, with the table set with fine china and glassware. The interior of the palace is also noted for its high-quality woodwork and rare period antiques.

Additional Information

Within the walls of the palace are a stable, kitchen, and gardens. Visitors will see a wheelwright demonstrating his craft in the stable area. The formal gardens feature manicured parterres and beautiful flower beds.

Bassett Hall

Waller and Francis Streets
Williamsburg, VA 23187-1776
(804) 229-1000

Contact: The Colonial Williamsburg Foundation

Open: March-Dec. 8:30 a.m.–8 p.m.; Jan.-Feb. 9 a.m.–5 p.m.

Admission: Adults $13 (free with Patriot's pass or Royal Governor's pass)

Suggested Time to View House: 2 hours

Description of Grounds: Extensive landscaped grounds and gardens with nature trails

Best Season to View House: Year-round

Number of Yearly Visitors: 950,000

Year House Built: c. 1780

Style of Architecture: Georgian

On-Site Parking: Yes **Wheelchair Access:** Yes

Description of House

Bassett Hall is closely linked with the restoration of Colonial Williamsburg. This modest, two-story white frame house was home to Mr. and Mrs. John D. Rockefeller for many years before they bequeathed it to this historic town with all of the furnishings intact. The house owes its name to Burwell Bassett who bought the property in 1800 and owned it for nearly forty years. Bassett was a nephew of Martha Washington and also served as a state senator and a Congressman.

The interior of this attractive home is displayed much as it appeared when the Rockefellers restored and furnished it in the mid 1930s. Mrs. Rockefeller was an early collector and enthusiast of American folk art, and while Williamsburg's Abby Aldrich Folk Art Center exhibits most of the collection, Bassett Hall displays selected pieces in the midst of the family's fine period furnishings.

Notable Collections on Exhibit

Bassett Hall exhibits more than 125 pieces of American folk art including weathervanes, chalkware, pottery, needlework, and more than seventy paintings and drawings.

Abram's Delight Museum

1340 Pleasant Valley Road
Winchester, VA 22601
(703) 662-6519

Contact: Winchester-Frederick County
  Historical Society
Open: April 1-Oct. 31, 9 a.m.–5 p.m.
Admission: Adults $3.50; children $1.75;
  students and seniors $3; family $8.75.
  Guided tours, annual candlelight tour
  (first weekend in Dec.); July 4th open
  house.
Suggested Time to View House: 90 minutes
Facilities on Premises: Gift shop
Description of Grounds: Lovely grounds
  surround the museum, visitors may
  walk through the restored English
  garden.
Best Season to View House: Spring and
  summer
Number of Yearly Visitors: 4,500
Number of Rooms: 13

Style of Architecture: Stone with
  Federal-style wing
Year House Built: 1754
On-Site Parking: Yes **Wheelchair Access:** No

Description of House

In 1732 the land was surveyed for Abraham Hollingsworth, a Quaker, who declared the site a "delight to behold" (hence the name). He built a log cabin on the present site and was one of the area's earliest settlers. His son, Isaac, built this massive stone house with walls two-and-a-half feet thick. The Hollingsworth family lived in Abram's Delight until the 1900s when it was closed after the death of Miss Annie Hollingsworth.

The original portion of the house is a two-story, three-bay, random rubble stone dwelling with two interior end stone chimneys and a gable roof. The house sits on a split-level stone basement which is accessible by both interior and bulkhead entrances. The open gable end is pedimented and has two attic-story windows. The front facade is made up of a central door flanked by a window on either side and all first floor bays have segmented stone arches above them. A two-story, slightly smaller, wing was added in 1800. This was constructed in a style similar to the main house. The objects on display in this house museum are associated with life in Winchester and Frederick counties prior to 1830.

Notable Collections on Exhibit

Included in the collection are three portraits of the Judge White family done by Charles Peale Polk. Also included in the furnishings are a plantation desk, a 1790 corner cupboard, a butler's desk, and pieces of china and silver from the Hollingsworth family.

Additional Information

The restored log cabin on the west lawn was not part of the original Hollingsworth homestead although it dates from the same period.

Stonewall Jackson's Headquarters

415 North Braddock Street
Winchester, VA 22601
(703) 667-3242

Contact: Winchester-Frederick County
Historical Society

Open: April 1-Oct. 31, 9 a.m.–5 p.m.; also
open weekends in March, Nov. and Dec.

Admission: Adults $3.50; children $1.75;
students and seniors $3; family, $8.75.
Guided tours, re-enactments, July 4th
open house with United Daughters of
the Confederacy acting as hostesses.

Suggested Time to View House: 45 minutes

Facilities on Premises: Gift shop

Description of Grounds: The front lawn
contains a historic cannon

Best Season to View House: Spring and
summer

Number of Yearly Visitors: 6,200

Year House Built: 1854

Number of Rooms: 11

Style of Architecture: Gothic Revival

On-Site Parking: Yes **Wheelchair Access:** No

Description of House

Although this house has had many residents over the years, none is more famous than Stonewall Jackson who used the building as his headquarters from 1861 to 1862. This first owner, Dr. William Fuller, a Winchester dentist, built the house in 1854. He later sold it to Lewis T. Moore (grandfather of actress, Mary Tyler Moore), in 1856. He invited General Stonewall Jackson to use his home during the 1861 winter campaign as a headquarters.

Stonewall Jackson's Headquarters is the first Civil War museum one comes to upon entering the state of Virginia from the North. The Gothic Revival stone cottage is unusual for the area. The wallpaper in the General's office is an exact reproduction of the original gilt paper which Jackson admired during his use of the home. Today, the museum is interpreted to honor Jackson's memory and contains many of his personal items.

Notable Collections on Exhibit

On display are Jackson's personal prayer table, initialed prayer book, and field glasses. Turner Ashby's pistol and saddle were donated to the museum by his descendants. The map-making instruments of Jedediah Hotchkiss are on display as well.

Additional Information

Most of the soldiers who died in the five Civil War battles fought in and around Winchester are buried at the Stonewall Confederate Cemetery within Mount Hebron Cemetery, located only eight blocks from the headquarters.

Carter's Grove Plantation

P.O. Box 210
Yorktown, VA 23690
(804) 898-3400

Contact: Colonial National Historical Park
Open: March-Nov., daily 9 a.m.–5 p.m.;
and during the Christmas season

Activities: Guided tours
Year House Built: 1750 to 1755
Style of Architecture: Georgian

Description of House

The mansion was named for the very wealthy planter, Robert "King" Carter. Carter bought the plantation for his daughter, Elizabeth, and she and her second son, Carter Burwell, inherited the property after the "King's" death. In his will, he stated that the estate should always be called Carter's Grove.

Carter Burwell hired architect David Minitree to build this impressive Georgian mansion which has been called "the most beautiful house in America." The mansion with its 200-foot facade is a masterpiece of Virginia architecture. The exterior features superior brickwork, while the interior boasts a great arch and stairway, fine woodwork, and a sophisticated floor plan. In the latter part of the 19th century, later occupants added a long Victorian-style veranda to the riverfront facade. Carter's Grove maintains many beautifully rooms furnished in the style of Virginia gentry.

Notable Collections on Exhibit

The main house showcases an excellent collection of furnishings ranging from the 17th through the 20th centuries including many beautiful pieces of decorative art.

Moore House

P.O. Box 20
Yorktown, VA 23690
(804) 898-3400

Contact: Colonial National Historical Park
Open: March-Nov., daily 9 a.m.–5 p.m.
Activities: Guided tours; self-guided
  battlefield tours
Year House Built: c.1710
Style of Architecture: Georgian

Description of House

The Moore House is most notably known as the place where negotiations between the British, Americans and French took place thereby ending the Revolutionary War. As a result, Cornwallis and his British army surrendered in defeat on October 19, 1781 in Yorktown. Over the years, the house has been occupied by several generations of the Moore family, descendants of Major Lawrence Smith, a prominent lawyer, frontier commander, and a somewhat unsuccessful leader of loyalist forces in Bacon's Rebellion of 1676. When he died in 1700, his large estate went to his second son and namesake who constructed the Moore House in the early 1700s. After Lawrence Smith Jr.'s death in 1739, the house and lands eventually passed to Augustine Moore who had married Lawrence's daughter, Lucy Smith. The couple lived at the estate until their deaths in the late 1700s. Augustine Moore left the house to his good friend General Thomas Nelson whose descendants kept the house until 1821. During McClellan's Peninsular Campaign against Richmond early in the Civil War, military action around Yorktown caused considerable damage to the Moore House. Shellfire damaged the house, and foraging soldiers later stripped away siding and other wood for fuel. The house remained derelict until it was repaired for the Centennial Celebration of the victory over Cornwallis in 1881. Fifty years later, in 1931, the National Park Service restored the Moore House to its original Colonial appearance.

Refurnishing of the house has done much to bring it to life. Period pieces have been used, most of which date between 1725 and 1775. A few items included in the furnishings are believed to have been in the house during the surrender negotiations.

Additional Information

Along with the Moore House, the nearby Nelson House also witnessed the famous 1781 Battle of Yorktown in 1781. Built by "Scotch" Tom Nelson in 1711, this unpretentious home was General Cornwallis's first headquarters during the siege of the town. After the house was heavily damaged (there are two cannonballs still visible in the walls), the general took refuge in an underground shelter. The Nelson House also played a role in the Civil War, by serving as a field hospital for wounded troops. In 1968, the National Park Service acquired the house and restored it to its original appearance.

West
Virginia

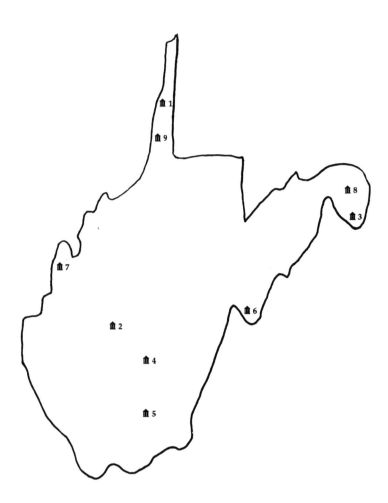

1. **Bethany College**
   Alexander Campbell Mansion

2. **Charleston**
   Governor's Mansion

3. **Harper's Ferry**
   Harper's Ferry

4. **Hillsboro**
   Pearl S. Buck Birthplace Home

5. **Lewisburg**
   Historic Lewisburg

6. **Mathias**
   Henry Lee's Cabin

7. **Point Pleasant**
   Mansion House Museum

8. **St. Martinsburg**
   General Adam Stephen House

9. **Wheeling**
   Mansion Museum

Alexander Campbell Mansion

Bethany College
Bethany, WV 26032
(304) 829-7285

Contact: Bethany College's Heritage Resource Center

Open: April 1-Oct. 31, Tues.-Sat. 10 a.m.–12 p.m.; Sun. 1–4 p.m.; other times by appointment

Admission: Adults $3; students (grades 1-12) $1.50; under 6 with parent free. Guided tours, audiovisual presentations; video: "Wrestling with God"; Christmas candlelight tour.

Suggested Time to View House: 1 hour

Facilities on Premises: Gift shop

Best Season to View House: All

Number of Yearly Visitors: 2,000

Year House Built: Begun in 1793

Style of Architecture: Country Farmhouse

Number of Rooms: 23 (18 open to the public)

On-Site Parking: Yes **Wheelchair Access:** Yes

Description of House

Alexander Campbell was an important leader in the emerging nation. A Scotch-Irish immigrant, Campbell became one of America's most renowned reformers and educators. He was the foremost spokesman for a religious reformation born near Bethany which became America's largest indigenous religious movement. Campbell was also the founder of Bethany College.

Campbell acquired the homestead from his father-in-law, John Brown, who had built the three-story east section of the house in 1793. In 1819, Campbell made his first addition. He enclosed the west porch as a hallway and added a large room with a dormitory above to house the Buffalo Seminary, the forerunner of Bethany College. After the seminary closed in 1823, Campbell divided the classroom into the master bedroom, or clock room, and the dining room. He carved the bedrooms for his growing family from the dormitory. A small brick section was added in 1836 to enlarge the dining room because so many visitors came to the home. This hexagonal brick study has a cupola signifying to Campbell that "his light—both physical and spiritual—came from above."

Most of the furnishings are original to the house and many were hand-made by John Brown, the builder of the house. Other furnishings are period pieces.

Notable Collections on Exhibit

The house contains Campbell family furnishings, including the bed in which Campbell died in 1866, his arm study chair, and many pieces built by John Brown, among them the cradle that rocked all fourteen of the Campbell children, a tall secretary and a walnut and mahogany veneered sideboard. Also featured is the Barclay Exhibit, a display of exotic fabrics and furnishings which Decima Campbell (Alexander's daughter) brought back from the Orient, Decima's paintings, and many of the Barclay family papers; copies of treaties, passport, beautiful Arabic documents written by the sultan of Morocco concerning the first treaty of commerce between the U.S. and Morocco.

Additional Information

Also on the grounds are a one-room schoolhouse and a smokehouse/springhouse. The Campbell Mansion was totally restored in 1989 and 1990.

Governor's Mansion

1716 Kanawha Boulevard
Charleston, WV 25305
(304) 348-3809

Contact: The West Virginia Preservation
Foundation
Open: Thurs.-Fri. 9:30 a.m.–11:30 a.m.
Activities: Guided tours of State rooms
Description of Grounds: Expansive,
tree-shaded grounds
Year House Built: 1924
Style of Architecture: Georgian
Number of Rooms: 30

Description of House

Ground was broken for this impressive mansion in 1924 and a year later it was completed. Governor Ephraim Morgan was the first to occupy the new official residence, one week before his term expired in 1925.

The West Virginia Governor's Mansion is an elegantly proportioned Georgian structure is set off by red Harvard brick and white Corinthian columns. Designed by Charleston architect, Walter F. Martens, the mansion is a study in refined grace, beginning with its two-story portico, supported by four Corinthian columns. The garage, service wing and garden were added in 1926 and twenty years later, the slate-covered mansard roof was added to conform to the original plans. The ground floor of the mansion houses the state rooms including the ballroom, the state dining room, the drawing room, and the library. The second floor is the private residence for the first family. Located on beautifully landscaped grounds, the mansion features an especially fine view of the Kanawha River.

Notable Collections on Exhibit

The ballroom features chandeliers that once hung in Scott's Drug Store on Capital Street in Charleston and a classic white mantel from an old Irish castle. The state dining room includes a circa 1820 banquet table with seating for twenty-two guests. The drawing room is graced by chandeliers from the old Kanawha Hotel in Charleston and a lovely mantel that is a replica from the President's Cottage at the Greenbrier Hotel in White Sulphur Springs. The library displays superior quality West Virginia hardwood in the Georgian-style butternut paneling.

Harper's Ferry

**Shenandoah Street
Harper's Ferry, WV
(304) 535-6029**

Contact: National Park Service

Open: 8 a.m.–6 p.m.; closed major holidays

Admission: Free. Audiovisual program, self-guided walking tours

Suggested Time to View House: 2½ hours for entire walking tour

Facilities on Premises: Visitor's Center, Gift shop

Description of Grounds: Park with historic town

Best Season to View House: Year round

Year House Built: c. 1790s

Style of Architecture: Varies

On-Site Parking: Yes

Description of House

It was here in Harper's Ferry at the confluence of the Potomac and Shenandoah Rivers that John Brown led his abortive attempt in 1859 to capture the arsenal for arms to free the black slave. After considerable bloodshed, the raiders were captured by U.S. Marines under Colonel Robert E. Lee and six of his followers were tried for treason, convicted, and hanged at Charles Town. During the Civil War, the town also played a crucial role as the Union troops regarded the location as key in protecting the safety of Washington, D.C. In 1862, General Stonewall Jackson finally captured the town and took over 12,000 prisoners before joining Lee at Antietem.

The park features several historic houses which have been restored to their original appearance. The two-and-a-half story Harper House is the oldest residence in Harper's Ferry. The stone dwelling was built in 1782 by Robert Harper. Visitors can also see the John Brown monument, which marks the original site of the firehouse where John Brown and his raiders made their heroic stand, and John Brown's Fort, at Old Arsenal Square which was the scene of John Brown's capture. There is also the Master Armorer's House to view, a mid 19th century house built for the chief gunsmith of the armory. The dwelling now houses a museum on the history of gunmaking. In addition, the federal arsenal and armory, built in 1796, are open to the public. Here, many of the muskets and rifles used in the War of 1812 and the Civil War were manufactured.

Pearl S. Buck Birthplace Home

P.O. Box 126
Hillsboro, WV 24946
(304) 653-4430

Contact: Pearl S. Buck Birthplace Foundation, Inc.
Open: Mon.-Sat. 9 a.m.–5 p.m.; Sun. 1–5 p.m.
Admission: Adults $3; students $1. Guided tours, special events.
Suggested Time to View House: 45 minutes
Facilities on Premises: Gift shop and book store

Best Season to View House: May-Nov.
Number of Yearly Visitors: 3,000
Year House Built: 1875
Style of Architecture: Dutch Colonial
Number of Rooms: 12
On-Site Parking: Yes **Wheelchair Access:** Yes

Description of House

Pearl S. Buck, the only American woman to receive both the Pulitzer Prize and the Nobel Prize was born here on June 26, 1892. The home was built by her grandparents. The Stultings came from Holland in 1847 to escape religious persecution. They eventually settled in Hillsboro and built their two-story home patterned after their Dutch home with wood and flagstone floors. One of their daughters, Caroline, married Absalom Sydenstricker. They went to China as missionaries. On one of their furloughs home, Caroline gave birth to Pearl Comfort Sydenstrickler. This author of *The Good Earth* would become one of America's most beloved writers.

The house was made with three layers of brick and then covered with "Jenny Lind" (vertical wood) siding. The interior features much of the original furniture and woodwork. There is an original Chinese Bible used by Pearl's father and an 1850 settee by John Belter.

Additional Information

In addition, the Sydonstricker Log House, Pearl Buck's father's boyhood home, has been moved to the grounds. There is also a cultural center planned to house the writer's original manuscripts.

Historic Lewisburg

105 Church Street
Lewisburg, WV 24901
(304) 645-1110

Contact: Lewisburg Visitor's Center
Open: 9 a.m.–5 p.m.; closed major holidays
Admission: Free. Walking tours
Suggested Time to View House: 2 and a
half hours for entire walking tour
Facilities on Premises: Gift shop
Description of Grounds: 236-acre national
historic district
Best Season to View House: Year round
Year House Built: c. 1800s and 1900s
Style of Architecture: Varies
On-Site Parking: Yes

Description of House

This historic town was originally named Camp Union, but came to be known as Lewisburg in honor of General Andrew Lewis, who organized the Virginia militia in 1774 against the Shawnee Indians. Some consider this battle the first of the American Revolution. Chartered in 1782, the frontier town prospered as a way-station on the James River and Kanawha Turnpike. Lewisburg was also involved in the Civil War. On May 23, 1862 the Confederate forces of Henry Heth clashed with the Union troops of George Crook, who would later become famous for his capturing of Apache chief Geronimo.

The center of historic Lewisburg has an unusually large number of old structures for such a small city, and the old part of town is now a National Historic District. There are over sixty 18th and 19th-century buildings of historic and architectural interest including the John North House, built in 1820, home to a town official. It now houses the collections of the Greenbriar Historical Society. Several log cabins are also still standing including the Thomas Gralton-Parr House from 1796; and a stately two-story house where General Robert E. Lee was entertained, the James Winthrow House which dates from 1818. The Winthrow House exhibits a fine display of regional antiques.

In addition to the many notable buildings, there are also several historic cemeteries of note. The Confederate Cemetery contains the remains of close to 100 unknown soldiers from the Battle of Lewisburg while the old cemetery next to the Old Stone Church is the final resting place for other notable citizens. Visitors can spend hours exploring this unique town, and learn the fascinating history which lives on to this day.

Additional Information

While not every home is open to the public, each June various houses are open for viewing by theme—call the Lewisburg Visitor's Center for more information.

Henry Lee's Cabin

Route 2, Box 24
Mathias, WV 26812
(304) 897-5372

Contact: Lost River State Park
Open: Sat.-Sun. 10 a.m.–6 p.m., Mon.-Fri.
  by appointment
Admission: Free
Suggested Time to View House: 30 minutes
Facilities on Premises: Recreational
  facilities located in park
Description of Grounds: The cabin is
  located in Lost River State park
  comprised of more than 3000 acres of
  beautiful woodlands and recreational
  activities
Best Season to View House: Summer-fall
Year House Built: c. 1810
Style of Architecture: Frame
Number of Rooms: 6
On-Site Parking: Yes

Description of House

Originally part of the massive land holdings of Thomas Lord Fairfax, this land was apportioned after the Revolutionary War. Successful military leaders were granted land for their service during the War, including "Light House Harry" Lee. Shortly after receiving the land, Lee built this simple two-story frame cabin as a summer resort. Harry's son, Charles Carter Lee, inherited the land and had cabins and a large boarding house built for the for the lodging of guests who came to partake of the widely reputed sulphur spring waters located here. Howard's Lick, as it was known, became a very fashionable social center of the day with the addition of music, dancing, riding and hiking.

Later, as the property passed through several hands, it finally reached the Carr family and through their efforts the resort reached its height. They enlarged the lodge, added bowling alleys, tennis courts, hot and cold sulphur baths, and telephones. The lodge was known as Lee White Sulphur Springs until the hotel burned and the resort closed. Today, visitors may visit the original cabin which is listed in the National Register of Historic Places and is preserved as a museum at the park.

Mansion House Museum

Point Pleasant Monument State Park
Point Pleasant, WV (304) 675-3330

Contact: Point Pleasant State Park
Open: April-Nov. Mon.-Sat. 9 a.m.–4 p.m.,
Sun. 1–5 p.m.
Admission: Free
Suggested Time to View House: 45 minutes
Facilities on Premises: Gift shop

Description of Grounds: The mansion is
located in state park with a monument to
a historic battle.
Best Season to View House: Spring-fall
Year House Built: c. 1796
Style of Architecture: Log
Number of Rooms: 8
On-Site Parking: Yes

Description of House

The historic area known as Point Pleasant, is located between the Ohio and Kanawha Rivers. Legend says that George Washington gave the area its name when he was surveying the region in the 1740s. A major battle between General Andrew Lewis and his troops and the Shawnee Indians took place here in 1774 at the instigation of Lord Dunmore, the governor of the colony of Virginia. Dunmore hoped that the battle would create an obstacle to Lewis's involvement in the Revolutionary cause. The tactic failed, and many consider this battle the first of the Revolution. Today, the park commemorates the battle, and the Mansion House exhibits materials related to this historic day.

The Mansion House is constructed of hand-hewn logs, and is considered the oldest structure in the Kanawha Valley. In addition to the exhibit related to the battle and the history of the region, the house also has a fine collection of Colonial furnishings. The parlor displays an impressive square piano, believed to be one of the first brought over the Alleghenies while the bedrooms are furnished with four-poster beds which are close to two centuries old.

Additional Information

The park features many other notable sites which commemorate the historic Battle of Point Pleasant. The centerpiece is an eighty-four-foot obelisk honoring the Virginia militiamen who gave their lives at the battle, while a statue of a frontiersman stands at the base. Smaller tables honor "Mad" Anne Bailey whose husband died in the battle, and Joseph Celoron de Blainville, a French explorer who claimed this area for his country in 1749.

General Adam Stephen House

309 East John Street
St. Martinsburg, WV 25401
(304) 267-4434

Contact: General Adam Stephen Memorial
Assoc., Inc.

Open: May-Oct.,Sat.-Sun. 2–5 p.m.

Activities: Guided tours and special
programs

Suggested Time to View House: 45 minutes

Description of Grounds: A stone smoke
house and log outbuilding have recently
been reconstructed.

Number of Yearly Visitors: 5,000

Year House Built: 1774

Number of Rooms: 8

On-Site Parking: Yes

Wheelchair Access: Yes

Description of House

When Adam Stephen built his house, he already had behind him a long
and illustrious dual career as surgeon and soldier, and had distinguished
himself as second-in-command to General Washington. Stephen also served
as the first High Sheriff of Berkeley County, as a member of the House of
Burgesses at Williamsburg, and later as a delegate to the Virginia General
Assembly, at Richmond. In the Revolutionary War he drove Dunmore out
of Norfolk, Virginia, and fought so well in the Battle of Trenton that he was
promoted to the rank of general. Later he was engaged in the Battle of
Princeton, Chadd's Ford, Brandywine and Germantown.

In 1770, General Adam Stephen acquired a 225-acre tract of land in
Frederick county, and he built upon it a sturdy limestone residence. Severely
rectangular and unembellished, this home of Martinsburg's founder to this
day crowns its rocky hill. The furnishings are appropriate and of the same
period as the house.

Mansion Museum

Burton Center
Wheeling, WV 26003
(304) 242-7272

Contact: Oglebay Institute

Open: Mon.-Sat. 9 a.m.–5:30 p.m.,
Sun. 1–5 p.m., closed Thanksgiving,
Christmas, Jan. 1

Admission: Adults $4; seniors $3.50; youths
(13-18) $3; children (under 12) free. Tours,
lectures, changing exhibits, annual
antiques show and sale, and "Festival of
Lights", call for schedule information.

Suggested Time to View House: 40 minutes

Facilities on Premises: Gift shop

Description of Grounds: The mansion is
located in a 1500 acre park with gardens,
greenhouses, and many recreational
facilities.

Best Season to View House: Spring-fall

Number of Yearly Visitors: 100,000

Year House Built: 1846 with additions

Style of Architecture: Greek Revival with
Neoclassical additions

Number of Rooms: 19

On-Site Parking: Yes

Wheelchair Access: Partial

Description of House

The Mansion House in Oglebay Park has changed considerably over the years with its different owners. Built in 1846 by Hanson Chapline, a wealthy doctor, the mansion was originally an eight-room farmhouse. The estate had seven different owners until Earl Oglebay, a successful industrialist, purchased it in 1900. A native of Wheeling, Oglebay made his fortune in iron ore mining and a shipping business based along the Great Lakes. Working with a local architect, Oglebay renovated the mansion to include a huge portico on the front of the house and a two-story wing on the north end of the building and the breakfast area in the dining room. Upon his death in 1926, he willed the estate to the city in order that it become a facility for education and recreation.

The mansion is a history museum which, through a series of period room settings depicts the development of the Wheeling area from the late 1700s through the 1800s. A Victorian parlor decorated with red upholstered furniture, bric-a-brac, and drapery represents the period from 1850 to 1900.

The dining room has Federal period furnishings including several Sheraton and Hepplewhite pieces and French Zubor wallpaper in the Eldorado pattern. The original dining room carpet is a hand-made reproduction of an 18th century French needlepoint. The master bedroom has an impressive canopy bed with a beautifully stitched coverlet made in Morgantown. Another smaller room known as the provincial room showcases Wheeling-made furniture including a handsome rocking chairs and a Franklin stove. The Waddington room is dedicated to the history of the Oglebay family and includes portraits, photographs, and family-owned furniture.

Notable Collections on Exhibit

The mansion displays an excellent collection of furnishings representing the house's many periods of occupancy. Of particular note is an Oglebay silver tea service made as a wedding gift for Sarita Oglebay with engravings depicting scenes from her life. In addition, the Glass Room exhibits a unique collection of glassware made by Wheeling companies and includes excellent examples of cut glass tableware, pressed glass items, and carnival glass. A gallery on the lower level of the museum hosts changing exhibits devoted to local, regional, and national decorative arts.

Additional Information

Visitors to the Mansion Museum should combine a visit to another notable Wheeling mansion, Willow Glen (on Bethany Pike). This unusual sandstone structure features interior decorations by Tiffany and Company and a dining room set that belonged to Jefferson Davis.

ℐ𝓃𝒹ℯ𝓍

🏛Kentucky

🏛 Louisianna

🏛 Mississippi

🏛 North Carolina

🏛 South Carolina

🏛 Tennessee

🏛 Virginia

🏛 West Virginia

🏛 Alabama

	Photo or illustration courtesy of
Arlington	Arlington Historical Association
Bellingrath Gardens and Home	Bellingrath-Morse Foundation
Bluff Hall	Marengo County Historical Society
Bragg-Mitchell Mansion	Bragg-Mitchell Mansion
Bernstein-Bush House	Museums of the City of Mobile
Carlen House Museum	Museums of the City of Mobile
First White House of the Confederacy	White House Association of Alabama
Hart House	Historic Chattahoochee Commission
Oakleigh Period House Museum and Complex	Historic Mobile Preservation Society
The Old State Bank	City of Decatur/Old Bank Board of Directors
Scott & Zelda Fitzgerald Museum	Scott & Zelda Fitzgerald Museum Association
Shorter Mansion	Eufaula Heritage Association
Sturdivant Hall	Sturdivant Museum Association
W.C. Handy House	Florence Historical Board
Weeden House	Twickenham Historic Preservation District Association

🏛 Florida

Audubon House and Gardens	Mitchell Wolfson Family Foundation
Bonnet House	John Pearce/Bonnet House, Inc.
Ca' d'Zan	John and Mable Ringling Museum of Art
Gonzalez-Alvarez House	St. Augustine Historical Society
The Henry Ford Home	City of Fort Myers
Historic Pensacola Village	Historic Pensacola Preservation Board
Little White House	Little White House Company
Old Settler's House	Manatee County Historical Commission, Inc.
Tampa Bay Hotel	Richard Thomas/Henry B. Plant Museum
The Wreckers Museum	Old Island Restoration Foundation, Inc.
Thomas Edison Winter Home	City of Fort Myers
Whitehall	The Henry M. Flagler Museum

🏛 Georgia

1847 John Fitz Jarrell Residence	Jarrell Plantation State Historical Site
Bedingfield Inn	Westville Historic Handicrafts, Inc.
Chief John Ross House	Chief John Ross House Association
Chieftains	Chieftains Museum, Inc.
Hofwyl-Broadfield Plantation	Georgia State Parks and Historic Sites
Indian Springs Hotel	Butts County Historical Society
Isaiah Davenport House Museum	Historic Savannah Foundation
Jekyll Island Club Historic District	Jekyll Island Authority-Museum Division
Johnston-Felton-Hay House	Georgia Trust for Historic Preservation
Little White House Historic Site	Georgia Dept. of Natural Resources
Oak Hill	Oak Hill and The Martha Berry Museum
Old Cannon Ball House	Sidney Lanier Chapter
The Old Governor's Mansion	Georgia College
Owens-Thomas Museum	Pamela Lee/Owens-Thomas House and Museum
Pebble Hill	Pebble Hill Foundation
Pemberton House (Heritage Corner)	Historic Columbus Foundation

	Photo or illustration courtesy of
Plum Orchard Mansion	Cumberland Island National Seashore
Rhodes Hall	Georgia Trust for Historic Preservation
Sidney Lanier Cottage	Middle Georgia Historical Society
Swan House	Atlanta History Center
Taylor-Grady House	Junior League of Athens
Telfair Mansion and Art Museum	Telefair Mansion and Art Museum
Tullie Smith Farm	Atlanta History Center
Vann House	Georgia Department of Natural Resources
Vickery House	The Dahlonega Club, Inc.
Westville	Westville Historic Handicrafts Inc.
The Wren's Nest	The Joel Chandler Harris Association, Inc.

🏛 Kentucky

1824 Centre Family Dwelling	Leslie Page/Shakertown at South Union
Adsmore Museum	Board of Trustees of George Coon Pub. Library
Ashland	Henry Clay Memorial Foundation
Berry Hill Mansion	Office of Historic Properties
Butler-Turpin House	Kentucky State Parks
Executive Mansion	Office of Historic Properties
Farmington	Historic Homes Foundation, Inc.
Historic Riverview at Hobson Grove	Hobson House Association, Inc.
Lincoln's Boyhood Home	National Park Service
Locust Grove	Historic Homes Foundation, Inc.
McDowell House and Apothecary Shop	McDowell Cambus/Kenneth Foundation
My Old Kentucky Home	Kentucky Department of Parks
Old Governor's Mansion	Office of Historic Properties
Thomas Edison House	Historic Homes Foundation, Inc.
Vest-Lindsey House	Office of Historic Properties
Waveland State Historic Site	Kentucky Department of Parks
White Hall	Kentucky Department of Parks
William Whitley House	Kentucky Department of Parks

🏛 Louisiana

Aillet House	West Baton Rouge Historical Association
Allendale Plantation Slave Cabin	West Baton Rouge Museum
Arlington Plantation	Gerald Cole/Arlington Plantation
Bayou Folk Museum-Kate Chopin Home	Assoc. for the Pres. of Hist. Natchitoches
Beauregard House	Jean Lafitte National Historical Park
Beauregard-Keyes House	Samuel Wilson/Keyes Foundation
Destrehan Plantation	River Road Historical Society
Gallier House Museum	Gallier House Museum
Grevemberg House	Gerald Cole/Louisiana Landmarks Soc.
Hermann-Grima House	Christian Woman's Exchange
Houmas House Plantation	Houmas House Plantation
Madewood Plantation House	Josh Tanner/Madewood Plantation House
Magnolia Mound Plantation	Magnolia Mound Plantation
Nottoway	Nottoway Plantation
Oaklawn Manor	Gerald Cole/Oaklawn Manor
Pitot House Museum	Louisiana Landmarks Society
Shadows-on-the-Teche	National Trust for Historic Preservation
Tezcuco Plantation	Tezcuco Plantation, Inc.
Williams Residence	Jan White Brantley/Historic New Orleans Collection

🏛 Mississippi

	Photo or illustration courtesy of
Anchuca	May Burns/Anchuca
Blewett-Harrison-Lee House	William Williams/Historic Columbus Found.
Auburn	Natchez Pilgrimage Tours/Auburn Garden Club
Beauvoir-The Jefferson Davis Shrine	United Sons of Confederate Veterans, Inc.
The Burn	The Burn/Natchez Pilgrimage Tours
Cedar Grove Mansion	Ted & Estelle McKay/Cedar Grove Mansion
Curlee House	City of Corinth
Duff Green Mansion	Duff Green Mansion
Dunleith	Rudi Holnsteiner/Natchez Pilgrimage Tours
Fortenberry-Parkman Farm	Mississippi Agriculture and Forestry Museum
Governor's Mansion	Misssissippi Dept. of Archives and History
The House on Ellicot Hill	Natchez Garden Club/Natchez Pilgrimage Tours
Lansdowne	Natchez Pilgrimage Tours
Liberty Hall	William Williams/Historic Columbus Found.
Longwood	Rudi Holnsteiner/Natchez Pilgrimage Tours
Magnolia Hall	Pilgrimage Garden Club/Natchez Pilgrimage Tours
Manship House	Mississippi Department of Archives & History
Martha Vick House	Martha Vick House
McRaven	McRaven
Monmouth	Pilgrimage Garden Club/Natchez Pilgrimage Tours
Rosalie	Rudi Holnsteiner/Natchez Pilgrimage Tours
Rosewood Manor	William Williams/Historic Columbus Found.
Rosswood Plantation	Rosswood Plantation
Rowan Oak	Rowan Oak/Oxford Tourism Council
Springfield Foundation	Historic Springfield Foundation
Stanton Hall	Rudi Holnsteiner/Natchez Pilgrimage Tours
Temple Heights	William Williams/Historic Columbus Found.
Waverly	Waverly Plantation
White Arches	William Williams/Historic Columbus Found.

🏛 North Carolina

Barker House	Historic Edenton
Bennett Place	N.C. Dept. of Cultural Res., Div. of Archives and History
Biltmore House	Biltmore Estate
Burgwin Wright House and Gardens	Nat'l Soc. of the Colonial Dames of America
Carl Sandburg Home	Carl Sandburg Home
Charles B. Aycock Birthplace	N.C. Dept. of Cultural Res., Div. of Archives and History
Cupola House	Historic Edenton
Dixon-Stevenson House	Tryon Palace Historic Sites and Gardens
Duke Homestead	Marian O'Keefe/Duke Homestead
Executive Mansion	Jerry Miller/North Carolina's Executive Mansion
Haley House	The High Point Museum
Haywood Hall	The Friends of Haywood Hall, Inc.
Hezekiah Alexander Homesite	The Charlotte Museum of History
Historic Bath	N.C. Dept. of Cultural Res., Div. of Archives and History
Historical Beaufort	Beaufort Historical Association
Horace Williams House	Chapel Hill Preservation Society
Hope Plantation	Jerry Miller/Historic Hope Foundation
Horne Creek Living Historical Farm	N.C. Dept. of Cultural Res., Div. of Archives and History
James Iredell House State Historic Site	Historic Edenton

	Photo or illustration courtesy of
James K. Polk Memorial	N.C. Dept. of Cultural Res., Div. of Archives and History
Joel Lane House	Joel Lane House, Inc.
John Wright Stanly House	Tryon Palace Historic Sites and Gardens
Marks House	Albemarle Stanly Co. Historical Pres. Comm.
The Mendenhall Plantation	Historic Jamestown Society, Inc.
The Michael Braun House	Rowan Museum, Inc.
Mordecai Historic Park	Capital Area Preservation
Old Salem	N.C. Dept. of Cultural Res., Div. of Archives and History
Owens House	Historic Halifax
Reynolda House	Reynolda Museum of Art
Richard Bennehan House	Stagville Center
The Sally-Billy House	N.C. Dept. of Cultural Res., Div. of Archives and History
Smith-McDowell House	Smith-McDowell House Museum
Snuggs House	Albemarle Stanly Co. Historical Pres. Comm.
Somerset Place	N.C. Dept. of Cultural Res., Div. of Archives and History
Thomas Wolfe Memorial	N.C. Dept. of Cultural Res., Div. of Archives and History
Tryon Palace	Tryon Palace Historic Sites and Gardens
The Utzman-Chambers House	The Rowan Museum, Inc.
Williams 'Glebe' House	Episcopal Diocese of East Carolina
Zebulon B. Vance Birthplace	N.C. Dept. of Cultural Res., Div. of Archives and History

🏛 South Carolina

Aiken-Rhett House	The Charleston Museum
Boone Plantation	F.S.S. Josephson/Boone Plantation
Drayton Hall	Paul Berwick/National Trust for Historic Preservation
Edmondston-Alston House	Middleton Place Foundation
George Parsons Elliott House	Historic Beaufort Foundation
Hampton Plantation	Hampton Plantation State Park
Hampton-Preston Mansion and Garden	Historic Columbia Foundation
The Harold Kaminski House	Historic Georgetown
Heyward-Washington House	The Charleston Museum
Historic Brattonsville	York County Historical Commission
Historic Camden	Historic Camden
Hopsewee Plantation	Hopsewee Plantation
Jennings-Brown House	Marlborough Historical Society
Joseph Manigault House	The Charleston Museum
Magnolia Dale	Edgefield County Historical Society
Mann-Simons Cottage	Historic Columbia Foundation
Middleton Place House	Middleton Place Foundation
Nathaniel Russell House	Historic Charleston Foundation
Oakley Park	The United Daughter of the Confederacy
Redcliffe Plantation	Redcliffe Plantation State Park
Robert Mills Historic House and Park	Historic Columbia Foundation
Thomas Price House	Spartanburg Co. Historical Association
Verdier House	Historic Beaufort
Walnut Grove Plantation	Spartanburg Co. Historical Association
Woodrow Wilson Boyhood Home	Historic Columbia Foundation

🏛 Tennessee

	Photo or illustration courtesy of
Andrew Johnson National Historic Site	National Park Service
Armstrong-Lockett House	Armstrong-Lockett House
The Athenaeum Rectory	Assoc. for the Pres. of Tennessee Antiquities
Belle Meade Plantation	Assoc. for the Preservation of Tenn. Antiquities
Belmont Mansion	Belmont Mansion Association
Blount Mansion	Blount Mansion
Carnton Plantation	Carnton Association, Inc.
Carter House	Assoc. for the Pres. of Tennessee Antiquities
Cragfront	Assoc. for the Pres. of Tennessee Antiquities
James K. Polk Ancestral Home	James K. Polk Memorial Association
Kingstone Lisle	Historic Rugby, Inc.
Oaklands Historic House Museum	Oaklands
The Pillars	Assoc. for the Pres. of Tennessee Antiquities
Ramsey House	Assoc. for the Pres. of Tennessee Antiquities
Rock Castle	Historic Rock Castle
Rocky Mount	Rocky Mount Historical Association
The Hermitage: Home of Andrew Jackson	Ladies' Hermitage Association
Woodruff-Fontaine House	Assoc. for the Preservation of Tenn. Antiquities
Wynnewood	State of Tennessee

🏛 Virginia

Abrams' Delight Museum	Winchester-Frederick Co. Historical Society
Adam Thoroughgood House	The Chrysler Museum
Agecroft Hall	Agecroft Association
Ash Lawn-Highland	Ash Lawn-Highland
Bacon's Castle	Assoc. for the Pres. of Virginia Antiquities
Bassett Hall	Colonial Williamsburg Foundation
Belle Grove Plantation	Belle Grove, Inc.
Berkeley Plantation	Berkeley Plantation
Boyhood Home of Robert E. Lee	Lee-Jackson Foundation
Buena Vista	City of Roanoke
Carlyle House	Northern Virginia Regional Park Authority
Carter's Grove Plantation	Colonial National Historical Park
Centre Hill Mansion	Petersburg Museums
The Claude Moore Colonial Farm	The Claude Moore Colonial Farm
Colonial Williamsburg	Colonial Williamsburg Foundation
Evelynton	Evelynton
The Exchange Hotel	Historic Gordonsville, Inc.
Gadsby's Tavern	Gadsby's Tavern Museum
Governor's Mansion	Colonial Williamsburg Foundation
Gunston Hall	Board of Regents of Gunston Hall
Historic Michie Tavern	Ed Roseberry/Historic Michie Tavern
Historic Sully	Fairfax County Park Authority
Hunter House Victorian Museum	Hunter Foundation
Kenmore	Kenmore Association, Inc.
Lee-Fendall House	Virginia Trust for Historic Preservation
Lloyd House	Alexandria Hist. Restoration and Pres. Comm.
Magnolia Grange	Chesterfield Historical Society
Mary Washington House	Mary Washington Branch of APVA

	Photo or illustration courtesy of
Maymont	Maymont Foundation
McClean House-19th Century Village	National Park Service
Mill House Museum	Historic Occoquan, Inc.
Monticello	Robert Lautner/Thomas Jefferson Memorial Foundation, Inc.
Montpelier	National Trust for Historic Preservation
Moore House	Colonial National Historical Park
Moses Myers House	The Chrysler Museum
Mount Vernon	Mount Vernon Ladies' Association
The Newsome House	John Warters/Newsome House Museum & Cultural Ctr.
Oatlands	Oatlands, Inc.
Point of Honor	Lynchburg Museum System
Pope-Leighey House	National Trust for Historic Preservation
Poplar Forest	The Corp. for Jefferson's Poplar Forest
Ramsay House	City of Alexandria
Red Hill	Patrick Henry Memorial Foundation
Riddick's Folly	Riddick's Folly, Inc.
Sherwood Forest Plantation	Historic Sherwood Forest Plantation
Smithfield Plantation	Assoc. for the Pres. of Virginia Antiquities
Stone House	Manassas Nationnal Park Service
Stonewall Jackson House	Historic Lexington Foundation
Stonewall Jackson's Headquarters	Winchester-Frederick Co. Historical Society
Stratford Hall Plantation	Richard Cheek/Stratford Hall Plantation
Upper Wolfsnare	Princess Anne County Historical Society
Weems-Botts Museum	Historic Dumfries Virginia, Inc.
The White House of the Confederacy	John Shirley/Confederate Memorial Literary Society
Wickham House	The Valentine Museum
The Willoughby-Baylor House	The Chrysler Museum
Wilton House Museum	National Society of the Colonial Dames
Woodlawn Plantation	National Trust for Historic Preservation
Woodrow Wilson Birthplace	Woodrow Wilson Birthplace Foundation, Inc.

🏛 West Virginia

Alexander Campbell Mansion	Bethany College's Heritage Resource Center
General Adam Stephen House	Gen. Adam Stephen Memorial Assoc., Inc.
Governor's Mansion	The West Virginia Preservation Foundation
Harper's Ferry	Eva Jakubowski
Henry Lee's Cabin	Lost River State Park
Historic Lewisburg	Lewisburg Visitors Center
Mansion Museum	Oglebay Institute